P9-BYO-052

The White House Tapes

OTHER BOOKS BY JOHN PRADOS

Lost Crusader: The Secret Wars of CIA Director William Colby

Operation Vulture

America Confronts Terrorism (ed.)

The Blood Road: The Ho Chi Minh Trail and the Vietnam War

President's Secret Wars: CIA and Pentagon Covert Operations from World War II Through the Persian Gulf

Combined Fleet Decoded: The Secret History of U.S. Intelligence and the Japanese Navy in World War II

The Hidden History of the Vietnam War

Valley of Decision: The Siege of Khe Sanh (with Ray W. Stubbe)

Keepers of the Keys: A History of the National Security Council from Truman to Bush

Pentagon Games

The Soviet Estimate: U.S. Intelligence and Soviet Strategic Forces

The Sky Would Fall: The Secret U.S. Bombing Mission to Vietnam, 1954

The White House Tapes

EAVESDROPPING ON THE PRESIDENT

John Prados

THE NEW PRESS

NEW YORK
LONDON

© 2003 by John Prados
All rights reserved.
No part of this book may be reproduced, in any form,
without written permission from the publisher.

Published in the United States by The New Press, New York, 2003
Distributed by W. W. Norton & Company, Inc., New York

ISBN 1-56584-852-7 (hc.)

Library of Congress Cataloging-in-publication data is available.

The New Press was established in 1990 as a not-for-profit alternative to
the large, commercial publishing houses currently dominating the book
publishing industry. The New Press operates in the public interest
rather than for private gain, and is committed to publishing, in inno-
vative ways, works of educational, cultural, and community value that
are often deemed insufficiently profitable.

The New Press, 38 Greene Street, New York, New York 10013
www.thenewpress.com

Printed in the United States of America

2 4 6 8 10 9 7 5 3 1

TO
Betty Lou
Who lived through it all

CONTENTS

ACKNOWLEDGMENTS

Most grateful thanks must go first to transcriptionists Ellen Pinzur and Kathryn Lewis, without whom the contents of the conversations included here would remain uncaptured. Transcription is an extremely difficult task, but with their added knowledge of the relevant history and political personalities, Pinzur and Lewis have helped make these transcripts more accurate still. Editor Diane Wachtell should also be acknowledged for her contribution to the transcripts, which caught additional text and helped to distill those edits we have made in the audio presentations.

At Minnesota Public Radio we must acknowledge Stephen Smith and Sasha Aslanian, who arranged to get a set of the relevant tapes, and then created improved versions on CD, both facilitating work on the transcripts and production of the CDs included here. Tom Mudge and Craig Thorson did much of the technical work. Kate Ellis did important research that is reflected in the CDs and in the documentary program compiled by American RadioWorks.

Archivists at the National Archives and various presidential libraries deserve credit for making available the tapes used in the project. At the Franklin D. Roosevelt Library this was Mark Renovich. At the Harry S. Truman Library the responsible archivist was Pauline Testerman. From the Dwight D. Eisenhower Library we received assistance from Kathy Struss and Herbert Pankratz. At the John F. Kennedy Library our helper was Allan Goodrich. From the

Lyndon Baines Johnson Library we received assistance from Linda Seelye and Regina Greenwell. At the Nixon Library Project of the National Archives we were helped by Ron Sodano. At the Gerald R. Ford Library we received help from Kenneth Hafeli. At the Ronald Reagan Library our assistance came from Steve Branch.

The Miller Center of Public Affairs at the University of Virginia also provided important assistance with tapes to Minnesota Public Radio. David Shreve there furnished material for the DAT tapes on Lyndon Johnson.

Major credit for this project belongs to its editor, Diane Wachtell of The New Press, who saw the need for a collection that enables Americans to actually *listen* to their presidents at work. Thomas Blanton of the National Security Archive deserves credit for encouraging the author to proceed on the basis of Wachtell's suggestion. The germ of this idea had resulted in the collection before you today.

Without these persons, the present collection would not exist. These persons deserve credit for the quality of this collection. I myself am responsible for its defects.

A NOTE ON TRANSCRIPTIONS

A number of points should be borne in mind concerning these or any other transcriptions of recorded conversations. The authoritative source should be seen as the tape, not the transcription. However, both the tape and the transcription are affected by external factors that limit our ability to understand the proceedings recorded. This is unfortunate, but it is also inevitable.

Sound recordings made by presidents were created using a wide variety of equipment and techniques, as indicated in our introduction. Many were not recorded on tape, but rather on plastic disks and belts. For the sake of simplicity, we refer to all of the recordings as "tapes." According to experts who have studied the White House recording systems, much of the equipment was off-the-shelf gear used for office dictation or general sound recording. Microphones and cables were often poorly installed, adding room noise and electronic buzzing to tapes. Low quality tape stock and slow recording speeds also reduced sound fidelity. The manner of recording also matters—recorders that were turned on manually to take down conversations have performed better than voice-activated systems, as the Nixon tapes attest.

With microphones placed in lamps, built into tables, recessed into walls or fireplaces—all to be unobtrusive—the layout of the recording environment ensured that persons on the tape were at different (and varying) distances from the microphones capturing their words. Lyndon Johnson's telephone tapes are some of the best precisely because LBJ and his companions in conversation were speaking directly into the telephone's microphone. Franklin Roosevelt's recordings are also pretty good, as the microphone was placed on top of his desk and people sat around it. Tapes done in the Oval Office have tended to be superior to ones recorded in the Cabinet Room, perhaps due to the smaller space or the different coverage by the arrays of microphones.

Things that happened during the recorded meetings also affect the tapes. Papers being shuffled on the desk or table, the sound of writing, things falling, the hum of air conditioners, JFK's rocking chair, people crossing their legs and hitting the underside of the table, noises in the room or outside it, power surges, machinery noise, gaps left when tape reels ran out and the record was picked up by another tape or recorder—any number of other possible sources of interference have reduced the quality of the recordings. In addition, there are sources of unintelligibility that arise from the discussions themselves. Soft-spoken people do not record as well, others slur their words. Frequently many persons in a meeting react at the same moment and speak over each other, masking individual remarks. All manner of interruptions occur. There is also the matter of ambient noise around the transcriptionists as they labored on these tapes.

Further problems with the tapes arise from the effects of age and their manner of storage prior to the moment when the tapes became a recognized resource and measures were taken to safeguard them. In combination with the quality of the original tapes—some of which, the joke is, were purchased at the drug store down the block rather than being professional-grade product—age and storage issues introduce hissing and other distracting sounds in the recordings we hear today. In addition, archivists, Nixon family members, and national security authorities who have deleted material from the tapes introduced substitute sounds (most commonly a loud buzzing noise or an audio tone) that interrupt the audio signal and may cause the ear to distort sounds heard immediately prior to and after such excisions.

Additional sources of error stem from the fact that only some of the voices that are heard here are known. We have frequently used memoranda of conversations describing the same meetings, notes, participants' memoir accounts or other secondary histories, knowledge of the subject and of the policy positions of participants, and biographies that identify the regional origins of participants to help identify the people speaking on these tapes. Despite the great care taken, there are persons who cannot be identified, and there may be instances in which our identifications are mistaken. For these we apologize in advance.

Transcription is not a science. Sometimes it has seemed much more an art. We have proceeded by assembling what information is available on each of the events recorded here, including tape guides from the archives, such papers as may exist detailing the conversations at the meeting, documents that were under discussion at the meeting, and profiles of the participants. In at least one case (March 26, 1971), this has involved filing specific declassification requests for documents under discussion. One conclusion we may draw in passing is that in every case we have seen, the tapes reveal much more that took place in these meetings than documentary records ever noted. The assembled materials both established the context for the tapes and furnished clues as we listened and transcribed.

Every person hears something different. Transcriptionists Ellen Pinzur and Kathryn Lewis did yeowomen work on these texts, and the recordings were also listened to by the author and the editor. Individual passages were often rewound dozens of times to try to glean just what was being said. This has been a very time-consuming process. Each of us contributed something, each of us heard words in places where only sounds were audible to another, or found places we could identify someone or something not evident to another. The transcripts were also compared with others covering the same events. We discovered that no two transcripts are entirely identical. For example, our transcription of the Nixon "Smoking Gun" tapes differs from that compiled by Senate Watergate investigators, which differed from the one done by Nixon tapes authority Stanley Kutler (as does ours also). Everyone heard something different. We apologize again to those who hear a different conversation from the one we did; we can only respond that this is our best reconstruction of what was said. Again, the tape itself is the authoritative source, and the transcripts should be viewed as an aid to listening.

USING THE RECORDINGS
AND GUIDEBOOK

The compact disks in this set were produced by American RadioWorks, the national documentary unit of Minnesota Public Radio. Many of the original tapes are of poor technical quality. Using the best recordings provided by each presidential archive, ARW improved the audio to the greatest extent possible. The recordings have been edited to serve as a companion to *The White House Tapes*. Some conversations have been edited to delete room noise or elide portions of conversations not on-topic. These edits are indicated by a brief silence. Portions of the tapes have been deleted for national security purposes; in the Nixon tape selections deletions were made in both the interest of national security and for reasons of personal privilege. These are indicated either by a brief tone or by a slightly extended period of silence.

In the transcripts we have indicated places where the words spoken were not discernable in several ways. Where a sentence or longer passage cannot be understood, we have used "[unintelligible]." Where the lost passage is a phrase or a few words, we have used "[word]" or "[words]." On occasion we thought we could interpret the missing word, but we were not sure or the word did not seem to make sense; in these instances we noted the guess within the "word" brackets with a question mark. Sometimes the word was not understandable, but it was clearly a name or place. In such cases we noted "[name]" and so forth. From time to time we also noted sounds within brackets, including telephones ringing or being slammed down, dogs barking, hammering, coughing, laughing, and so on. Where a number of persons speak at the same time we have noted "[voices overlap]."

To the extent possible we have identified persons referred to by the speakers on these recordings. Identifications appear in brackets when the individuals are first named. From time to time speakers refer to something or make a point that needs clarification (and occasional refutation) and these items are explained in notes that are gathered at the end of the book.

Each presidential selection begins with an overview commentary by the author which sets the stage for the conversation. These commentaries describe the background events that led to the conversations and show the importance of the discussions the presidents decided to record. The commentaries explain who is participating in the conversations and what role these talks play in larger events. At times, the commentaries also reflect on what happens in the conversations and the significance of decisions made or rejected. In short, the commentaries furnish the background necessary to put presidents' tape recordings in their proper light.

The White House Tapes

Introduction

In recent years, Americans have been tremendously fascinated with the discovery that their presidents made secret audio recordings of themselves while they were in office. The existence of such recordings came to light for the first time on July 16, 1973, during the Watergate hearings, when Nixon presidential assistant Alexander P. Butterfield revealed that the Oval Office and the Cabinet Room, as well as other White House and presidential locations, were wired with microphones linked to a sound recording system. Americans, who had heard for months of Nixon administration wiretaps on journalists, current and former officials, persons on a Nixon "enemies list," and at the Watergate, were electrified at the realization that the president had bugged himself too. These recordings ultimately yielded evidence of Nixon's participation in an obstruction of justice that led to his resignation from the presidency.

Apart from their political consequences, the Watergate tapes created an intense interest in presidents' use of sound recordings, and it quickly emerged that Nixon's practice had been more the norm than the exception. Almost immediately, official custodians of John F. Kennedy's presidential records disclosed that JFK had also made tape recordings, and archivists working with Lyndon B. Johnson's records confirmed the same for him, both as vice president during the Kennedy administration and while president. Later came news that Franklin D. Roosevelt, Harry S. Truman, and Dwight D. Eisenhower had each made some sound recordings while in office. As Betty Sue Flowers, present director of the Lyndon Johnson Library of the National Archives, has put it, "There's a bunch of poetry there." Flowers said she meant that "the human voice itself has qualities that when someone is talking you get into the heart, so for me the essence of poetry is that direct, that direct connection with the soul of a human being, and I don't know anything better than tape to get you right into the heart."[1] Perhaps it is this idea of hearing the hearts of presidents that accounts for the fascination Americans have had with sound recordings made by their leaders.

Although obtained using different kinds of equipment under a range of recording protocols, what most of these tapes have in common is the fact that they were made without the knowledge of the individuals (apart from the presidents themselves) who were being recorded. Figures from Martin Luther King Jr. to foreign heads of state and members of presidential administrations, including Robert McNamara, Melvin Laird, and McGeorge Bundy, participated in what they undoubtedly felt were private conversations with American presidents, while being taped without their knowledge or consent. Their statements of belief, use of facts, and expressions of opinion are what they wanted the president to accept, not their posturing for posterity. Indeed this is the real stuff of history.

This collection samples that history widely. Where possible we have tried to select tapes from each president that show him at work, not simply performing ceremonial tasks. We have selected both domestic politics and foreign policy issues. Our domestic selections have been primarily civil rights, and for foreign policy the Vietnam War; we have provided snapshots of different presidents working the same problems. We searched for key incidents or moments, discovered whether these were the subjects of the tapes, then listened to the tapes to ascertain their audio quality and suitability. The result is a captivating series of listening portraits of modern American presidents.

Presidential concern with public opinion polls dates from the infancy of that technique, as Franklin Roosevelt demonstrates in a conversation strategizing for the 1940 elections. FDR's comments on Hitler, Mussolini, and the Japanese threat in the Pacific shed an interesting light on pre–World War II U.S. policies. Roosevelt's comments on various ethnic groups in that conversation, and on African Americans in another, evoke a different era and sensibility. John F. Kennedy's 1963 meeting on the eve of a coup to overthrow the Diem government in South Vietnam, the last possible moment the United States could have backed out of a fateful choice for war, is a stunning revelation.

Lyndon Johnson on Vietnam and the Gulf of Tonkin show the march to war in Vietnam, while Richard Nixon's 1971 meeting on the war demonstrates how difficult the problems had become. Kennedy and Johnson on civil rights comment at key moments in the struggle. Richard Nixon and Billy Graham in 1972 offer disturbing perspectives on a range of social issues, and Nixon and H.R. Haldeman in the "Smoking Gun" conversations permit us to listen to a talk that brought down a presidency. Ronald Reagan offers his explanations of the Iran-Contra affair as well. Moments from the presidencies of Harry Truman, Dwight D. Eisenhower, and Gerald Ford complete the collection.

Although books and conferences have discussed the existence of these tapes and several projects are currently underway to put all declassified presidential recordings on the Internet, access to the recordings themselves until now has not been readily available. To date, for an American to listen to the recordings included in this collection has required a combination of detailed historical knowledge, a significant travel budget, audio recording expertise, and superhuman hearing. The tapes are stored at presidential libraries across the country or at the National Archives. To uncover them one would have to know what to look for and have a clear sense of what events might be covered on tape. Finding the tapes, a number of which have no finding aids, would be just the beginning. In the case of the Nixon tapes, duplication services are awkward and the only alternative is to bring one's own recording equipment. Audio quality for many of the tapes is poor. Speakers are not identified nor is historical context provided. Even with these drawbacks, to purchase individual copies of the conversations included in this collection would cost upward of $200.

The difficulties obtaining and understanding these recordings stand in inverse proportion to their importance as historical records. William Doyle, author of *Inside the Oval Office: The White House Tapes from FDR to Clinton*, calls the tapes "fly-on-the-wall drama of the presidents as executives in action behind closed doors, providing glimpses of the flesh-and-blood humanity of the executives who sat behind the Oval Office desk." Stanley Kutler, Watergate historian and transcriber of *Abuse of Power: The New Nixon Tapes*, calls them "an unprecedented view of a man in the cockpit of the presidency." Deborah Leff, director of the Kennedy Library, refers to the act of listening to the tapes today as "eavesdropping on history," and Philip Zelikow, director of the Miller Center of Public Affairs at the University of Virginia, which has embarked on an ambitious effort to transcribe the entire set of taped records of both John F. Kennedy and Richard M. Nixon, calls the sets of tapes the "most unique evidence of the working of a government in all of recorded history."[2]

The White House Tapes marks the first time copies of these remarkable artifacts of our collective history have been made widely available to the American public in a form that enables them to listen in on the presidents.

* * *

Audio recordings became possible in 1877 when Thomas Edison invented the phonograph. His device captured spoken words by etching sound vibrations onto a tin cylinder. Edison filed for a U.S. patent on December 24, 1877. In 1889, Danish engineer Valdemar Poulsen combined an electromagnet with a steel wire to make sound recordings. Poulsen's telegraphone, as he called the machine, received a U.S. patent on November 13, 1900. These two technologies—grooved records and electromagnetic impulses—would become the two most widely used methods of twentieth-century recording and playback: records and tapes. Early tape recorders were custom built and suffered not only from primitive microphone technology but also from the quick popularity of vinyl disc recordings, the music reproductions that expanded the horizons of player pianos to make possible a wide range of sound reproductions.

By the 1930s wire tape recorders were becoming available commercially, but, equally important, the notion of using magnetism to record sounds was adapted in other contexts. In Hollywood, the "talkie" began in 1929. These featured a vinyl disc played in conjunction with the movie until engineers devised ways of using magnetism to record sounds directly onto the film itself. As long as voice recordings were limited to steel wire on a reel, storage capacity made it impractical to collect conversations on any large scale. The film recording technique substantially increased the duration of the soundtrack that could be stored on a reel, thus making it possible to collect substantial amounts of conversation. By 1940, the Radio Corporation of America (RCA) had begun experimenting with equipment that used film but recorded only a soundtrack, not pictures.

It was then that Franklin Delano Roosevelt began to record some of his speeches and fireside chats. As the chief executive who innovated the use of regular press conferences to shape public perceptions, FDR had an interest in assuring the accuracy of quotes taken from his public appearances. Since many of these press conferences were held off the record, and the presence of a stenographer could suggest to reporters that their access was not so privileged after all, White House stenographer Henry Kannee argued successfully for recordings as an alternative. The idea of placing microphones in the Oval Office then seemed a natural extension.

In the summer of 1940, the White House contacted RCA, and FDR met privately with corporate executive David Sarnoff. The RCA film recording device was licensed from a Chicago sound engineer named John Ripley Kiel. Summoned to Washington, D.C., Kiel spent several days installing a system with a microphone hidden in a lamp on FDR's desk and another in a telephone. Wires led to the large (three-and-one-half-feet high and almost two feet wide) device, called a Continuous Film Recording Machine, which was placed in a cabinet downstairs, in a room usually used to store gifts to the president. The machine had the capacity to hold twenty-four hours of sound on a reel, with switches that could be turned on by both President Roosevelt and stenographer Kannee. It also had a setting for activation by sound. A press conference held on August 23, 1940, became the first event recorded by President Roosevelt.

Of fifteen hours of existing Roosevelt tapes, two-thirds consist of recorded speeches, and the remaining third covers six meetings, one telephone call, and fourteen press conferences. Unfortunately, the sound quality on most of these is fair to poor, and the phone tape contains only FDR's side of the conversation, which was with Secretary of State Cordell Hull on September 4, 1940. FDR's final Oval Office recording dates from October; the last item among the Roosevelt tapes is a radio speech from January 1941. For this collection we have selected an FDR meeting with African American leaders on September 27, 1940, and another he held with House of Representatives chieftains Sam Rayburn and John W. McCormack, held on October 4. These selections meet some of our criteria for inclusion—to see presidents actively at work and to have good audio fidelity. Roosevelt also ranges the gamut from domestic politics and an election campaign to the world problems of Hitler, Mussolini, and the Japanese aggression in Asia.

Roosevelt stopped taping after only a few months. Some speculate that the president's purpose in taping was to compile records of the final months of his second term, which might have been FDR's last had he lost the 1940 election. It is equally possible that the quality of the tapes was simply not good enough to interest Roosevelt in continuing the practice. Printed references in newspapers and some books about FDR secretly taping his meetings during World War II do not correspond to the holdings in the Roosevelt Library. The recording film on FDR's machine when it passed into the hands of his successor was the same one that had been there when he recorded in 1940.

President Roosevelt passed away while still in office on April 12, 1945, to be succeeded by Vice President Harry S. Truman. Roosevelt's RCA machine was still in place and Truman learned about it during his first days in office. Truman did not like the idea of taping, but tried the system out at a press conference on May 23. After listening to the result he told stenographer Jack

Romagna, "I sure don't want to have anything to do with that."[3] A few other fragments of President Truman's work meetings were taped, less than three hours in all, of events between 1945 and 1947, out of a total of about ten hours of tape. Much of the Truman material consists of conversations with friends or even among unknown workmen laboring to fix up the Oval Office. Truman had the entire system ripped out at that time. He continued to record his own speeches, and the audio film from the FDR machine was apparently sent to the Roosevelt Library. In 1973, coincident with Watergate, archivists at the Roosevelt Library found the ten tape items actually pertinent to Truman's presidency. Archivists forwarded the Truman recordings to the Harry S. Truman Library in Independence, Missouri. Overall there are a little over nine-and-one-half hours of private Truman tapes, of very poor sound quality. In contrast, and illustrating the extent to which recording had become established for general public information purposes, President Truman recorded some 800 speeches. Here we have fragments of telephone calls with friends and government officials, including Secretary of State George C. Marshall and Treasury Secretary John Snyder. We have included the only Truman tape known to have originated after 1945, in which Truman's concerns range from Kansas City politics to appointments at the State Department.

Dwight D. Eisenhower achieved fame as a general years before he came to the presidency, leading the invasion of Normandy in World War II. Both as a staff officer in the U.S. War Department and later as a top commander, General Eisenhower writes that he made use of sound recordings from which memoranda of conversation were compiled.[4] These relied upon microphones linked to Dictaphone Dictabelt machines, using a rubber or plastic belt as the material upon which sounds were recorded. An early entry into the office recording world, the Dictaphone had become a relatively mature technology by the 1920s. FDR used one at times, and by the middle and late 1940s, they were the most advanced system available. Ike left the military to become president of Columbia University in 1949 and is also said to have had a Dictaphone recording system there, in his office in Low Library. At the White House, communications specialists recommended to Ike that he install a Tycoon Soundscriber machine, which makes recordings on discs similar to vinyl records. Ike did that but he later installed Dictaphone Dictacord A2TC. (One of the Eisenhower tapes consists of a secretary instructing Ike in the use of the Dictaphone machine.) The equipment was the responsibility of White House Communications Agency technicians John Waybrant and Al Duffy.

Papers kept by President Eisenhower's personal secretary, Ann Whitman, indicate just over two dozen occasions when the equipment was actually used by Eisenhower while he was president, all prior to the spring of 1959. The recordings made by the machines were overlooked until much later, though journalists mentioned Eisenhower's taping in articles in 1979 and 1982. The Eisenhower Library found a few of the discs but could not read them. Five belts for the Dictaphone were discovered among the Eisenhower papers in the 1990s, apparently by grandson David Eisenhower while he was at Abilene doing unrelated research, but none of these were the important meetings Ike had put on his Soundscriber. When the recordings were uncovered, the Eisenhower Library had no workable Soundscriber machine for the discs, and the Dictaphone Company no longer had equipment compatible with the belts Ike had used. Archivists secured help from the Johnson Library, where there were also machines, which had been restored with parts from IBM. IBM had subsequently taken over the company that manufactured the Soundscriber. Apparently the Johnson Library was able to play Eisenhower's belts and convert them to cassette tape recordings, upon which the Eisenhower tapes are now based. The Nixon Library Project at the National Archives happened to have a working Dictaphone. The audio quality of the Eisenhower tapes is quite bad, often with only brief snatches of understandable conversation, and the surviving tapes do not include the important conversations. What happened to those tapes remains unknown. We have included a conversation on international treaties and U.S. law between Eisenhower and a prominent Democratic senator, Walter George, which took place in January 1955.

Meanwhile technology continued to advance. During World War II, German engineers created a recorder which for the first time used plastic magnetic tape, the medium in all modern taping equipment. The California-based Ampex Corporation attempted to create an analogous system, and a commercial recorder on this principle was delivered to the American Broadcasting Company in April 1948. By the 1950s advanced materials such as mylar and celenar had been adapted to create durable magnetic tapes. Use of these tapes on a reel-to-reel recorder had, by the late 1950s, evolved to the point that dependable machines were limited only by the supply of recording tape.

Quite soon after he took office, President John F. Kennedy blundered into a major misadventure, that is, the Central Intelligence Agency attempt to invade Cuba using a group of Cuban exiles recruited in the United States. Differences developed over what advice the Joint Chiefs of Staff had given Kennedy prior to the failed covert operation. Desire to avoid similar situations in the future is the explanation *Newsweek* magazine offered in a 1983 article purporting to explain why JFK felt he needed a taping system. *Newsweek* cited as its source Kennedy private secretary Evelyn Lincoln,[5] who supervised the taping system.

Two separate Kennedy taping operations were established: one recorded office proceedings; the other telephone calls and private notes the president dictated for Lincoln. The office taping system was actually designed and installed by Secret Service agent Robert Bouck, chief of the Protective Research Section of the White House detail, whose tasks normally included electronic sweeps in the West Wing offices, protecting Kennedy against bugs or eavesdropping devices placed there by others. As Bouck recalls, JFK wanted accurate records of discussions on certain subjects, including U.S. policy toward Russia.[6]

Bouck designed the system; the Army Signal Corps, which ran the White House Communications Agency, bought the equipment for cash from a local electronics shop. Bouck installed it during the summer of 1962 while JFK vacationed at the Kennedy family compound in Hyannisport, Massachusetts. With help from another Secret Service agent, Chester Miller, Bouck placed one microphone in the kneehole of President Kennedy's desk in the Oval Office and others in unused recesses for light fixtures in the Cabinet Room. A reel-to-reel Tandberg tape recorder was located in a storage room in the basement directly under Evelyn Lincoln's office; it was connected to the mikes by wires passed through the floor. The microphones had their own batteries for power, similar to the miniature devices used by intelligence agencies at the time. They had enough sensitivity to pick up sounds within a radius of fifteen feet, but since people talking could be anywhere in the rooms, the voices on tape are often faint and overpowered by ambient noise. President Kennedy personally controlled the system by using a switch. One switch was located in his desk in the Oval Office, and in the Cabinet Room, the switch was at JFK's chair, under the table. Later Bouck placed a third switch in the Oval Office, on the coffee table by the fireplace, for when Kennedy moved to the less formal arrangement of sofas and chairs in that part of the room.

Bouck and Miller personally operated the equipment. At some point they supplemented the original tape recorder with another machine wired in tandem to continue taping when the reel ran out in the first one. When a tape was used up, a light signal came on in the West Wing security office, and the Secret Service agents threaded a fresh tape onto the recorder. The president first recorded three meetings, concerning the economy and nuclear testing, on July 30, 1962. The last recorded meeting was on November 7, 1963—a wide-ranging session that included talk of plans for the Democratic convention upcoming in 1964, troubles in developing certain new aircraft and the associated defense contracts, wheat sales, and other matters.

The separate Dictaphone system was linked to the common phone line in President Kennedy's office, as well as to the telephone on Evelyn Lincoln's desk. This was a commercially available model using red plastic belts (sometimes called "sleeves"). The machine itself and the spare belts were located in a locked cabinet close to Lincoln's desk. Kennedy would press a switch to activate a light on his secretary's desk, and Evelyn Lincoln would start the Dictaphone recorder. It is not known whether JFK could operate the recorder directly from his own desk. Used belts were placed in a safe in the outer office. Mrs. Lincoln believes the system was installed by the telephone company (without Secret Service participation) while the president was vacationing in Newport, Rhode Island. Kennedy made three such visits over weekends in late August and early September 1962. The earliest recorded telephone call occurred on September 10, 1962. The last recorded telephone calls took place on October 29, 1963, the same day President Kennedy held the meeting on Vietnam that is included in this collection.

The day Kennedy was assassinated, November 22, Agent Bouck entered the Oval Office and Cabinet Room and dismantled the taping system. The Dictaphone linked to the telephone line was apparently left in place. The Kennedy tapes turned over to the National Archives in 1976 included conversations at 325 meetings (totaling approximately 248 hours) and in 275 telephone calls (about 12 hours). In 1998 the Kennedy family gave the Archives two dozen more dictabelts containing four additional hours of telephone conversations, which had become separated from the set before it was originally turned over.

Only President Kennedy himself, Mrs. Lincoln, and the Secret Service agents are known to have been aware of the taping systems initially. Presidential aides Kenneth O'Donnell and David Powers are also thought to have had knowledge of the system. National Archives officials at a conference at the Kennedy Library in February 2003 mentioned documents recently found that confirm Robert F. Kennedy's knowledge of the tapes as well. Bobby Kennedy knew of them by the mid-1960s at the latest, since he gave Evelyn Lincoln instructions about transcription. Miller Center historians believe that by 1963 Robert Kennedy and his private secretary were already aware of the tapes. These historians also state that knowledge of the taping system attributed to Kenny O'Donnell and Dave Powers, which is supported by presidential library archivists, is based upon stories they think apocryphal. When the existence of the Kennedy tapes was extensively reported in 1982, the president's surviving brother, Senator Edward M. Kennedy, said he had not been cognizant of the tapes at the time. Neither had Ethel Kennedy, Robert's wife, even though Bobby made subsequent use of the tapes for a memoir of the Cuban Missile Crisis.

Officials such as Robert McNamara, McGeorge Bundy, George Ball, and General Maxwell D. Taylor all professed ignorance. Secretary of State Dean

Rusk reported that he knew that at least some meetings were being recorded: "There were many times when a microphone was on the table. We knew we were being recorded."[7] McNamara, Ball, Taylor, and Rusk all agreed that they assumed they were on the record at these meetings. "History was unfolding," McNamara averred. "I'm happy to live with what I said."[8] George Ball, who served as undersecretary of state under Rusk, told the Washington Post: "Frankly I think it is a good idea in some of these meetings to make a clear record of what is said. . . . There basically isn't any privacy when you're a government official talking to a president."[9]

We have included a Kennedy meeting on the occasion of the march on Washington by African Americans in August 1963, one of the largest public demonstrations until that time, when the participants discuss racial issues and the status of proposed civil rights legislation which became the landmark Civil Rights Act of 1964. On the foreign affairs side, we have Kennedy's national security meeting of October 29, 1963, at which JFK and his top officials ponder the prospects for a military coup in South Vietnam to overthrow the government of Ngo Dinh Diem. The Saigon leader was murdered in the coup on November 1. Just three weeks later President Kennedy would be assassinated during a trip to Dallas, Texas.

Lyndon Baines Johnson became president on the afternoon of the Kennedy assassination, taking his oath of office on Air Force One during the flight back to Washington. He arrived at the White House in the early evening and began a full day as president the morning of November 23. Within twenty-four hours, President Johnson had ordered an overhaul of the White House telephone system. From that moment until January 1969, LBJ was on the phone constantly, crafting political coalitions, stage managing legislation, needling his advisers, seeking information on every subject from the Kennedy assassination inquiry (Warren Commission), to the Vietnam War, to civil aviation agreements with Russia. JFK had been known for his use of the telephone, but LBJ was master of the medium. There was no important business of the United States that avoided President Johnson's telephone touch.

Taping calls would be a key feature of the Johnson method. He spoke later of the value of the tapes for writing memoirs, but President Johnson went out of his way to have secretaries compile notes and simple transcripts of the calls contemporaneously,[10] at least suggesting he had current use for the material. The dictabelts with the recordings were entrusted to Johnson secretary Mildred Stegall. She recalled that the president repeatedly emphasized that no one was to have access to the dictabelts and estimates that LBJ would ask her twice a year or so whether the material was safely locked away, a practice Johnson continued until his death in 1972.[11]

Little is known of the specifics of the system. Johnson is thought to have continued to use John Kennedy's phone recorders, but he must have been able to activate the system himself because staff do not report having done this. At various times Johnson made use of the Dictaphone machines, Soundscribers, and a third type known as the Edison Voicewriter. Richard Nixon, with whom Lyndon Johnson spoke about tape systems, reports that LBJ's phone system covered his office, his bedroom in the White House family quarters, Camp David, the LBJ Ranch in Texas, and his office in the Federal Building in Austin.

President Johnson taped as many as 9,300 telephone calls: 800 calls were taped in a little over a month in 1963, no fewer than 4,600 in 1964, 1,780 in 1965, 1,240 in 1966, 350 during 1967, and another 540 in 1968, for a total of more than 400 hours, compared with 16 hours of Kennedy phone tapes. The pattern of Johnson's taping also speaks to an intention to make contemporaneous use of the records. During the early years, Johnson did the most taping; as LBJ's political problems sharpened, and the Vietnam War weighed more heavily, he did much less.

Richard Nixon wrote that he heard a story through the White House grapevine, concerning LBJ and Robert Kennedy: Bobby had been his brother's attorney general and continued in that job for some months under President Johnson until taking a leave of absence as their relations, always touchy, gradually deteriorated. According to this story, LBJ met Bobby privately to tell Kennedy he would not be selected as candidate for the vice presidency on a Johnson ticket in 1964. (Robert Kennedy actually ran for a New York seat in the United States Senate in 1964 and won that election. He never returned to the administration.) Johnson immediately sent out the tape for transcription, but the entire tape proved to be unintelligible. A technician supposedly concluded that Bobby had carried some sort of interference device in his jacket pocket. The story is salacious but there is no evidence that LBJ's offices were wired for sound at that time.[12]

Heroic measures of preservation have made the treasure trove of Johnson recordings available to Americans. When the dictabelts were dug out from the vault during the 1970s and 1980s, they were found to be in very poor condition, quite apart from the difficulty of finding working original machines. Many were wet from condensation and also physically deteriorated. Experts discovered they could dry the tapes out by stretching them between tissue paper, to absorb the moisture, then baking them. The process permitted a tape to be played just one more time, and the Johnson Library used that last run to transfer the audio to new tapes.

Like JFK before him, President Johnson also eventually had a taping system put in to record proceedings in the Cabinet Room and in the hideaway office next to the Oval Office, but this was not until January 1968. The White House Communications Agency did the work, placing two microphones in the Little Lounge (as the side office was known) and drilling lapel pin–size mikes into the Cabinet Room table. The activation switches were in a control panel on LBJ's desk in the lounge, and at his place in the Cabinet Room. The microphones fed into a mixer and then a reel-to-reel tape recorder located in the basement. President Johnson apparently did not begin using the system until the summer of 1968. That August the Russians invaded Czechoslovakia when they feared the Czechs were weakening in their ideological fealty to communism, and LBJ turned the tapes on when his top advisers met to consider how to deal with the crisis. From then through the end of his administration, Johnson recorded about 200 hours of meeting tapes.

We have selected a variety of Johnson telephone calls for inclusion on two of the most important issues of his presidency—civil rights and Vietnam. LBJ talks with FBI director J. Edgar Hoover about missing civil rights workers in Mississippi, wondering if they have simply disappeared. Here too we hear LBJ wrestling with what to do about Vietnam during the phase when he made decisions to increase American involvement in the war. At times, such as when LBJ spoke with Walt Rostow in early March 1964, the president expresses doubt. At other moments Johnson forges ahead. The coverage ends on August 4, 1964, the dramatic day when civil rights and Vietnam melded into one huge headache when the FBI found the bodies of slain civil rights workers at the same time as LBJ decided to bomb North Vietnam.

Richard Nixon reports that, right from the beginning, he intended his administration to be the best chronicled in history.[13] During the transition, President Johnson talked to Nixon about the taping system and extolled its virtues as a resource for ensuring accurate material for memoirs. H.R. Haldeman, Nixon's chief of staff, who has compiled the most extensive account of the origins of the new president's own taping system, writes that he cannot recollect whether Nixon learned of the system from LBJ or from FBI director J. Edgar Hoover.[14]

In any case, on inauguration day they found taping equipment in what had been the Little Lounge (which would be Haldeman's initial office in the West Wing), hidden in the upper part of a closet near the fireplace. President

Nixon ordered all the taping gear ripped out. But Nixon's desire to document his work remained. That became the point of departure for a long process of trial and error. Nixon disliked note-takers at his meetings (according to Haldeman this dated from the Eisenhower administration, when, as vice president, Nixon was forced to take along State Department note-takers for meetings during his foreign trips), fighting this even at the beginning when Haldeman insisted. The president argued that note-takers interfered with free discussion. The next expedient was to have Nixon himself make notes, or have staff debrief the president and make notes immediately after a meeting. But the president was tightly scheduled and these methods were doomed from the start. Another alternative was to have staff right outside the room question participants as they left meetings, but this proved awkward and provided one-sided accounts. Yet a further possibility became having trusted staff make so-called "color" memoranda after the meetings. Haldeman, John Ehrlichman, Henry Kissinger, and others all did this, but the color memoranda were more about trappings than content.

President Nixon and Haldeman then came up with the idea of relying upon Army General Vernon F. Walters, whom they felt might be capable of producing meeting memoranda that covered not only tone and color but also might have a virtually complete account of content (Walters had been a favorite of Nixon's since translating for the then–vice president during a visit to South America in 1958). Walters, who performed many tasks for the Nixon administration, including setting up Henry Kissinger's secret negotiations with North Vietnam, turned this proposal down cold. Haldeman recalls he "naively" met General Walters to make this request: "He drew himself up and inflated himself to full general-size height and breadth, inserted his array of medals right in front of my nose, and said, 'I am a general in the United States Army, I am a commander of troops. I am not a secretary to anybody.' "[15] (It may be amusing to note that Walters functioned essentially as a staff aide and translator, serving as staff officer and attaché, and had not held a troop command since 1942, when Lieutenant Walters landed in North Africa with the 9th Infantry Division.)

The Nixon White House was still fumbling for a solution in late 1970 or early 1971 when the president learned that Lyndon Johnson had told others that Nixon was foolish not to have some recording mechanism. President Nixon now made what became a fateful decision to go ahead.

At first Nixon wanted the same kind of system LBJ had had, which the president could turn on or off at will. "Mr. President," Haldeman recalls he told Nixon, who was not adept with machinery, "You'll never remember to turn it on except when you don't want it, and when you do want it you're always going to be shouting—afterwards, when it's too late—that no one turned it on."[16]

Nixon agreed to have a taping system that was mostly voice activated. Haldeman gave the assignment to his special assistant Lawrence M. Higby, who shuffled the work over to Alexander P. Butterfield. The latter recalls that Haldeman, disdainful of the military who ran the White House Communications Agency, told him later the same day, "Don't have the military do it!"[17] Since Butterfield liaised with the Secret Service, the arrangement was logical enough. It was the Technical Security Division of the Secret Service that did the installation. The setup in the Cabinet Room would be manually controlled, turned on by Butterfield, who sat in the Cabinet Room, or when he was alerted by a red light at his desk. When a meeting began, Butterfield would turn on the switch (some taped records, like the selection here from March 1971, are incomplete, quite likely because Butterfield was late to the machinery). Only Nixon, Haldeman, Higby, Butterfield (Stephen B. Bull replaced Butterfield in February 1973 and also belongs in this group), and the Secret Service were aware of the existence of the taping system.

The Secret Service wired five microphones into President Nixon's desk in the Oval Office and one more on each side of the fireplace at the opposite end of the room. In the Cabinet Room, there were two microphones under the table near the president's chair. All the lines fed into mixers and then Sony reel-to-reel tape recorders. The taping system went into operation on February 16, 1971. On April 6 at Nixon's request the Secret Service expanded coverage with four microphones in the president's hideaway office in the Old Executive Office Building, and wired in the telephones there, in the Oval Office, and in the Lincoln Sitting Room of the family quarters. On May 18, 1972, Camp David was added, with a microphone in the president's study at Aspen Lodge, and two more on phones on his desk and on the table in the middle of the room. The Aspen taps were placed on Butterfield's initiative and were removed in March 1973.

President Nixon apparently had second thoughts—at the eleventh hour. On April 9, 1973, Nixon instructed Haldeman to shut down the entire system, but later that day he took back the order. Instead he told Haldeman he wanted the system converted from voice activated to manually controlled. "For reasons I cannot remember, Nixon's order was not carried out," Haldeman writes.[18] The taping system, voice activated as before, remained in operation until two days after Alexander Butterfield revealed its existence to Senate Watergate investigators. All the tapes from all the systems add up to almost 4,000 hours of audio coverage, dwarfing the output of all previous presidents put together.

The great imponderable of Watergate is, of course, why Richard Nixon did not simply destroy the tapes. Nixon obviously knew what questionable conversations had taken place in the Oval Office, and he also knew that audiotape records of those meetings existed. Until July 1973 there was no subpoena for that material, and the tapes could have been destroyed with impunity. By his own admission Nixon had listened to some tapes a month earlier, reminding himself of the sensitivity of this material. In a televised interview with British journalist David Frost in September 1977,[19] President Nixon said he did not believe the existence of the tapes would become public, and that if he had destroyed them it would have appeared he had something to hide. Nixon expanded upon these remarks in memoirs published in 1978. Therein he writes he had felt that staff members such as Alexander Butterfield would have claimed executive privilege before revealing anything about the tapes.

In April 1973, just two weeks before the forced resignation of Chief of Staff Haldeman, Nixon reported he had actually had a long conversation with Haldeman about the tapes, which ended with his instructions to keep only the tapes bearing on a few episodes of the Vietnam War and to destroy the rest. Haldeman resigned before he could carry out this order. Once Nixon had been informed that Senate investigators and the special prosecutor were aware of the tape system, it had become too late. Nixon's lawyers agreed the tapes could no longer be safely destroyed. Lying on a hospital bed several days after the Butterfield revelation (Nixon had had an attack of a blood circulation disease), the president wrote himself a note on a yellow legal pad: "Should have destroyed the tapes after April 30, 1973."[20]

The taping system selected by President Richard Nixon produced some of the worst audio reproductions. The sound activation feature made the whole process highly dependent on microphone sensitivity. As voices rose or fell, their pitches changed, or as they became softer, the tape recorders might suddenly stop, or they might start up at the sound of room noises. Many tapes pick up in midphrase or word, or maddeningly start and stop. At the meetings, where the recorders were activated by someone who was not a participant, a premium was placed on Alex Butterfield or Steve Bull being in place at the right moment. These issues further complicated the standard problems of people being far away from the microphones. The recording equipment itself, though more sophisticated than that used by earlier presidents, proved unable to overcome these difficulties.

Both Nixon and Haldeman report they were conscious of being on tape at first but soon forgot all about this. Nixon claims in his memoirs that he never listened to any of his tapes until June 4, 1973, when, under pressure from the Watergate investigations, he went to check certain facts he knew would be on tape. The Nixon tapes also raise the issue of entrapment: listeners must bear in mind that often Nixon knew the tape was on when others in the room did not. At the time of the Christmas bombing in the Vietnam War (December 1972), Henry Kissinger recounts that he had an unusual talk with Nixon where the president kept asking him questions designed to elicit replies suggesting that Kissinger had come up with the whole idea, which had turned into a huge political firestorm. John Dean, who managed the Watergate cover-up for Nixon for some months after it began, felt from the way the president asked leading questions to which both of them knew the answers and the kinds of things Nixon brought up, that his conversation with Nixon of April 15, 1973, was being recorded. Dean's offhand comment about recording to Senate Watergate investigators is in fact what began the unraveling of the presidential tapes story. This issue of making a record exists for every president who used tapes, and Nixon's recordings, the first to be revealed, immediately suggested the question. Another related question that listeners need to take into account: the possibilities that arise when it is the superior who knows the tape machine is running but subordinates do not. Kennedy-Johnson era officials were comfortable with this situation, but the basic structure of discussions under such conditions contains inherent possibilities for entrapment.

Following on the heels of President Nixon's painful experience, Gerald R. Ford's attitude toward taping seemed very different. As Ford wrote in his memoirs, "One of the first decisions I'd made as President was to ban any 'bugs' or secret electronic recording devices either in the Oval Office or anywhere else in the building. The idea that anyone on my staff would tape another person without that person's knowledge or consent was unconscionable, and I made sure that everyone knew my feelings about it."[21] Aides to Ford recount that he told his senior assistant, Bob Hartman, "I want to be damn sure all that stuff is out of here," within hours of assuming the presidency on August 9, 1974. That was a Friday. On Monday, August 12, Gerald Ford addressed a joint session of Congress and made a point of saying there would be no taping or bugging in his administration. President Ford personally seems to have stuck to that intention.[22] Indeed, in a taped conversation with Henry Kissinger, included in this collection, Ford takes pains to let Kissinger know they are being recorded, and to ask his permission to proceed.

Yet, despite his public posture on wiretaps and their kin, it seems highly likely that, following the practice of the six presidents before him, someone in the Ford administration actually did engage in extensive taping. President Ford's paper records are replete with verbatim transcripts of meetings of every sort—with foreign leaders, with cabinet advisers, with congressional figures, sessions of the National Security Council, and more—that appear to have been made from such recordings. The standard explanation has been that notetakers constructed the meeting records. However, at least one of these transcripts, typed in the form common to draft documents before they were finalized, bears the notation "end of tape 1." It is impossible to know who did the taping or how extensive the practice was, but the evidence seems to argue that the Ford White House taped events and then destroyed the tapes as soon as paper records had been created. In any event, only two audio recordings made by President Ford in office survive, and they are both included here.

* * *

Throughout the decades when presidents employed dictabelts and tape machines to make audio records of their private conversations, a parallel series of developments took place with respect to photographic records, beginning with still photos and progressing on to film and video over the years. The visual medium has its own story, one that goes back at least as far as the Kennedy years, and involves an unusual and virtually unknown unit within the White-House community.

Although officials could find no records dating earlier than the spring of 1960, according to lore, as early as 1949 President Harry S. Truman asked the military for a photographer who could be assigned permanently to record presidential activities. The Navy responded by detailing a senior enlisted man, a chief petty officer, to the White House under the general supervision of the president's naval aide.[23] This practice continued through the Kennedy administration; Yoichi R. Okamoto, who served Lyndon B. Johnson, was the first official photographer on the White House staff. Prior to that all pictures of presidents were taken by these military photographers, or by newsmen and newswomen. By Kennedy's time the practice had settled down to a routine—the naval detailees were assigned by the aide, took their pictures, then developed and processed them at the Naval Photographic Center in Washington, D.C.

There was no formal authority for the photo work. The Navy budgeted neither extra money nor additional personnel to the photographic center to cope with White House demands. When the situation was first reviewed in 1961, the Navy concluded that there was no prohibition against the work either, and that the president's request as armed forces commander in chief was sufficient reason to continue the photo services. But Jack Kennedy was a great consumer, demanding photo coverage for all manner of trips and events, and the Naval Photographic Center, a unit of about one hundred persons, soon groaned under the burden of meeting the requirement. By 1963 the center was telling Navy authorities that up to fourteen enlisted personnel were necessary to do the White House photography, and they were often on call twenty-four hours a day, making it impossible to use the sailors for other Navy work. That year the center spent almost $50,000 on White House pictures and movies, triple the amount of Dwight Eisenhower's last year. The center asked for more money and people in October 1963.

Under Johnson, the demands increased. Costs for film and equipment rose. LBJ's employment of Okamoto as White House photographer took some of the pressure off the Navy, but in 1965 the task still consumed the full-time labor of four to six sailors. At least the authority issue was settled — in December 1964 the Naval Photographic Center was instructed by its parent command, the Navy's Bureau of Weapons, to provide the White House photo services.

Going into 1965 the Navy photo staff at the White House expected to be asked more frequently about motion pictures. In fact by August 1966 the staff was doing *only* movies, and with Okamoto's still photo unit up to speed, only three sailors (two of them part time) were required for the still photography work. This proved a temporary reprieve, however. Johnson political assistants were mapping out more movies they considered necessary, and the Naval Photographic Center was asked to send five more people to the White House for movie work. They could either assign more sailors or hire civilian employees. In mid-1968 the Naval Photographic Center was given extra money to complete all of LBJ's movie work before the end of his term in office.

Just as he had originally dismissed LBJ's audiotape system, President Richard Nixon at first had no use for Johnson's movie operation. In February 1969, Nixon ordered the movie unit disbanded altogether. But the abolition held for barely six months. In September 1969, the White House asked that a news reel camera crew be available on standby to film significant events upon request. This meant re-creating the twenty-four-hour film capability. Thereafter requests multiplied along with the scope of the film coverage demanded, until the effort peaked at the time of Nixon's 1972 electoral campaign.

President Ford continued to make use of the film unit, though to a lesser extent than Nixon. The Navy had a two-person team on hand at the White House daily to cover "photo ops" and sent a three-person film crew along on all presidential trips. Ford's use of the unit increased dramatically during his last year, which included the 1976 election, which he lost to James Earl Carter.

On the technical front, in the meantime, videotaping technology had overtaken film, and by the time Jimmy Carter was president-elect and making his transition into the White House, recommendations were to switch to videotapes. When the costs were analyzed, however, the conversion seemed quite expensive, and Carter made do with film coverage. Six sailors were assigned to the film unit in his day. During the Carter years, the Navy film crew continued working with 16mm movie equipment. They shot about 2 million feet of film, recording ceremonies, presidential trips, state dinners, and occasional bill signings. Carter specifically kept them out of meetings, and if a couple made it to film, they were inadvertent or recorded with no sound.

President Ronald Reagan brought the photo unit into the video age, and elevated it to levels of importance that make the unit central to this collection of presidents on tape. Reagan sanctioned the conversion to video, at a cost of more than $300,000. The unit's personnel increased from six to nine persons, then to eleven, but costs for film processing were radically reduced, permitting the photo shop (at least theoretically) to run for about the same amount of money. Final conversion to videotape took place in January 1982. The object was to provide complete documentation of the president's activities, including White House functions, all domestic and foreign travel, and as much of his personal life as Reagan would allow. This unit is the source for the Reagan audio tapes we include here, which were made from the audio portions of videos done by the Navy photographers.

Although decision documents and official papers frequently refer to the purposes of all this photographic coverage as historical and educational, and references abound to depositing items in the National Archives and presidential libraries, in fact the film programs were executed almost entirely at the behest of the presidents' political advisers. For Ronald Reagan this involved the press secretary and the White House director of television. "Educational purposes" were supposed to include supplying tapes of presidents upon request to the public, but the video unit was exempted from this function in March 1982.

The video operation was supervised by a deputy special assistant to the president, Edward V. Hickey, in the White House Military Office. Under a long-service civilian manager named Joseph Holmes, who passed away early in the Reagan administration, then successors Mary Jane Regan and Elizabeth Board, the unit took its assignments from the president's press secretary or his chief of staff—people like Larry Speakes, James A. Baker III, or Donald Regan. The film unit had an office on the fourth floor of the Old Executive Office Building, but its main offices were in Anacostia Naval Station, in the building that houses the White House Communications Agency. Usually two video crews were on duty at the White House each day to give the unit the ability to cover multiple functions. Holmes (or his successors) usually worked from 8:30 A.M. to 6:00 P.M., with the important starting point a nine o'clock session between the video crew chiefs and the presidential communications people to go over Reagan's schedule and decide what to cover and how. At the communications office, Dave Fisher always looked out for the video unit, making sure they got calls ahead of the press, sometimes a month in advance, ideal camera positions, and space on the aircraft for trips.

The film unit typically covered everything the press covered and some things they did not. At the events to which the media *were* admitted, the naval video unit typically stayed on longer, a little after the standard "photo opportunity," and so might catch a little of the conversation around the table at the start of a meeting. The video unit sent crews to Ronald Reagan's California retreat, Rancho Cielo, much more frequently than the media, and it covered the president's Saturday radio speeches, which the press did on only one occasion. The naval crews were also sent to Camp David numerous times, where the media were rarely permitted. Most important, the naval video crews recorded certain "closed" events where the media were not allowed. For example, when Reagan ran for reelection in 1984, the video unit recorded the president's practice sessions for the televised debates he would have with Democratic candidate Walter Mondale.

Products of the video unit reflected the administration's political aims far more than any educational or historical purpose. One early film was *Sunrise at Montebello*, a ten-minute documentary about President Reagan's participation at a summit conference among leaders of the largest industrialized nations. The film would be billed as testing Ronald Reagan's mettle, though for anyone who knew much about what goes on at these pro forma Group of Seven (later Group of Eight) summits, the premise was rather laughable. Another film was *The Gipper Comes Home*, a half-hour narrated by California's Pat O'Brien on President Reagan's speech to the graduating class at Notre Dame. *Peace through Strength* was a similar half-hour documentary built around Reagan's visit to the aircraft carrier U.S.S. *Constellation* at her home port of San Diego, California.

There were documentaries on President Reagan's first 200 days in office, on the rechristening of the battleship *New Jersey*, and on a civil rights speech to the National Black Republican Council. And there were "state visit" documentaries, which were built around foreign leaders' visits to Washington and were usually given to that person as a souvenir. Seventeen of these videos were created between 1982 and 1984. The most typical product of the video unit would be weekly compilation tapes of President Reagan's appearances, screened for a White House audience on Thursday afternoons. Political operatives would select snippets of video they could use for their particular projects.

Most of the Reagan tapes mirror those recorded by other media who covered the news conferences and official functions, though the naval photographers often got a little bit more because they could stay a little longer. Although the film and video tapings were never a secret from those being recorded, former Reagan administration officials have said they soon grew accustomed to the presence of the naval video crews and paid them no mind. That resulted in some tapes such as the last one included here—the closest thing Reagan produced to the inner office tapes of Kennedy, Johnson, and Nixon. In this conversation between President Reagan and his incoming national security adviser, Frank C. Carlucci, Reagan outlines his key public actions during the Iran-Contra affair, putting the president's own words—quite literally—on the record for history.

In the meantime, the White House video unit has served through the administrations of George H.W. Bush and William J. Clinton. A political fundraising scandal that briefly beset President Clinton in 1997, revolving around his use of White House coffee hours for soliciting contributions, was brought on by activities on White House camcorders that were running while the president went about his business. Both Bush and Clinton maintain they have no Oval Office audiotapes.

*　　*　　*

How all the various tapes of the presidents have come to be available to Americans is a story in its own right. When Senate Watergate investigators and the special prosecutor sought release of the Nixon tapes, Nixon asserted a claim of executive privilege, arguing that conversations involving the president were automatically protected from disclosure. As political pressure built, President Nixon tried to head off the legal case by producing transcripts of some of the tapes himself, but this gambit proved unsuccessful. The Supreme Court ruled in mid-1974 that the tapes had to be released. Congress quickly passed a law making the Nixon records, including tapes, property of the United States (and followed in 1978 with the Presidential Records Act, making all records of subsequent presidents part of the national patrimony).

In late 1974, soon after leaving office, former President Nixon sued to assert ownership of his tapes and other records, and in 1975, Watergate defendants also won a ruling that any release of these materials should be held up at least until their legal appeals had been exhausted. By October 1976, the Watergate criminal cases had come to an end and the United States Court of Appeals ruled that the tapes could be copied, broadcast, or reproduced. This ruling, in a new suit brought by broadcast media, applied to some sixty-three hours of tape that had been listened to by juries in the cases, about half of which had also been used by congressional investigators. Richard Nixon's lawyers argued that the former president would suffer mental anguish from release of the materials, that release violated his privacy, and that the audiotapes were different and susceptible to far more offensive uses than written transcripts of the same material. That case went to the Supreme Court, which found against Nixon in 1976. From May 1980 until September 1984, it was possible to listen to excerpts of the Nixon Watergate tapes at the National Archives in Washington.

The former president used a similar argument in another suit that pertained to the full range of his tapes, and lost that suit in 1979 and at the appellate level in 1982. The Supreme Court let that ruling stand late the same year by not accepting the case for review. President Nixon did succeed in establishing one legal point, however, which was that there was a distinction between official material on the recordings and personal comments mixed into the same conversations (listeners will discover that the Nixon tapes contain numerous deletions of conversation deemed personal). That meant reviewing all Nixon tapes for the presence of personal material, including those previously open to the public. Nixon did lose a subsequent court case that sought to reserve to himself the power to decide what was a valid personal deletion. Those determinations were made by the Archivist of the United States until 2002, when an executive order by President George W. Bush reserved decisions to the sitting president.

Additional legal action focused on the question of original ownership of the records, on which hinged the issue of compensation to the former president. Federal courts agreed with Nixon, who passed away in April 1994. The Nixon estate abandoned efforts to keep the tapes under wraps, reaching an agreement with the National Archives in 1996 that enabled progressive release of the tapes. But a final suit demanded that all personal and private tapes (believed to total about 819 hours out of about 3,700) be returned to the family. The National Archives at one time estimated that as many as 17,000 edits would be necessary to cull personal material out of the official tapes. The Nixon estate valued the records at more than $200 million but eventually settled for $18 million.

Only those presidents who held office after 1978, when Congress passed and President Jimmy Carter signed the Presidential Records Act, created their tapes (primarily video by this time) understanding that these were the property of the United States. That group includes Ronald Reagan, George H.W. Bush, William J. Clinton, and George W. Bush. Previous incumbents, during the "audio era," owned their records but deeded them to the United States. Nevertheless the 1982 court decisions confirming public access to the Nixon tapes were taken as marching orders by officials holding custody of earlier presidents' tapes. Virtually all the presidential tapes we have today have been made available since 1982, as the direct or indirect result of the Watergate litigation.

Although the Kennedy tapes remained property of the family, they were held in trust by the National Archives. President Kennedy's former secretary Evelyn Lincoln moved to the National Archives with the tapes and worked there until 1965, putting the slain president's records in order and, on the tapes, attempting to compile some logs and lists, as well as transcripts requested by Robert F. Kennedy (some of which he used for his book *Thirteen Days* on the Cuban Missile Crisis). The Kennedy materials moved from Washington to a federal records center in Waltham, Massachusetts, in three shipments in 1965, 1969, and 1971. The tapes most likely formed part of the first shipment. Archives officials report that until 1975 they did not have the combinations to the safes in which the tapes were stored. The family deeded the records to the United States in February 1965, but the tapes, not understood to form part of this gift, remained in control of their representatives until 1973.

When Watergate brought the whole issue of tapes to public attention that year, and the Kennedy Presidential Library publicly revealed the existence of Kennedy tapes, the Kennedy dictabelts were also restored to their place in the set. The remaining recordings were transferred to National Archives control in stages, a process completed when the Library changed the combinations on the safes containing the materials on August 15, 1975. In May 1976, an addendum to the deed of gift formally completed the transfer of the tapes to the National Archives, of which all the presidential libraries are part. After extensively logging and listing of the Kennedy tapes and separating out private materials, in early February 1982 the Kennedy Library made public a list of 325 meetings and 275 telephone conversations that President Kennedy had recorded.

The Library at first intended to create transcripts of all the tapes before opening them to the public. Archivists actually did create a few transcripts, the most extensive being a set regarding the 1962 troubles at Mississippi State University (Ole Miss) surrounding the integration of that school by means of the enrollment of James Meredith. But Kennedy Library officials soon realized the enormity of the task of transcribing all this material and abandoned the effort. In 1982 former national security advisor McGeorge Bundy piqued public interest in the Kennedy recordings by making transcripts of some of President Kennedy's meetings during the Cuban Missile Crisis, in connection with historical conferences reconsidering that event. Bundy's use marked the effective opening of the collection to the public.

At the Johnson Library, the existence of tapes was also confirmed at the time of the Watergate disclosures about Richard Nixon's audio recordings. Library director Harry R. Middleton took custody of the Johnson tapes on January 29, 1973, with the stipulation that these were to remain in the vault for fifty years, and the instruction that Middleton should listen to the tapes and decide which ones ought to be preserved and which destroyed.

Middleton, who worked assiduously to open up all the records of Lyndon Johnson's presidency, listened to some tapes and could not see why all of them should not enter the public domain. The court decisions on the Watergate tapes became a motivator. Middleton went to Washington and convinced National Archives officials of the desirability of opening the tapes and then spoke to the Johnson family. Lady Bird Johnson cooperated in the effort (daughter Linda Johnson Robb says she would have opposed opening the tape but that she was not asked). In February 1982, the Johnson Library made public transcripts of taped conversations Johnson had had before becoming president. Another stimulus was a subpoena served on the Johnson Library in connection with the lawsuit titled *Westmoreland* v. *CBS*, also around 1982, which required the Johnson Library to furnish all materials relevant as evidence in the suit, which included the tapes.

Continuing controversy over the assassination of John F. Kennedy, which led to the President John F. Kennedy Assassination Records Collection Act of 1992, again required the opening of records for a specific purpose. The Johnson Library responded by releasing recordings and transcripts of telephone calls President Johnson had made in the weeks immediately after the Kennedy assassination. These were made available in installments beginning in October 1993. Thereafter the Library continued to open tapes, proceeding chronologically. At this writing the tapes President Johnson made are open up through the fall of 1965.

The selections in this set are intended to offer a sample of recordings made by the eight presidents, from Roosevelt to Reagan, whose records are in the public domain, and who used audio and/or visual recording equipment in private settings while in office. To assemble them, I visited the Kennedy Library in Boston; the Johnson Library in Austin; the Eisenhower Library in Abilene, Kansas; the Nixon holdings at the National Archive in Washington, D.C.; the Ford Library in Ann Arbor; and the Reagan Library in Simi Valley. Because many of the recordings are not logged or indexed, I relied heavily on conversations with archivists at each of these institutions and at the Roosevelt, Truman, Carter, and Eisenhower libraries, for help in identifying and procuring the most substantive and most audible recordings. I also made extensive use of primary sources, including presidential appointment books, secretaries' notes, and contemporaneous memoranda of meetings and conversations, as well as transcriptions of some conversations previously done by congressional investigators on scholars. Examples from both the domestic realm and foreign policy are included for each president, where available; several of the selections from Lyndon B. Johnson's presidency are from August 4, 1964, a day on which the president was called upon to cope with foreign and domestic crises simultaneously.

The recordings in this collection mark the first time the public at large will be privy to the sounds of their presidents at work, from an FDR strategy session on integrating the military, to the anger in President Johnson's voice as he takes Walt Rostow to task for a press leak regarding U.S. strategy in Vietnam, to the incredible machinations of the so-called "Smoking Gun" tapes of June 23, 1972, which brought down Nixon's presidency. If Andrew Carnegie or Jack Welch hadn't just written about themselves but had recorded their daily business, the results could not be more interesting. In this quintessential primary source on American governance, we see how this country is truly run.

JOHN PRADOS
Washington, D.C.

Franklin D. Roosevelt

SEPTEMBER 27, 1940: PRESIDENT ROOSEVELT MEETS WITH AFRICAN AMERICAN LEADERS

Among the longest, most intense political struggles in American history has been that of African Americans striving to end segregation and win their rights. During the Great Depression era of the 1930s, the social welfare measures enacted by Franklin Roosevelt's administration were among the first major federal assistance programs to benefit African Americans. To take 1937 as a benchmark, that year 20 percent (390,000) of Works Progress Administration (WPA) employees were African Americans, as were 10 percent of Civilian Conservation Corps (CCC) enrollees. There were 10,000 African American children in WPA nursery schools, 5,000 instructors teaching African Americans to read and write, 35,000 minority students helped by the National Youth Association in high schools and colleges, schools for African Americans being built in the South, and low-income housing being built throughout the land. Nevertheless, segregation remained entrenched, not only in the South. For example, African Americans in the CCC were concentrated in their own camps. Much remained to be done.

As war clouds gathered over Europe and in the Far East, and the United

States began expanding its armed forces and gearing up the war industry, civil rights leaders started to focus on the persistent segregation that existed in those sectors as throughout society. In the U.S. Navy, with some 81,000 sailors in 1932, there had been just 441 African Americans. The numbers were higher by 1940 — as will be seen in the conversation that follows — but the true situation was even more dismal than the low numbers indicate, for opportunity was virtually denied to African American seamen. In the Army, African Americans had long been concentrated in just a handful of units. Four regiments of infantry and cavalry (a regiment of infantry typically consisted of about 3,300 men, with roughly 1,000 in a cavalry regiment) in the Regular Army and three in the National Guard made up the sum total of African American participation, with several of them at skeleton strength. Only a few African Americans had ever graduated from West Point, and none from the Naval Academy. The only high ranking African American officer was Colonel Benjamin O. Davis Sr., even as war approached and America's military buildup created a huge need for leaders. Beyond that was the question of participation of African Americans in defense industries.

At the same time, the importance of African American political participation was growing. A shift in voting away from the Republican legacy of Abraham Lincoln and to that of the Democrats had helped elect Franklin D. Roosevelt in 1932. Four years later, Walter White of the National Association for the Advancement of Colored People (NAACP) felt justified in sending a paper to the White House arguing that, with FDR's second election coming up, African American votes could prove decisive in no fewer than seventeen states. In the 1940 election, with President Roosevelt trying for an unprecedented third term, the African American constituency had assumed such weight that FDR's opponent, Republican Wendell Willkie, made his own bid for African American support.

What President Roosevelt could do for African Americans was very much on the table in 1940. Legislation to outlaw lynchings, and on other civil rights issues, had failed in Congress in recent years, victim to the ability of segregationist die-hards to filibuster. Roosevelt felt boxed in by political factors such as his need for southern Democrats. First Lady Eleanor Roosevelt, a committed New Dealer and a strong supporter of civil rights, increasingly figured as FDR's ambassador to the African Americans. Her actions would be crucial in the events leading up to the Oval Office meeting recorded here.

Stymied on other fronts, African American leaders in the 1940 campaign concentrated on participation in the national defense. That summer, depressed with their circumstances in the Navy, fifteen African American mess attendants aboard the cruiser *Philadelphia* had published a complaint in a Pittsburgh newspaper. For their efforts, the seamen were court-martialed and drummed out of the service with dishonorable discharges. Other African Americans trying to enlist or to become pilots were turned away from recruiting stations or training programs.

On September 14, 1940, the Congress passed a bill creating the Selective Service system, the first peacetime draft of Americans into the armed forces in U.S. history. The law provided for drafting 800,000 Americans and specified there should be no restriction as to race in the process. Of course this conflicted with the reality of African Americans in the military, who numbered only 2 percent of the force in 1939 (4,700 of almost 500,000, with just two officers), and for whom, though the War Department had theoretical plans to increase participation, there were no practical provisions. On September 16, the annual convention of the overwhelmingly African American Brotherhood of Sleeping Car Porters passed a resolution appealing to President Roosevelt, Congress, and the War and Navy Departments to eliminate discrimination in military service and defense industries. Eleanor Roosevelt attended this New York convention and dined with the Brotherhood's president, A. Philip Randolph. The African American leader had sought a meeting with Roosevelt but had heard nothing. Eleanor intervened directly with FDR and an Oval Office meeting was arranged for September 27.

The African American leaders who came to the White House that day included Randolph, Walter White of the NAACP, and T. Arnold Hill, former head of the National Urban League. They met with President Roosevelt and a full panoply of top officials of the War and Navy Departments. Secretary of War Henry L. Stimson[1] and Secretary of the Navy Frank Knox were both in attendance. As the following conversation demonstrates, the senior officials were well aware of the problems, but barely willing to seek solutions. President Roosevelt talked about improvements, but did not see past the traditional style of segregated units of African Americans. His suggestion of more African American bands on Navy ships was particularly laughable. One wonders how Randolph, White, and Hill managed to stay quiet in response to some of this palaver. One indication of their frustration lies in the fact that they had brought along a paper that sketched out how integrated Army units could be formed, but would not leave it with President Roosevelt. It is noteworthy that in spite of this deadlock the African American leaders continued to urge their followers to vote Democrat in the 1940 elections.

Progress did follow the September meeting, but it flowed largely from administration embarrassment and public pressure. First, the White House put out no comment on the meeting for almost two weeks. When it did, on October 9, Press Secretary Steven Early read a War Department statement declaring only that African Americans would be accepted for pilot training and that segregated Army units would be formed in all branches of the service. Early intimated that the African American leaders had agreed with this policy. The Early statement brought a joint denial by Randolph, White, and Hill, who accused the Roosevelt administration of betrayal. President Roosevelt responded with a public letter in late October which indicated that he regretted the misinterpretation and stated that what the group had agreed upon at the September 27 meeting was that African Americans would be enlisted for all aspects of military service, including combat roles. Not long afterward, Colonel Davis received a promotion to brigadier general.

For Philip Randolph the frustrations boiled over. On a railroad tour through the South to visit the divisions of his union in early 1941, Randolph began to call for African Americans to march on Washington. He issued his official call from New York headquarters on January 15. An outpouring of African American determination followed. Where Randolph had originally envisioned a march by perhaps 10,000 African Americans, it soon seemed there could be 25,000 or more. By June, Randolph foresaw as many as 100,000 protesters. The event was scheduled for July 1. President Roosevelt strenuously attempted to head off this demonstration, sending at different times as emissaries the head of the National Youth Association as well as Eleanor Roosevelt. On June 18 he held another White House meeting with Philip Randolph and Walter White, with both Frank Knox and Henry Stimson definitely in attendance. On June 25 President Roosevelt signed Executive Order 8802 on Fair Employment Practices, establishing a Fair Employment Practices Commission (FEPC) with the authority to prevent discrimination in employment in war industries. Randolph called off the march on Washington.

The exigencies of World War II inevitably brought African Americans to a new level of participation in the U.S. military. Before it ended there were 900,000 African Americans in uniform, 7,000 of them officers. There were African American achievements on the battlefield on land, at sea, and in the air. The Navy commissioned its first combat vessel entirely crewed by African Americans in 1944. It abolished separate training for African Americans in all Navy schools and programs in June 1945. Nevertheless, full integration of the armed forces would be left to FDR's successor, Harry S. Truman. On June 26, 1948, President Truman issued Executive Order 9981, which provided for such integration. Although as late as the Korean War there would still be Army units entirely made up of African Americans, these became vestiges of the past rather than the military norm.

The Fair Employment Practices Commission (FEPC) functioned very effectively throughout World War II. No funds were appropriated for it after the end of the war, however, and the FEPC passed out of existence on June 30, 1946. Re-creating the FEPC and making it a permanent institution of government became a key goal of the civil rights struggle in subsequent years, as will be seen again in the John F. Kennedy civil rights recording in this collection.

Franklin D. Roosevelt

September 27, 1940, 11:15 A.M.

Meeting in the Oval Office with Walter White, Philip Randolph, Secretary of War Henry L. Stimson, Assistant Secretary Robert P. Patterson, Navy Secretary Frank Knox, and Arnold Hill

Philip Randolph: Mr. President, it would mean a great deal to the morale of the Negro people if, uh, you, you could make some announcement on the role the Negroes will play in the armed forces of the nation, [word] make known

President Franklin D. Roosevelt: [speaking over Randolph] We did it the other day.

Philip Randolph: [continuing] in whole [word] defense set-up.

President Roosevelt: We did it the other day, when, when, when my staff told me of this thing.

Philip Randolph: If you did it yourself.

President Roosevelt: Yeah, yeah, yeah, yeah, yeah, [talking over Randolph].

Philip Randolph: If you were to make such an announcement, it would have a tremendous [continues through President Roosevelt talking] effect upon the morale of the Negro people all over the country.

President Roosevelt: [speaking over Randolph] Now, I'm making a, a national defense speech around the, ah, twentieth of this month about the draft as a whole and the reserves, and so forth. I'll bring that in.

Philip Randolph: It would have a tremendous effect because I must say, that the, uh, it is an irritating spot for the Negro people. They feel that they, they are not wanted in the, in the various armed forces of the country, and they feel they have earned the right to participate in every phase of the government by virtue of their record in past wars for the nation. And consequently, uh, without regard to, uh, political complexion, without regard to any sort of idea whatever, the Negroes as a unit and they are feeling that they are being uh, shunted aside, that they are being [unintelligible] and that they are not wanted now.

Voice: I [words unintelligible] the other day that other [word] are trying and trying when [words unintelligible] the reach the highest [unintelligible]. The Negro is trying to get *in* the army. And, and, he's trying to get *in*, in fact.

President Roosevelt: The first level of the main, the main point to get across is in, ah, building up this, uh, draft army, the selective draft—that we are not as we did before so much in the World War [World War I], confining the Negro in to the non-combat services. We're putting him right in, proportionately, into the combat services.

Philip Randolph: Well, we feel that's something.

President Roosevelt: Which is something. I mean, you now know, it's a step ahead. [Words] what we want, it's a step ahead.

Walter White: Mr. President, may I suggest another step ahead? It has been commented on very widely in Negro America, and that is that we realize the practical reality that in Georgia and Mississippi

President Roosevelt: Yeah.

Walter White: . . . it would be impossible to have units, of uh, where people's standard of admission would be ability but what's going to matter in places like New York, Massachusetts, Illinois, Pennsylvania, Negroes and whites go to school together, they play on the same athletic teams; for example, if [name, his] grandson and my boy are classmates at the Ethical Culture School and [unintelligible] and uh, yet when it comes to the Army [words] they say, well Negroes are not good enough, they've got to be shunted aside.

I'd like to suggest this idea, even though it may sound fantastic at this time, that in the states where there isn't a tradition of segregation, that we might start to experiment with organizing a division or regiment and let them be all Americans and not black Americans and then white—working together.

Now, there are a number of reasons why I think that would be sound, ah among them that I think it would be a practical work of democracy and I think it would be less expensive and less troublesome in, in the long run.

President Roosevelt: Well, you see now Walter, my, my general report on it is this—that the thing is we have to work into this. Now, for instance, you take, take, the, the divisional organization, what are your new divisions? About 12,000 men.

Assistant Secretary Robert Patterson: Fourteen.

President Roosevelt: Yes, and twelve, fourteen thousand men. Now suppose in there that you have, one, ah, what do they call it? What do they call the gun units. Artillery?

Assistant Secretary Patterson: [unintelligible]

President Roosevelt: What?

Assistant Secretary Patterson: [unintelligible]

President Roosevelt: One battery, with Negro troops, and officers, there in that battery, uh, like for instance New York, and another regiment, or battalion, that's a half of a regiment, of Negro troops. They go into a division, a whole division of 12,000. And you may have a Negro regiment, you would, here, and right over here on my right in line would be a white regiment in the same division maintain, maintain the divisional, organization, the divisional organization. Now what happens? After a while, in the case of the war those people get shifted from one to the other. The thing that sort of [unintelligible] you would have one, one battery out of a, out of a regiment of artillery, ah, that would be a Negro battery with, a white battery here and another Negro battery, and, and gradually working in the field together. You may back into what you're talking about.

Walter White: What we're suggest is that in fact [unintelligible] we can work [words] meeting the reality [unintelligible]

Philip Randolph: And I think, Mr. President, to supplement, if I may, the position of Mr. White, uh, it is that idea is working in the field of organized labor. Now, for instance there are unions where you have Negro business agents

President Roosevelt: Sure

Philip Randolph: Whereas, 90% of the members are white.

President Roosevelt: Yeah.

Philip Randolph: And you also, you even have Negroes who are parts of unions in Birmingham, Alabama, in the same union with the whites. [Roosevelt mumbles] And if it can, if can work out on the basis of democracy and the, in the trade unions, it can in the Army. And

President Roosevelt: Yes. You take the Hudson River where, where Judge Patterson and I come from we have a lot of brickworks.

Philip Randolph: Oh yes

President Roosevelt: Up around Fishkill, the old brickworks. Heavens, they have the same union.

Philip Randolph: Exactly.

President Roosevelt: There are the white workers and the Negro workers in those brickworks.

Philip Randolph: Quite so.

President Roosevelt: And they get along no trouble at all!

Philip Randolph: Quite so, and when they come out of their union and into the Army, well now there isn't much justification for separating them, don't you know. Uh, Colonel Knox, ah, as to the Navy, what, ah, is the position of the Navy on the integration of the Negro brigades?

Secretary Frank Knox: Well, you have a factor in the Navy, which is not present in the Army, and that is that these men live aboard ships. And if I said to you that I was going to take Negroes into a ship's company [words] to the Negro. In the worst [unintelligible]. And you can't have separate ships with multiple Negro crews because every Navy man has to be interchangeable.

President Roosevelt: If you had a northern ship and a southern ship it'd be different. But you can't *do* that. [laughs]

Secretary Knox: [words] with the President's suggestion on some way of providing a way [words] to serve the Navy without raising the question that comes from putting white men and black men living together in the same ship.

President Roosevelt: Well, I think the proportion is going up, and one very good reason is, that in the old days, ah up to two years ago, up to the time the Philippines Independence Act, effectively [words] 75 or 80 percent of the, ah, mess people on board ship, uh, were Filipinos, and of course, we're taking in no Filipinos now, for the last, what is it? Four years ago, two years ago?

Voice: Two years.

President Roosevelt: We're taking in no Filipinos whatsoever, and what we're doing, where we're replacing them with, uh, with colored boys [words] mess captain and so forth, and so on. And in that field they can get up to, ah, the highest rating of a chief petty officer. The ah, the, the head mess attendant, ah, who's aboard a battleship is a chief petty officer. Which is, which is, which is, which is.

Philip Randolph: Is there at this time, a single Negro in the Navy of officer status?

President Roosevelt: Yes.

Secretary Knox: There are 4,007 Negroes out of a total force at the beginning of 1940 of 139,000 [unintelligible]. They are all messman's rank. [Voices overlap]

President Roosevelt: I think, another thing, another thing Frank, about, uh, I, forgot to mention, I thought of it about, oh, a month ago, and that is this: We are training a certain number of musicians on board ship. Ah, the ship's band, and there's no reason why we shouldn't have a colored band on some of these ships, because they're darn good at it. And that's something we should look into.

Voices: [unintelligible]

President Roosevelt: It will increase the opportunity, that's what we're after.

Voices: [unintelligible]

President Roosevelt: They, they may develop a leader of the band.

Voices: [unintelligible]

President Roosevelt: Fine, fine.

Walter White: . . . gentleman [word] millionaire, I believe that. Uh, but, there are two main, uh, points, that had fairly great, ah disturbing influence on me, though: one [words] tries to set down as briefly as possible, in a memorandum showing the things that concern Negroes most. There is discrimination in the Army and in the Navy, and the armed forces the Air Corps, in the matter of [word] though, [words] in the labor in the navy yards, and particularly in industry which has contracts for the national defense program. I've just completed an article, I hope it's the last draft, for the *Saturday Evening Post*, which I gather you know about,

President Roosevelt: Yeah, yeah.

Walter White: But in Pensacola, for example, there is a, an apprentice school, which gives a very fine course, four-year course, a free and two dollars in any expense [unintelligible], and no Negro is allowed to go into it, into that.

President Roosevelt: Well.

Walter White: Um, and apprenticeship is tremendously important.

President Roosevelt: For flying, ground work?

Secretary Knox: Flying, ground crews. [Voices overlap. FDR says, "Good."]

President Roosevelt: I think we can work on that. Get something done on that.

Secretary Knox: [words] We would be able to come up with [words]. We have a lot of colored help in the navy yard. I [words], I was up in Watertown last Monday, Boston, Monday, and uh, uh, there were many colored people there.

Walter White: But most of them are limited, the unskilled.

Secretary Knox: Well, [unintelligible, voices overlap]

Assistant Secretary Patterson: Right now the cartridge case factory is [words], there is a lot we didn't know. In Charleston, South Carolina, they practically ousted all skilled and semi-skilled Negroes.

President Roosevelt: In Charleston?

Assistant Secretary Patterson: In Charleston, yes.

[Voices overlap]

Philip Randolph: [words] comprehend these matters is an acute form of racism.

[Voices overlap]

Walter White: We just don't have [words] and it's nobody's brief to know too much about it. [Words] Uh, Patterson is specific. We have nobody in there

Secretary Henry Stimson: That's why, what I, what's his name? Tobias?

President Roosevelt: Tobias, yes.

[Voices overlap]

President Roosevelt: And of course, on the, on the development of this work, we've got to have somebody, I think we, for instance in, in the Navy, you ought to have somebody in the office

Voice: But we have that

President Roosevelt: Who will look after it. What [responding to last comment]?

Voice: We have that, indeed last time [words, FDR interjects, "Good, where"] or more [FDR interjects, "Yeah, yes, yes," after a few words in each case] awakening the needs

Voice: But we

President Roosevelt: [Interrupts] And right in the Navy Department, in the old days, I had a boy, who was out here [word] by the name of Pryor. Do you know Pryor? He used to be my colored messenger in the Navy Department. He was only a kid. I gave him to Louis Howe, who was terribly fond of him. Then when he came back here in '33, Louis Howe said to me, "The one man I want in the office is Pryor." Well, Pryor now is one of the best fellas we've got in the office, and he handles all my [words] from the Department of Justice, from all of them, he's quite, quite good, he summarizes very quick.

Voice: You've never let me meet him.

President Roosevelt: What?

Voice: You've never let me meet him.

President Roosevelt: You should meet [the] man. Good boy! I'm talking about the old days, we kept a, clerk in the Navy department and I used *him*, people went to him with any kind of question, can we do this, can we do that, can we get another opening there. And do a very, very great service. I think you can do that in the Army and the Navy. Get somebody, there that will act as the, well as a hearinghouse.

Secretary Knox: An assistant secretary, and responsible to the secretary.

Walter White: I want to see you about that. [Voices overlap, Knox apparently does not reply, laughter]

Voice: Putting this out

Voice: He's giving, he's giving what you call the silent treatment. Ha, ha, ha. [laughter]

Philip Randolph: We took the liberty of putting this out. We finished just in time to get one set [FDR interjects, "Yeah"], in which we tried to give you the benefit of the, of the points [FDR interjects, "Yeah"] which are most important, uh, what they're most worried about. And these are — I'm not going to leave them here, you've got enough reading matter — uh, petitions from eighty-five American Legion and Veterans of Foreign Wars posts from California to Maine protesting against discrimination.

President Roosevelt: Yup, yup, yup, yup.

[Meeting breaks up into several side conversations.]

President Roosevelt: I had entirely forgotten about the possibility of a Negro band, to increase the opportunity. The more of those we can get, a little opportunity here, a little opportunity there.

Walter White: [words] feel when I hear we've been loyal. You know, in the last war — when they were worried about protecting Woodrow Wilson [FDR interjects, "Yeah"] — they had only Negroes protecting the White House.

President Roosevelt: I know it, I know it.

Walter White: I've been trying to get

President Roosevelt: Yeah. Well, of course, my letters are increased a bit from twenty threatening letters a day to nearly forty. But I feel all right! Ha, ha. Goodbye.

Philip Randolph: You're looking fine, Mr. President, and I'm happy to see you again. Well, I'm proud to say that people don't like me too. Even in Congress.

President Roosevelt: Bye!

Voices: Goodbye, Mr. President.

OCTOBER 4, 1940: PRESIDENT ROOSEVELT MEETS WITH SPEAKER SAM RAYBURN AND REPRESENTATIVE JOHN McCORMICK

Politics has the front seat in any presidential election. For Franklin D. Roosevelt in 1940, this dictum was especially true because FDR was seeking an unprecedented third term as president. His conversation on October 4, 1940, with two key Democratic leaders, House Speaker Sam Rayburn and House Majority Leader John McCormick is typical of this sort of encounter. (It can be compared here with Richard Nixon's 1972 conversations with Billy Graham and H.R. Haldeman, later in the collection.) President Roosevelt's Oval Office meeting occurred at an unusual moment in time, however, during the early months of World War II. The war raged at full intensity in Europe, and in the Far East Japan was conducting its own war in China. The United States was not yet in the war, although U.S. participation remained a major political issue. In fact, U.S. entry into the war, and the third term issue were the central matters at dispute in the campaign.

President Roosevelt promised to keep the United States out of the war. In his view, America was the "arsenal of democracy" and could help Great Britain defeat Germany through sales of weapons and munitions. Roosevelt's conversation here opens on this very point, with the president telling the legislators how he would react if Adolf Hitler's Germany demanded that the United States halt its arms shipments to England. Aside from the interest in FDR's brief comment on Hitler, Mussolini, and Japan, the salience of the political issue of U.S. participation is clear when Roosevelt begins to speak of the number of American voters who might object to the numbers of planes, anti-aircraft guns and other weapons being exported out of fear the United States might need these for its own defense.

Roosevelt's commentary leads quite directly into a discussion of the press, particularly the news versus editorial policies of the *New York Times*. The press was a particular problem for FDR in the election of 1940, when almost 80 percent of the nation's newspapers endorsed his opponent Wendell Willkie. (Of the rest, less than 10 percent actually came out in favor of FDR.) Although President Roosevelt mentions reaching out directly to the American people — he refers to a planned campaign speech — up until the final weeks of the campaign FDR appeared mostly at military bases and defense industry plants. It was Willkie who covered the country, traveling more than 30,000 miles to deliver 500 speeches in thirty-four states.

In this conversation, FDR accuses Willkie of using the tactics of fascism, making and repeating promises as if they were truths. In fact, the Republican candidate ran on a platform that accepted much of the New Deal, arguing that it could be administered more efficiently. Here Willkie departed from traditional Republican positions, perhaps a consequence of the fact that he was a former Democrat (Willkie had actually contributed money to FDR's first presidential campaign and had been a delegate to the Democratic National Convention in 1924). The Willkie campaign favored a constitutional amendment to limit presidents to two terms in office, and on the international front pledged to resist Hitler. Also coming in for some criticism here, at the behest of John McCormick, is FDR's opponent in the 1936 election, Kansas Republican Alf M. Landon, who is castigated for a statement that FDR was trying to drag the United States into the war. Landon had actually played a key role in the nomination of Willkie, who had been a dark horse candidate, when he broke a deadlock at the Republican convention by throwing his support to Willkie.

The comments at this meeting on ethnic groups in America and on opinion polls, along with President Roosevelt's analysis on the progress of the campaign, furnish a vivid snapshot of the opinions of key players just about a month before the election of 1940. Representative McCormick's view of how New England would go on election day proved mostly accurate, except that FDR lost in Maine and Vermont. Wendell Willkie ran strong in rural America, but Roosevelt would carry every city larger than 400,000 except Cincinnati. Overall, President Roosevelt received 27.7 million votes to Willkie's 16.8 million. As for World War II, the United States ended up in the war anyway, just over a year later, when Japan attacked the American base at Pearl Harbor.

Franklin D. Roosevelt
October 4, 1940, 11:00 A.M.
Meeting in the Oval Office with House Speaker, Sam Rayburn and
House Majority Leader, John W. McCormick

President Franklin D. Roosevelt: You would of course [Unintelligible]

Speaker Sam Rayburn: [Inaudible] a chance to vote for [Unintelligible]

President Roosevelt: And you see, look here now. I've now spoken to Frank [Probably Frank Knox] about these things. The Prime Minister of Japan has just given out an interview, which may or may not be true because they may deny it this afternoon, to the Scripps-Howard, uh, the, the INS papers, in which he says that Japan would regard it, as an act of war, if we were to give aid and comfort to any of the enemies of Japan. Now what d'ya mean, what's the word attack mean? I don't know. It's perfectly possible, not the least bit probable, I mean it's a, it's a, Jack Garner [John Nance Garner, the Vice-President] would say it's a one in ten shot, that Hitler, Mussolini and Japan united might, ah, feel if they could stop American munitions from flowing to England—planes, guns, anti-aircraft guns, ammunition and so forth—that they could lick England.

Now they might send us an ultimatum, if you continue to send anything to England, we will regard that as an attack on us. [Raps on desk] I'll say, I'm terribly sorry. We don't want any war with you. We have contracts, and under our neutrality laws any belligerent [coughs] has a right to come and buy things in this country and take them away. They'll thereupon say, well if after such and such a date you are continuing to ship munitions to England—and planes—we will regard you as a belligerent.

All right, what have we got to say on that? They have [unintelligible]. I'll say, I'm terribly sorry. We don't consider ourselves a belligerent. We're not going to declare war on you. If you regard us as a belligerent, we're frightfully sorry for you, because we don't. Now, all that we can say to you is that, of course, if you *act* on that assumption that we're a belligerent, and make any form of attack on us, we're going to defend our own. We're going to defend our own. And nothing further.

Representative John McCormick: In other words, they [unintelligible] and uh, they're trying to stop you. [unintelligible]

President Roosevelt: Now if that happens, of course, there will be, I mean if that situation takes place, we'd say we're not a belligerent, we're not fightin' ya, we're not at war with ya, but we decline to change the laws of the United States. We're going to defend ourselves, and our present policy of neutrality. [unintelligible] Now, there will be in this country if that happens a great deal of [clears throat] scared feeling, panic. There will be a lot of people that'll say "My God, we ought to keep some of these planes back here. We haven't got enough of these planes to defend ourselves. We ought not to send every other plane over to England. We haven't got enough anti-aircraft guns for Boston, and New York and Washington D.C." Sure it's perfectly true. And there'll be a demand that we pull right in, inside of ourselves, and keep everything we're making for our own defense. [Inaudible mumbling, not FDR] And that's just what they want to do.

Now this morning [sound of rustling paper, as in opening a newspaper] you know, uh, there was a terrible attack on Lehman [Herbert Lehman, governor of New York], because of what Lehman said—it's perfectly true—that the Axis powers, there's no question about it, would give anything in the world to have me licked on the fifth of November. And *The Times* yet, the morning comes out with one of those editorials, what, what, Lehman said, well how did he get that, well what do you mean? That the Axis powers, [unintelligible] Why you're insinuating, that ah, ah, they, they are taking a coercive appearance in our, in our, local affairs and that they and Willkie have some kind of an arrangement. And Lehman said no, I heard such a thing about they and Willkie having an arrangement, I am merely making the statement [FDR knocks on the desk] that they [word] want our defeat. *The Times* says wait, are [word] saying a dreadful thing like that?

This morning, front page of the *Times*, [name] Matthew warned October 3, while the *New York Times*, moreover, this is about this meeting of Hitler and Mussolini, moreover, and I, this ought to be used, I don't know if Steve [Steven Early, presidential press secretary], Steve was going to tell Jimmy [probably Senator James Byrnes, D-NC] about it in the Senate, I don't know if he gets in, the House gets in. Moreover, the Axis is out to defeat President Roosevelt, not as a measure of interference in the internal policies of the United States, but because the President's foreign policy, and because of everything for which he stands in the eyes of the Italians and Germans. The coming United States election is realized to be of vast importance to the Axis, therefore, the normal strategy for the Axis to do something before November 5th that would somehow have a great effect on the electoral campaign. Now, that isn't substantiation for what Lehman said

Representative McCormick: He's allowing for more.

President Roosevelt: What?

Representative McCormick: He's riding for more.

President Roosevelt: Riding from wrong?

Representative McCormick: And they didn't say anything about Landon's statement where he deliberately accused you, I thought he, I was fired with him because I had a very high regard for him. I didn't think Landon would stoop so low, as even for political reasons, to ah, to make the statement, that, the deliberate statement, that you were trying to drag the United States into war. You saw that statement didn't you Mr. President?

President Roosevelt: Sure, sure.

Representative McCormick: That was vicious.

President Roosevelt: [Exclamation] You know, ah, I mean that's a damn good thing [inaudible] took the front page of the *Times* against the editorial page of the *Times*. [laughs] which is very amusing. Ah, I would give anything in the world to get that fella licked. Of course, the trouble with Willkie, as you know, his whole campaign, the reason he's losing, he's losing, strength, is that he will say anything to please the individual or the audience that he happens to be talking to. It makes no difference what he's promised first. Well, [unintelligible] come in and say, "Now, Mr. Willkie, please will you, if elected, do thus and such?" "Of course I will." Then somebody else comes in and he'll say, "Of course I won't."

Representative McCormick: That is much the easiest thing [words].

President Roosevelt: What [words].

Voice: [unintelligible].

Speaker Sam Rayburn: Of course the people that, that nominated him, wanted him to come out and say, what [word] you want [unintelligible] religion

President Roosevelt: Sure

Speaker Rayburn: But by God, yesterday [McCormick interrupts and speaks over Rayburn]

Representative McCormick: The NBC

President Roosevelt: Yes

Speaker Rayburn: The day before you said that, uh, the right thing to do [dinging noise] without amending the law, is to ah [words] uncertain.

President Roosevelt: [sighs] Matter of fact this is a comedy. The, uh, uh, several weeks ago she know, uh, she said, "You know what, Mr. Willkie and I are in New York, well, I'd like to get your reaction. She reminds me of a carnival barker, one of those men, who, you know, is [word] you but wants to get you in, to get some money. You know she's not [word] you as long as she gets your money.

Old Sam Rosenman [Judge Rosenman, an intimate adviser of FDR's] was in this morning. I was fixing up with him, going over the final draft for a little dedication speech tomorrow, a [word] schoolhouse. And he got awful blurry, said you know half and another fella [words], you were right, Willkie is using, the tactics of Hitler. Fascism. Hitler's [word], and that's based on the iteration and reiteration of the same things, so often that after a while people come to believe it. "I'm going to put nine million men at work." [Words] That night, "I'm going to put nine million men at work" That's very, very nice. And after he said it thirty or forty times, if you say not, "I'm going to make a real issue about this [unintelligible] And you find that Willkie's proposals are going to put nine million men to work, now vote for him. It's the iteration, promise, promise, promise, every single morning, noon, and night. Same thing. People after a while get to believe it. And of course, on the strategical end of things, I said in, [place name—a reference to an FDR speech] I said, you watch these polls, you watch the Republican timing of this campaign, I think the polls couldn't talk him into quitting, they're going to show Willkie, ah, in pretty good shape. But the bottom line is then they're going to put him through a bad slump, bad slump, so that I'll be well out ahead on the first of October, and my judgment is that they are going to start Willkie, pick em up, pick em up, pick em up, from the first of October on.

Well you know what a horse race is, it's like, what they're going to do is have their horse three lengths behind coming round into the stretch and then in the stretch, in the first hundred yards he gains a length, in the next hundred yards he gains another length, and give people the idea that this fella still can win, he got time to win, he can nose off the other horse. Rare psychology.

Well, I don't know, whether that's their game, but I'm inclined to think it is. I'm wrong on my dates. They didn't start the 1st of October, next Sunday in the Gallup poll, we'll have a great many too many votes handed to us, five hundred. Great many too many.

Representative McCormick: Well, I kind of

President Roosevelt: They're giving us New Hampshire, they're giving us Massachusetts and Rhode Island, they're trying to put Connecticut in the ballot box

Representative McCormick: There's one underlying thought that I think you, ah, focus on. I think the descendants of the early Anglo-Saxons, they're great Americans, don't particularly love England, but they hate Hitler.

President Roosevelt: What?

Representative McCormick: Now I find up our way a trend among people that never voted, a Democrat, they're voting for President Roosevelt.

President Roosevelt: Yes.

Representative McCormick: They're not voting for any other Democrat.

President Roosevelt: No.

Representative McCormick: We had men, [word], we had cases of men who are, ah, ah, lifelong Republicans. They're deserting the Republicans on foreign affairs.

President Roosevelt: Yes, I know.

Representative McCormick: Because they know that, that, that you're the expression of their views.

President Roosevelt: Yeah. And they ought, and this is the wish is mother to the thought, that old Anglo-Saxon element, composed most of the undergraduates of Harvard College, and also New England. I'm hoping they'll offset the Italian defection.

Representative McCormick: You can send [name?]

President Roosevelt: I think

Representative McCormick: They'd risk my plan

President Roosevelt: I'm speaking on the 12th of October.

Representative McCormick: There's a weakening there, and I, I said to them, I said, listen [inaudible whispering]

Speaker Rayburn: In case they want to speak to him, he said he thinks that the Speaker, the leader would like to know what he might

Representative McCormick: What kept him [words], you know?

President Roosevelt: I think it's going to make a difference. I'm talking on Columbus Day, about Columbus being an Italian, a splendid nation, contributed so much to all of our civilizations, fine stock. So forth, and so on. Like the Latin Americans, the Spanish Americans. I think they'll begin to come back. I had a talk

Representative McCormick: I know they, they, eventually stand out [words]

Speaker Rayburn: Use of [word] in the, he'd probably [words]

President Roosevelt: Yeah, Yeah, Yeah.

[Voices overlap]

Harry S. Truman

UNKNOWN DATES, 1947–48: PRESIDENT TRUMAN, TELEPHONE CONVERSATIONS

President Harry S. Truman made some limited use of the recording equipment that Franklin D. Roosevelt had installed. Truman disliked the system, which may have contributed to little record keeping at the White House in relation to the president's recordings, and as a result there are no certain dates that can be given for these Truman conversations. Due to the equipment, President Truman is the only person whose voice is heard, save for a short exchange between the chief executive and Presidential Secretary Matthew Connelly at the beginning of our second recording. The subjects discussed enable us to put the conversations in either 1947 or 1948.

The first conversation concerns universal military training and selective service, the latter known more familiarly as the Draft. Men had been drafted into the armed forces from 1940 until 1945, when draft calls ended with the termination of World War II. Before that happened there began a project within government to design a unified military, combining the War and Navy Departments into the Department of Defense that still exists today. Universal military training became a feature of this postwar reorganization after October 23, 1945, when President Truman appeared before a joint session of Congress and advocated military unification as well as universal training. Truman repeated the call for universal training in his 1946 state of the union address. The concept was that all American men between the ages of eighteen and twenty would be given basic military training during a period of one year of service. They would remain civilians during that service, would not be assigned to any of the armed forces, and would return to civilian life with the completion of their training. In case of war the cadre of trained Americans would then enable the military to expand quite rapidly.

With the end of World War II an American triumph, the need for military service seemed remote, and the problem of the day more one of reducing the wartime military establishment of 12,000,000 persons to new peacetime levels. Universal military training was not popular and went nowhere. Military reduction, on the other hand, went rapidly enough, so that by early 1947 the armed forces were down to 1,500,000 in strength. President Truman did not give up. In February 1947 he asked for legislation that became the National Security Act of 1947, which created a Department of Defense, along with the present National Security Council, the Central Intelligence Agency, a separate Air Force, and a Marine Corps of fixed size and characteristics. There was some consideration of making universal military training part of this package, but ultimately it did not figure in the program. Instead, in a Princeton University commencement speech on June 17, President Truman again called for universal military training. He had favored universal training, Truman once said, since he himself had joined the National Guard before World War I.

Only days before Truman's Princeton speech, a fresh issue reached the agenda when Secretary of State George C. Marshall, in another commencement speech (at Harvard), advocated economic recovery assistance for Europe in the wake of the war. This initiative became known as the Marshall Plan. After study by expert panels, Truman appeared before a joint session of Congress on March 17, 1948, to ask for approval of funds for the Marshall Plan, as well as universal military training and the temporary re-enactment of selective service. Immediately after this speech, Truman went to New York where he made the same points at a dinner of the Sons of Saint Patrick at New York's Hotel Astor.

In Truman's first recording here, he is clearly speaking with someone, presumably a congressman, who can help him with the passage of universal military training. President Truman's reference to the Marshall Plan dates the conversation after June 1947. The date is more likely sometime after March 1948, however, because the president also refers to the Draft with his mention of selective service. That "emergency" request was part of his St. Patrick's Day message. In addition, Truman says that the occupation forces in Germany are short by 10,000 troops, a condition which was much more critical in 1948 due to growing crisis there, which led to the Berlin Blockade starting in June. Congress passed the Selective Service Act in June 1948, after which America had a peacetime Draft. Universal military training was never approved by Congress.

In his second conversation included here, President Truman is engaged in the standard business of the Oval Office, much as Lyndon Johnson is in the telephone calls at another point in this collection. Here Truman discusses an ambassadorial appointment with Senator J. Howard McGrath, who is the chairman of the Democratic National Committee. Given the tenures of the two individuals mentioned as ambassadors, this conversation also very likely occurs in 1948 when pleasing McGrath, who would be crucial in Harry Truman's campaign for election that year, would have been especially important to Truman.

Harry S. Truman
Telephone Conversations and a Brief Meeting
at Unknown Dates in 1947 or 1948

[Unless otherwise noted, the speaker is President Harry S. Truman in all cases.]

Hello, are you [unintelligible]

Well, he told me, he told me, told me about it. And I told him, told him that, ah, we are far from a universal training plan and, and selective service, and a selective service request was made, ah, ah, the emergency one, [unintelligible] the U.S. seems to be impotent. And if you can get, ah, swift action on selective service it would be exceedingly helpful to the Marshall Plan.

Well, why don't you get through with uh, with selective service and then, ah, go right to work on the universal training because we got to have it, [name], there's no ifs or ands about it.

You've always been [resourceful?], and you and I have been in agreement on that, but you handle this thing so it gits the most done in the least time.

Uh huh.

That's right.

That's right. Oh no, it's, must be, that's actually the reason, the only reason I ask for selective service is because we need the men. Uh, we're, the, the occupation forces are short by probably ten thousand men now and we're, and we're in a dangerous position with that, uh, same [words].

Alright, alright.

But, ah, don't, don't, don't go [get?] immersed in trading with [word] because we always keep working and trying to get that, but then get the other as quick as you can, because we need the men. But thank you, thank you.

Sound of telephone hanging up.

*   *   *

Matthew J. Connelly (presidential appointments secretary): [Name, then several words, apparently advice that Senator J. Howard McGrath (D-RI) wants to discuss the matter of this ambassador] Butler[1] of Australia. Butler's been doing the same thing. [Words] count for Australia.

President Harry Truman: Mm hmm.

Matthew Connelly: McGrath just wants to know for his own [word] what he might say to him.

President Truman: What have you told him, McGrath?

Matthew Connelly: [unintelligible]

President Truman: Yeah

Matthew Connelly [into telephone]: Put it through. [Connelly then speaks directly to the caller]: Senator, the President would like to talk to you.

President Truman: Hello Howard. I think I talked to General Marshall[2] and to Lovett[3] about, ah, ah Butler in Australia and ah, we couldn't get him into, ah, [words] because what's his name up there.

Atherton[4] has got about, ah, it seems to me, about a year to serve and then he's on the retirement list, ah, and then I've been trying to get, ah, arrangements made for Butler to come, close, close to home here. And I think we're going to get him in one of those South American countries or Central America, ah, very shortly.

No, they're working on it, working on it. But tell him if he'll just be patient and we'll get it done. And also tell him I have a letter from the Foreign Minister of Australia, and I forget what they call him, they call him, the secretary for external affairs, in which he paid him [Butler] a very high compliment, and said he was becoming very fond of him, eh. He had some trouble when he went down there in the first place. And, ah, that kind of set the pace, but they're coming around to our way of thinking, but I think we'll get it straightened out before we get through.

[Audio glitch covers name] was here to see me this morning. I was trying to get him to agree that appointment of that [unintelligible] in New York, and he wants to talk with you. He acted real surprised when I talked with him about it. Of course, I wanted to report to you. He said he'd like to talk to you before I did it [presumably before Truman named the person to the position he was thinking of], so we'll get him in here and then we'll talk some more about it.

All right, all right, you know how I feel. Huh?

Well I think we'll get him in South or Central America [tape cuts out] very shortly[5]

Inside the next [inaudible — tape cuts out]

Yeah, all right. We'll do it just that way. Well, I didn't have time to get hold of you this morning.

Yeah, I think that's very good. We'll do it. Bye.

Dwight D. Eisenhower

JANUARY 7, 1955: PRESIDENT EISENHOWER MEETS WITH
SENATOR WALTER GEORGE ON THE BRICKER AMENDMENT

Among the most contentious issues to arise during the early part of the Eisenhower administration was the question of presidential treaty-making powers. Those who opposed international involvement by the United States had a variety of motives. Some were traditional isolationists; others, in these months when the costly and frustrating—and United Nations–sponsored—Korean War was still hot, felt that international commitments pulled America into unwanted entanglements. Still others feared that presidents were too free to make treaties and agreements, pointing to the prewar and wartime diplomatic maneuvers of President Franklin D. Roosevelt. A variant of that view held that treaties impinged on American life and mores. (Article VI of the Constitution provides that the "supreme Law of the Land" consists of the Constitution, laws passed by Congress and signed by the president, and "all Treaties made, or which shall be made, under the authority of the United States.")

Ohio Senator John W. Bricker, a lawyer and former governor, espoused the last view—he argued that America was becoming a victim of "socialism by treaty." U.N. agencies regulating labor, health, and other issues, and such multilateral agreements as the International Convention on Human Rights, were seen by Senator Bricker as insidious agents of change. Bricker sought to curb this perceived danger, and he induced the Republican stalwarts of the Senate Foreign Relations Committee to hold several months of hearings on treaty powers in early 1953. That June, Bricker induced sixty-two Senate colleagues to co-sponsor an amendment to the Constitution of the United States that would specifically regulate treaty-making powers. What became known as the "Bricker Amendment," Senate Joint Resolution 1, provided that any part of a treaty which conflicted with the U.S. Constitution would be nullified, that Congress would have the power to regulate all executive agreements (a form of international convention that was an alternative to a treaty), and that treaties could become effective as law in the United States only through separate legislation.

Though Senator Bricker was a Republican like President Eisenhower, and though the huge number of co-sponsors of his resolution (which included many Democrats) indicated parliamentary strength sufficient to pass an amendment to the Constitution, Eisenhower remained steadfastly opposed to the initiative. There was significant public support for the resolution—congressional mail ran nine-to-one in favor and groups advocating Bricker's position included the American Bar Association, the U.S. Chamber of Commerce, the Committee for Constitutional Government, the American Legion, the Daughters of the American Revolution, and the Veterans of Foreign Wars. President Eisenhower himself recalled that, "for a time there was a tremendous emotional surge on the country, and this was in itself a matter of grave concern to me."[1]

Advised by Secretary of State John Foster Dulles and Attorney General Herbert Brownell, Eisenhower defended treaty powers as necessary to the conduct of foreign relations, and saw future chaos in a system where the Congress, as well as individual states, could nullify provisions of treaties agreed to by the nation. Ike also reports that he found a disparity between the emotional public outcry and the positions of informed experts, most of whom opposed the Bricker amendment. For the most part, the president worked behind the scenes. Eisenhower met with Senator Bricker in mid-June without result. He then announced his opposition to the Bricker amendment, or at least Bricker's version of it, publicly.

The president had Herbert Brownell draw up a more palatable text, and Ike then convinced Republican majority leader Senator William F. Knowland to propose the alternative legislation, which Knowland did on July 22, 1953. Knowland's version limited the Bricker restrictions to treaties and did away with what Ike termed the "which clause"—a provision that only legislation which would be deemed valid in the absence of a treaty could effect the transformation of treaty clauses into domestic law. Knowland's version also contained a major concession to the president—it made a simple majority (rather than a two-thirds vote) sufficient for treaty ratification. The other key achievement of Ike's behind-the-scenes maneuvers was keeping the legislation from a floor vote until August, when the Senate adjourned for the year.

President Eisenhower's most unusual ally in the struggle over the Bricker amendment was the chief of the opposition in the Senate, minority leader Lyndon B. Johnson of Texas. Senator Johnson passed key information to Eisenhower through John Foster Dulles and marshaled votes to keep the legislation from being railroaded through Congress. According to his biographer, Robert A. Caro, LBJ had concluded that the Bricker formula would tie the hands of all future presidents and that that was unacceptable.[2] Caro recounts that during the Senate's recess, Lyndon Johnson spent a great deal of time considering how to defeat the Bricker amendment while appearing to his own constituents and financial backers to have favored legislative limits on presidential authority. LBJ apparently conceived the idea of having a Democrat, Senator Walter George, propose yet a third version of the amendment that would make a Democratic proposal the focus of action, split the Republican Party, and continue to garner popular support while being more moderate than the alternatives. In this view of Senator Johnson's thinking, it was also necessary that the new version of the Bricker initiative come close to success while ultimately failing.[3]

In late December 1953, senators returned to Washington for their next legislative session. Lyndon Johnson held a key meeting with Walter George. There LBJ prevailed upon Senator George to think about changing from his posture of support for the Bricker amendment to one of introducing a new resolution. According to some of Johnson's advisers, Senator George had agreed to do so before their encounter ended.

On January 27, Senator Walter George introduced his own amendment language. It provided simply that no treaty could supersede the Constitution, and that no international agreement other than a treaty could become the law of the land without an act of Congress. Senator Bricker rejected this formula and set the stage for confrontation. Politics took their course, and all the maneuvering came to a head less than a month later. In a vote on February 17, the Senate rejected one of the most restrictive clauses of Senator Bricker's original amendment. On the 25th, the full Bricker amendment failed to pass by a vote of forty-two to fifty. It now had fewer supporters than the number of senators who had originally co-sponsored the legislation. The Knowland version was then replaced by Senator George's amendment. On February 26, 1954, the

George amendment failed also. Because two-thirds of senators had to approve a constitutional amendment, even though George garnered sixty votes for his bill, that fell short of the required margin among the ninety-one senators voting. The Bricker controversy was almost over. On March 1, President Eisenhower told the Republican congressional leadership at one of the regular meetings he had with them that the Bricker debate had become a thing of the past.

Unfortunately for the president, Ike's optimism proved premature. On January 6, 1955, Senator Bricker re-introduced his bill, again as Senate Joint Resolution 1. President Eisenhower's sensitivity on the matter is suggested by the fact that he had Senator George in to see him the very next morning. The official reason for their meeting may have been more or less ceremonial, for George, one of the grand old men of the Senate and already chairman of the Foreign Relations Committee, had been elected to be president pro tem (presiding officer in cases where the vice-president is absent) on January 5. However, their actual meeting had nothing to do with parliamentary niceties and everything to do with the Bricker amendment.

In their conversation Eisenhower went over much of the same ground that had figured in the debates of 1953–54. Walter George agrees to reflect Ike's viewpoint, talk to Senator Bricker, and take certain soundings. He does not promise to introduce any alternative resolution as he had done the year before. Nevertheless, George emerges as Eisenhower's ally in these key maneuvers. In fact, Senator George did not propose any alternative to the Bricker amendment, and by the beginning of March the press was aware of, and commenting on, the senator's refusal to engage.

Nevertheless, the political landscape had shifted since the earlier struggle over the Bricker amendment. Thanks to the results of the 1954 elections, Lyndon Johnson was now Senate majority leader and could ensure a rocky road for Bricker's bill. By 1955 there was nothing like the public support for this legislation that there had been. Backing of the American Bar Association was undercut when smaller lawyers' groups came out in opposition to the amendment, and a series of Supreme Court decisions in cases involving an American soldier stationed in France, and the interpretation of a U.S.-Canadian electric power agreement, reminded the public that there were advantages to having treaty provisions be part of U.S. law. Public advocacy groups also emerged especially to fight the Bricker amendment, notably the Committee for Defense of the Constitution by Preserving Treaty Powers.

President Eisenhower restated his opposition to the Bricker amendment at an April 1955 news conference, and felt confident enough of the lay of the political land this time that when a subcommittee of the Senate Judiciary Committee under Senator Estes Kefauver opened hearings on the amendment, Ike ordered Secretary of State John Foster Dulles not to testify. Dulles broke the appointment he had made to appear before Congress. When Dulles did show up a few weeks later, after quiet negotiations between Kefauver and the administration, it was to say he no longer favored the amendment that he had supported in 1952 before Eisenhower was elected. The president, as he had in 1953, stated at another press conference that he was willing to go along with a less expansive version of the Bricker amendment, but neither Senator George nor Knowland (now minority leader) would offer such a resolution. Lyndon Johnson, Walter George, and other opponents of the legislation had merely to move behind the scenes within the Senate, and the Bricker resolution never even came out of committee. This great debate was over.

Dwight D. Eisenhower with Senator Walter F. George in the Oval Office, January 7, 1955, 11:30 A.M.

President Dwight D. Eisenhower: Well, Senator, how nice of you to come in.

Senator Walter George: [Unintelligible words] How are you today?

Voice: Where is the [word] at?

Senator George: I'd like you to know that I lost that platform yesterday, as my name was so thin it was definitely, ah, ah, [words] and see what it's like. [Eisenhower laughs]

Voice: [Word—"pending"?].

Dwight D. Eisenhower: That's right.

Senator George: Yes.

President Eisenhower: I find that when I, when I dictate, I get up and I walk around.

Senator George: If you can walk around, why you can certainly [words].

Voice: That's right. You never get tired.

President Eisenhower: The, ah, first of all, I ah, just want to say, how [words] of ah, the reports I get from ah [name] as to how, ah, well you are to work with difficult [word], indeed especially those [words], and I would be remiss if I stuck to . . .

Senator George: Well, uh, thank you very much.

President Eisenhower: The, ah, what I wanted to talk to you about a bit is this confounded Bricker Amendment, which I see coming up to cause, trouble again. I've *always*, of course, been strong in the conviction—I believe that any treaty or any executive agreement which violates our Constitution oughtta be null and void. I'm perfectly willing to say that. I've never yet ah, and I've lived with this now for almost two years, I've never yet found any language that goes beyond that, which can satisfy this disposition without, in my opinion, dangerously weakening the position of our country. Even in its, some of its aspects bring us close to a French sort of thing, where no executive has, there's no executive in France who knows whether he has responsibility.

Senator George: All right. All right.

President Eisenhower: And we want, of course, all [words]. And I, I agree, I, I am ah, I am ah, I think Senator Bricker is perfectly honest in his, opinions, in his convictions. He's seen some abuse of power by the executive, which we all do.

Senator George: Yes, that's true, that's quite true.

President Eisenhower: But some abuse of power Senator, [words—"I did"?] occur in *any* three-cornered government under conditions of 'em all. If there's a weak executive and a strong and uh rather er unified legislature we can have uh, uh, circumstances arise that [words]. We can have the judiciary

Senator George: Yes.

President Eisenhower: Invigorated judiciary elects any laws they [volume surge] ever [words—"had printed"?]

Senator George: That's right.

President Eisenhower: Or you're [unintelligible]. So, we have little, uh, ups and downs, little valleys and peaks, and by and large I think our Constitution has brought us along pretty well through a hundred and seventy-seven years, *and* I'm perfectly willing to [words] Section One[4] of that [words] resolution. But when they take this plain [words] thing further along, I find so far I have not been able to go along with it.

Now, I wanted, to have this little talk, so that, I could, assure you, that there is absolutely nothing personal about my, view from office. I

Senator George: Oh [voices overlap, words "not exaggerating" are audible].

President Eisenhower: And it's, ah, I have listened, I have listened to every side, I've had them, the opposing people, sitting in front of me here. I've had Senator Bricker, and senator, and ah, Mr. Dulles and the Attorney General. Mr. [name], he was [words] long ago. I have listened without airing my convictions. Matter of fact I think I was the first one that ah, I think Mr., Senator Dulles, first one to mean um, um, I mean, ah Secretary Dulles at first didn't even want Section One because he thought that now they'd have to find a new meaning for that. Why did they put that in? I said, "I'll vote for Section One," and I think the entire, everything, that I know of now, sees that ah, that we ought to do something definite to show that we're not trying to set the thing or the executive agreement above our Constitution. But the others, when we go beyond that, I just don't know. I, I really get the feeling that, I know, that we had a long talk just last year.

Senator George: Yes. Yes.

President Eisenhower: And um, and I know that coming from the judiciary, you believe that the only step [words]. But you are not only president pro tem, but you are certainly the most, uh, highly respected senator in the Senate.

Senator George: You don't mind if I smoke?

President Eisenhower: Oh, no sir. Have you got matches?

Senator George: Yes, I've got matches.

[From this point through the end of this approximately twenty-five-minute-long recording there is constant noise interference, as if a soundtrack previously

recorded on this disk is also present on the current recording, with machine noise in addition. We will present only a few excerpts of the later portion of the conversation.]

President Eisenhower: I would hope that because of your judicial background that ah, you would think this matter over, be sympathetic, and see whether we couldn't [words] a goal. [Words] I feel it's necessary to go try to appeal to the country to keep legislators from approving it. I would, uh, hope and expect that we could have an honest meeting of the minds and, uh, trust, not [word] ourselves, we, uh, we [words] but I think, trust the several branches of the government to, uh, work together through the years and not let one, or three or four instances, ah, [unintelligible].

Senator George: I can appreciate your attitude about it, Mr. President, and that you're concerned about it. Frankly. Now last year, uh, we did have a talk, and, uh, I agreed with your position. I refused to go along with the rest of the resolution. [Unintelligible].[5]

[This meeting may have been attended from the beginning by others (witness the voice in the first few moments), or else just before this portion of the conversation President Eisenhower and Senator George are joined by other men. These likely include White House chief of staff Sherman Adams and congressional liaison General Wilton B. Persons, or his assistant, Bryce N. Harlow. Several unknown persons participate in the conversation from this point onward.]

President Eisenhower: We can very [word] actually take a look here, but I've got a letter to the point, from New York. It's from a prominent lawyer saying, "If you want me to head a citizens committee against the Bricker amendment I'd start now." Well I said I wouldn't like to do it now.

Senator George: Don't do it now.

President Eisenhower: No, I won't do it now.

Senator George: Let's see if this committee in Congress can do it.

President Eisenhower: Well, uh, I, uh

Senator George: See if it can't be voice-bagged.[6] See that's duplicates now. I don't know what the House committee would do, about ending this. At any rate, but it wouldn't be bad if it comes into the Senate.

Voice [murmur]: Yeah.

Voice: Who's got the House Judiciary [Committee chairmanship]?

Senator George: Uh, um, [mumbles names to himself] no, ah, not to the man I've been sending to

Voice: Who?

Voice: [name: "Woldman"?]

President Eisenhower: Is it [same name]?

Senator George: Yeah, I wouldn't know. Uh.

President Eisenhower: [Noise distortion] this point.

Senator George: Yeah, I did get to that, at a big briefing. He's a strong guy.

President Eisenhower: He's a good man.

Senator George: He's qualified. [Pause] Then there's [name], and he's pushed it halfway through his committee. He's gone [word] when we're at it together.

President Eisenhower: I like them both.

Senator George: Yes. Well, I'll do [Eisenhower speaks over George] what *I* can, I'll do what I can [Voices overlap. Eisenhower's comments are not distinct among the noises, except he leads with "Well, I have" and then "I should think that if"].

Voice: It will, will privately solve itself.

[Voices continue to overlap, several at the same time]

President Eisenhower: [Words] investigating. Waiting until next week will lead to a great important meeting.

Voice: Was he here before? [Voices overlap]

Senator George: I think I'll, I'll be, that I'll call you Monday. Yes, it was, uh

Voice: Well, I'll tell you, what he might do, uh, is, uh, just speak, uh, informally to Senator Kilgore [Senator Harvey Kilgore, D-WV, chairman of the Senate Judiciary Committee, which had jurisdiction over the Bricker bill], saying

Senator George: Well, I can do that, I would do that, one other man on that committee I would speak to, and I will speak to Senator Bricker. I'll say let's discuss this, I know you agree with his [words].

President Eisenhower: I personally feel now, being that [words]. He has made a commitment to somebody.

Voice: Well, he was just on the point of when he [word] was last year.

Senator George: Yes.

Voice: Especially [word].

Senator George: Yes.

Voice: Then he suddenly got to know, remember that time when he just turned around 100 percent? And I'm sure that [name] believes [words] percent, in there [dog barks].

Senator George: Well, the, they came over here, some of them, in fact, one of them, and, uh, [word] backwards being good. What they wanted was something else. [Voices overlap, city "Wichita" audible.]

Voice: Yeah, that [words].

Senator George: They wanted it to [word — "attend"?] to the matter but they wouldn't, they didn't own [words].

Voice: I'll do what I can.

Voice: Thank you very much, Mr. President. [Voices overlap]

Senator George: And, uh, I should like, uh, for an [words].

President Eisenhower: *Any time* that you want to call me on the phone or drop [word], I'll always [words — "position outside things for you"? — more]

Voice: Kenny?

Senator George: This being important, then, you want to live with it?

President Eisenhower: I, uh, I do both things in my life. It, It's just too [word — "complicated?"]

Voice: I'll be there. [Words] Every incident. It just helps you with work. Anytime you want to come visiting.

Voice: Thank you very much.

John F. Kennedy

AUGUST 28, 1963: PRESIDENT KENNEDY MEETS WITH CIVIL RIGHTS LEADERS

As a senator in the late 1950s, John F. Kennedy had expressed support for equal rights for all Americans, and voted for civil rights bills in 1957 and 1960. These flawed bills had not accomplished much not only because they had limited goals to start with, but also because the prospective laws had been watered down in an effort to secure the backing of less committed legislators. One permitted the Justice Department to intervene to enforce school desegregation; the other permitted department lawsuits in voting rights cases (thus creating the basis for Attorney General Robert F. Kennedy's legal actions during his brother's presidency). Running for president in 1960, Kennedy joined with twenty-three other Democratic senators in a pledge to seek new civil rights legislation early in the following session of Congress. Elected with an important assist from African American voters, Kennedy in office proved much more cautious, and relied instead on Bobby Kennedy's legal efforts and on such executive actions as appointing judges, obliging government agencies to promote more minorities, or extending the mandate of the United States Civil Rights Commission. President John F. Kennedy sought no actual legislation in either 1961 or 1962. African

American and other progressive leaders kept encouraging the president, but JFK feared that a congressional fight over civil rights could imperil his overall legislative agenda.

During that time, Kennedy could not but be aware of the seriousness of the equal rights struggle. African Americans in the South had grave difficulties registering to vote. Most schools remained effectively segregated. Job discrimination continued to be a huge problem. The president's brother, Attorney General Robert Kennedy, involved himself in many local efforts to enforce the civil rights provisions (by mid-1963 there had been forty-two lawsuits filed, as opposed to ten under the Eisenhower-era Justice Department) that were on the books. President Kennedy became directly involved in the 1962 desegregation of the University of Mississippi (Ole Miss) when courts ordered that student James Meredith must be permitted to enroll; JFK had to order out U.S. Marshals and federalize Mississippi National Guard troops to protect Meredith and ensure his right to register for classes. In November 1962 JFK issued an executive order prohibiting discrimination in federal housing practices such as issuing home loans, a measure recommended by the Civil Rights Commission in its report of the previous year. But in May 1963 municipal authorities in Birmingham, Alabama, broke up civil rights marches with fire hoses and dogs, igniting a torrent of protest. Then on the night of June 12 in Mississippi, African American activist Medgar Evers was murdered, further inflaming passions. A succession of marches and protests throughout the nation continued for months. In the South no fewer than 14,000 civil rights protesters would be arrested during that season of demonstrations.

Meanwhile, President Kennedy had begun to move more forcefully. On February 28, 1963, he sent a message to Congress decrying racial conditions, and he made at least two speeches, including a nationally televised one on June 12, recognizing both the legitimacy of the protests and the need for action on civil rights. A week later he proposed a civil rights bill to Congress, but one with provisions along the lines of those mentioned in February, which civil rights leaders considered inadequate. The legislation did, however, contain two items for which activists had long struggled—provisions to ensure equal accommodations in public housing, and to write into law the Fair Employment Practices Commission (FEPC), intended to prevent job discrimination. The latter had been created by executive action as early as 1941 by President Franklin D. Roosevelt to head off a march on Washington threatened by African American leader A. Philip Randolph, head of the Brotherhood of Sleeping Car Porters. The FEPC had prohibited discrimination in hiring in defense industries during World War II. Interestingly, one of the few meetings ever recorded on the primitive equipment President Franklin D. Roosevelt had installed in his Oval Office, in September 1940, had included Randolph and concerned integration, principally in the armed forces.

President Kennedy's delay in drafting civil rights legislation reflected real fears on the fate of such a bill if sent to Congress. Vice President Lyndon B. Johnson, formerly the Democratic majority leader in the Senate, not only a master of the Congress but a man truly committed to forging a new relationship among the races, had the same fears. In one of LBJ's few recorded pre-presidential conversations, he talked with President Kennedy and aide Theodore Sorensen about the civil rights bill. That was on June 3, 1963, several weeks before Kennedy actually let the bill out of the White House. "You haven't done your homework," LBJ had said, "On public sentiment, on legislative leaders, on the opposition party, or on the legislation itself." Vice President Johnson advised Kennedy to hold up the bill until he had enacted other parts of his legislative program to build momentum and grease the gears of Congress. He thought JFK ought to personally head South to Mississippi, Texas, or Louisiana a few times, and give speeches pointing at minority individuals stating that if he was going to have to order these people into battle he had to at least make it possible for them "to eat and sleep in this country," as LBJ put it to Sorensen. To Kennedy he said, "I'd move my children through the line and get them down in the storm cellar and get it locked . . . and then I'd make my attack."[1]

On June 22, 1963, three days after submitting his draft bill, President Kennedy held a meeting at the White House with a number of key civil rights leaders. Among them were Randolph, Roy Wilkins (whom Kennedy biographer Arthur M. Schlesinger Jr. believes JFK respected most of all), James Farmer of the Congress on Racial Equality (CORE), and Martin Luther King Jr. They told the president that African American leaders were planning to march on Washington, possibly to lay siege to the Congress until they got passage of civil rights legislation. Both President Kennedy and Vice President Johnson, who headed an administration panel on civil rights, warned of the political realities on Capitol Hill that stood in the way of a law. JFK maintained that the wrong kind of demonstration, especially any protest that led to violence, could have an effect the opposite of that desired. Reverend King argued that protest would dramatize the issue, mobilize support outside the South, and permit people to express their legitimate grievances in a disciplined, non-violent way. Kennedy reiterated the importance of his own problems with the Congress and emphasized the need to stay in contact, which sounded like little help for the civil rights leaders, but he told a press conference some weeks later that peaceful assembly to seek redress of grievances was in the great tradition of American democracy.

The president's concerns did influence preparations for the march. The idea had initially been conceived in Birmingham as a literal March on Washington — 8,000 protesters enraged by the events of a few months before to walk the 1,200 miles from that Alabama city to the capital. Bayard Rustin of CORE convinced the planners to shift focus, and the concept changed to a March on Washington for Jobs and Freedom that would bring together African Americans and civil rights supporters nationwide in a rally at the Washington Monument. Randolph backed the concept. Although the executive directors of the Urban League and the National Association for the Advancement of Colored People (NAACP), Whitney Young and Roy Wilkins, were at first reluctant, they too lined up behind the march. Major organizations working on the march included CORE, the Urban League, the NAACP, the Southern Christian Leadership Conference (SCLC), the Student Non-Violent Coordinating Committee (SNCC), and the National Council of Negro Women. Also participating were the National Council of Churches under Eugene Carson Blake, who had acquired some notoriety as a white leader arrested during a civil rights demonstration in Baltimore (he was also Dwight D. Eisenhower's own pastor), the United Auto Workers under Walter Reuther, the American Jewish Congress under Rabbi Joachim Prinz, and the National Catholic Conference for Interracial Justice under Mathew Ahmann.

Though sponsors worked to ensure a peaceful gathering, both national and local authorities feared violence. The Army and Navy alerted 4,000 troops at Fort Myer and Anacostia Naval Air Station, and thirty helicopters flew up from Fort Bragg to be in readiness. The 13,000 police and security people put on the streets included 350 Washington firemen, despite their union's objection to this mobilization. The city banned liquor distribution for the duration. The city expected up to 70,000 demonstrators from out of town, and between 10,000 and 25,000 Washingtonians to participate in the march. Asa Philip Randolph told reporters in advance that organizers had taken extensive measures to prevent violence. "Human beings are fallible," Randolph declared, "but these people are not coming here to discredit themselves."[2]

The March on Washington for Jobs and Freedom proved an enormous success. Streets that had been eerily empty early in the morning were jammed by noon. Even the police estimated the crowd at over 200,000 and there were others who put the number as high as 500,000 Americans. The crowd was entirely peaceful. They listened to speeches and honored activists from Rosa Parks to Mahlia Jackson. The worst conflicts concerned who would be permitted on the speaker's podium (regrettably, no women were allowed to make major addresses). Martin Luther King Jr. electrified the crowd with his now-famous "I Have a Dream" speech.

Even before the March, leaders had been scheduled for meetings on Capitol Hill and at the White House. The congressional convocation took place before the main rally, with figures such as Speaker of the House John McCormick. The session with President Kennedy, which makes up our oral selection, took place at 5:00 in the afternoon. The group that met with Kennedy at the White House included Roy Wilkins, A. Philip Randolph, Walter Reuther, Whitney Young, Floyd McKissick (substituting for James Farmer), John Lewis (of the SNCC), Eugene Carson Blake, and Reverend Martin Luther King Jr. As he had in June, Vice President Lyndon Johnson also attended this meeting, which lasted a little over an hour.

President Kennedy greeted King effusively, citing his own words to the crowd on The Mall. The president had already told Lee White, his associate special counsel for civil rights, how impressed he had been by King's rousing address. Our oral selection begins following introductions and some light banter, with Roy Wilkins's presentation. The meeting centered on the civil rights legislation Kennedy had proposed which was now before Congress. Philip Randolph pressed his contention that African Americans needed special treatment and training to make up for their disadvantaged status, arguments he had made publicly elsewhere. There was conversation throughout the meeting about the Fair Employment Practices Commission (FEPC), which the African American leaders wanted made permanent and strengthened. Walter Reuther pressed for strengthening Title III of the bill to enable the attorney general to litigate denials of civil rights, not merely on cases of refusal to desegregate schools. President Kennedy, as he had in June, emphasized the difficulty of securing a favorable vote in Congress for the bill if it contained the stronger provisions. Kennedy presented a lengthy roll call analysis (which we have omitted) of the probable votes in the House and Senate, the gist of which was that the bill needed to pick up about sixty Republican votes to pass the House, given the Southern Democrats and others who could be expected to vote against it. In the Senate JFK believed there were more votes against the bill than in favor of it, though possibles could tip the scales for a civil rights law. There were not enough votes, however, to prevent an opposition filibuster that would keep the bill from coming to a vote at all. Roy Wilkins presented a different view, as did words from Speaker McCormick, who is quoted as believing that a stronger bill passed in the House would put pressure on the Senate.

The meeting went back and forth over the issues of jobs, the FEPC, and prohibitions on discrimination in housing and public accommodation, all of which were central to demands of the day for racial equality. Kennedy and Lyndon Johnson spoke their warnings but were not really opposed to these things. Others had more dire warnings—that violence would ensue if civil rights action did not follow.

At 6:15 P.M., just after their meeting had concluded, President Kennedy issued a public statement he had first read to the march leaders: "We have witnessed today in Washington tens of thousands of Americans—both Negro and white—exercising their right to assemble peaceably and direct the widest possible attention to a national issue . . . this Nation can properly be proud of the demonstration that has occurred here today. The leaders of the organizations sponsoring the March and all who have participated in it deserve our appreciation for the detailed preparations that made it possible. . . . The executive branch of the Federal Government will continue its efforts to obtain increased employment and to eliminate the discrimination in employment practices, two of the prime goals of the March. In addition, our efforts to secure enactment of the legislative proposals made to the Congress will be maintained."[3]

John Kennedy died, cut down by a sniper's bullets, before the civil rights law became a reality. Lyndon Johnson made the law's passage a priority, and its most controversial sections would indeed be its provisions on equal employment opportunity and equal access to public accommodation. The House of Representatives passed the bill in February 1964, but a filibuster dragged on in the Senate for months. At various times, President Lyndon B. Johnson discussed progress with most of the same African American leaders who had been at the White House for the August 28, 1963, meeting (including Wilkins, Randolph, Young, and King). The crack in the wall finally came in June 1964, when Republican minority leader Senator Everett Dirksen ended Republican support for the filibuster. The Omnibus Civil Rights Act of 1964 passed the Senate by a vote of 71 to 29 in late June and would be signed by LBJ on July 2.

John F. Kennedy
August 28, 1963, 5:00 P.M.
Meeting in the Oval Office on Civil Rights with Vice President Lyndon B.
Johnson; Attorney General Robert F. Kennedy; Reverend Martin Luther King
Jr.; A. Philip Randolph, President, Brotherhood of Sleeping Car Porters; Roy
Wilkins, Executive Secretary, National Association for the Advancement of
Colored People (NAACP); Walter Reuther, President, United Automobile
Workers (UAW); Whitney Young, Executive Director, National Urban
League; Floyd McKissick, National Chairman, Congress of Racial Equality
(CORE); Rev. Dr. Eugene Carson Blake, President, National Council of
Churches; John Lewis, Chairman, Student Non-Violent Coordinating
Committee (SNCC); and others not identified

Roy Wilkins: Say that you're right. We think that change the *character* of it is
one of the prime factors in, in turning it into an orderly protest to, uh, *help*
our government rather than a protest against our government, which I think
you'll agree that is psychologically important. And the mood and attitude of
the people there today pleased all of us, without exception. Uh, they came, uh,
I said, facetiously over the radio, but so truly; I told them you'd be here, but
you never told me until day before yesterday. [Laughter; Wilkins speaks through
it] And you didn't tell me until today, when you said, "Didn't you know I was
coming?" [laughter] A man said to me, "We have fifty people here from Port-
land, Oregon, NAACP,"⁴ and I said, "Well he might tell [name] about it." But
I said, "Oh, we were so busy getting here." [Laughter]

Well, anyway, I think that's the reason the report should have indicated
there might not be enough. But, uh, our, both our advisors and our inward
confidence told us that we would have a minimum of 100,000 here. And then,
of course, as you saw some of the television programs, I don't have to spend a
lot of time on this. In fact, I don't have to spend any time at all because, if you
could say so, sir, you're politically astute, you realize that people there this
afternoon were expressing their deep concern from their home community,
from the grassroots, uh, for the advancement of civil rights legislation, yes; but
for a change in the climate that will affect their daily lives. Uh, we who come
to you occasionally and to the Congress, uh, intermittently, and say what our
people want, uh, I say our people, and I trust the interracial character of this
because, I mean, all the people who believe in justice and who feel that the
government should function, uh, to bring about justice — those of us who come
to you and say, "Our people want this and we want that, we think so-and-so
ought to be done." Understandably, you might feel, uh, at times, that this is a

program dreamed up by the leaders, or at least pushed by them for some motive of their own with hopes that they have backing.

We think today's demonstration, if it did nothing else, and I think this was principle thing it did, showed that people back home, from the small towns, big cities, the working people, men who gave up two days' pay, three days' pay, paid $30 and $40, $50 and $100, who flew from Los Angeles, $300 round trip, to come here. It means that *they*, and not Martin Luther King, or Roy Wilkins, or Whitney Young, or Walter Reuther, uh, have dreamed up this civil rights business. They, they feel it in their hearts, enough come here and show by their presence, to you and to the Congress, what they hope their government will do. It fell to my lot, sir, in this afternoon of superlative oratory, to be the one to deal rather pedantically and pedestrianly with the, with the hard business of legislation. And the other gentlemen were free to soar into the wild blue yonder. And they did so soar.

But I dealt with the legislation, and of course, this must be of concern to you. We, uh, we would like to be included in your package, which is now being submitted by the House Judiciary Committee, an FEPC [Fair Employment Practices Commission] bill, for the reasons that Walter [Reuther] has outlined in all of our speeches more eloquently by Walter and by Philip Randolph because they're so familiar with the way we feel. But Walter, uh, realized that the Negro is *terribly* underemployed; and while we do not hope, and do not believe that an FEPC bill will correct all of this, it will help to relieve, uh, some of the tension, it will open up some opportunities and, best of all, it will arouse a hope that if they *do* qualify, that race, religion, and nationality will not act to bar them from the job.

HR405 has been reported by the House Education and Labor Committee and has been, uh, given to Mr. Schuler in the House Judiciary Committee, and that Mr. Schuler has said that, that, uh, if possible, he would include it and it would be given every consideration. We have been assured that in the subcommittee on the Judiciary Committee in the House, there are now 6 votes out of the 11, which would include the FEPC bill in the package as reported out to the floor and which would include also the, uh, controversial Part 3 language from the 1957 bill, uh, which, uh, and I include, of course, in that bill.

And today when we talked this morning with Majority Leader McCormick [John McCormick, D-MA, was Speaker of the House in 1963]; he reminded us that he had voted for Part 3 in 1957, and I believe, sir, indeed, you did also. And he reminded us also that the House had passed an FEPC bill on at least two occasions. And he said that he felt that he could assure us, if the committee reported these two items as parts of the package, that they would pass the House.

This means that the House would be given an opportunity to pass upon it, and gives, in his, uh, opinion, it would pass. He's a veteran of the House, they don't have to dwell on that. And it would mean that the issue would then be presented to the Senate. And we believe that both of these Houses ought to be given the opportunity to say "No" on these matters. We do not believe, and we do not share the apprehension of some people, that to include these two items would do damage to the chances of the rest of the Bill.

Now, Mr. Dirksen [Senator Everett Dirksen, R-IL] was explaining that it had been reviewed. He told us he would support all, all of your package except Title II. And he told us there was one little word there, and Mr. Dirksen is very good with words, he said, uh, "I have not changed my opinion as yet, or, I, I still have the opinion," I don't think there was any promise there that he might change his mind.

Unidentified Voice: His mind wasn't closed.

Roy Wilkins: Yes, he did change his mind a bit, but like always—thank you, thank you, thank you, he did say his mind wasn't closed. Uh, so that this is the, really, the sum total of our conferences with the Congressional leaders. Mr. Mansfield [Senator Mike Mansfield, D-MT] was his usual careful and courteous self, uh, restricting himself to his, uh, duties as Majority Leader and, uh, being careful not to, uh, infringe upon anything else; he, he did imply in a couple of cases that his personal values might not always agree with some of the official acts that he performed. But nowhere did we get, uh, I think, Gentlemen you'll correct me, nowhere did we get a cold shoulder on this matter, nor even political machine-like consideration, Mr. President.

So we are, we are encouraged to believe, sir, that if the, uh, uh, right word could go to the right people who seem receptive to the strengthening, uh, measures that, that we urge, uh, at least they would pass the House. This would be of great encouragement, would throw the matter straight into the lap of the Senate. Now, there isn't any [unintelligible] going on the Hill, Mr. President, we, we are in school desegregation which occupies a lot of our attention; public accommodation, we take for granted that we'll get something on it. It's spoken of as controversial but that means only that it's emotional, we feel. It seems to us incontrovertible that, uh, citizens of the United States must be accorded this, uh, right in, uh, to go freely and, uh, to enjoy public accommodations. On school desegregation, there is a limitation on the authority of the Attorney General in the present draft. And he is empowered to proceed in cases where the complainants are indigent; first place, you must have complainants; the second place they must be indigent. We feel that if nothing else is done to this section, if it is not strengthened in any other way, at least that limitation oughtta be removed. And the Attorney General ought to be empowered to proceed on his *own* recognition of the situation, which is that nine years have passed [since the landmark case *Brown v. Board of Education of Topeka, Kansas* decided by the U.S. Supreme Court on May 17, 1954] and many school districts have not acted, and there ought to be a *prima facie* case for the Attorney General of the United States to proceed whether he's got a complaint or not, whether it came from a rich family or not a rich family, but a well-to-do family or a poor family.

I think, if I, I've summarized this, uh, but if you have any, uh, other suggestions that the. President might, uh, that I've omitted, it, I'll be happy to hear you add them.

Philip Randolph: Well, Mr. President, we also want to supplement, uh, the statement made by Mr. Wilkins, who is an expert on the legislative situation. That, uh, emphasis needs to be placed on the inclusion of the Fair Employment Practice Bill in the package that you presented to the Congress. It will need Presidential, uh, backing, Presidential imprimatur, in order for it to receive the recognition that it deserves. Uh, there's the matter of, uh, fair employment we know must also be linked up with *full* employment, and we know also that full employment is conditioned by the rate of economic growth. Uh, but we also feel that there needs to be today because of the, uh, incredible position of the Negro worker, uh, whose real unemployment is two-and-a-half times that of the white. Uh, and, er, who represents a disproportionately large number in the so-called hard-core of unemployment in this country, because of the being the first fired and the last hired. There, there seems to us that something ought to be done to help them get jobs now; uh, for instance, we have thousands of, uh, Negro workers who can't even read. And, uh, are not in a position to even acquire skills and training, uh, even though, uh, we know that, uh, today in the job market you are not going to be able to sell, uh, muscle-power any more to any great extent because of the march of science, technology and [unintelligible] automation.

Now, uh, inasmuch as the Negro worker is handicapped in selling his labor pow—power in the national job market, because of, uh, racial bias and because of the lighted fuse.[5] Uh, we, uh, feel that some, uh, uh, that is public works ought to be, uh, developed. Uh, unless that is done, uh, they're going to be thrown underneath, because as we look at the problem, uh, it, it just seems almost insoluble, uh, when you have a society that's becoming increasingly mech — mechanized and already where skills and training are indispensable and you have hundreds of thousands and millions of people, uh, that, that can't even be trained because of the lack of the fundamental equipment of being able to read.

But, now, uh, therefore, we, we, we need some crash not [unintelligible], training program that, uh, even if it's not going to reach a large segment of, of the black workforce. Uh, in addition to that, uh, and I think that, uh, we talked of it some time ago in, uh, some of the conferences here, uh, the, the teen-agers constitute a grave problem. Because, uh, they're dropping out of school, and it is estimated that 75% of the group now in school will not graduate, will not finish high school. And yet, a high school graduate is necessary to be included in a friendship-training program. So that, uh, if they're dropping out of school and, uh, they're incapable of going into a friendship-training program to get training, we'll just, uh, where are we going? We're up against a terrific problem. And not only are they dropping out of school and, uh, unemployed, but they're running out of hopes. And I come up against the young teen-agers from time to time and, uh, I, uh, may suggest to you that they present, uh, almost an alarming problem. Because they have no faith in anybody white; they have no faith, uh, in the Negro leadership; they have no faith in, in, in God; they have no faith in the government. In other words, they believe that the hand of society is against them; and this is the situation that you find with respect to Negro youth in the various centers of the country. Uh, we suggest the only way to meet this situation is to, uh, compel them to take training; uh, some time to acquire some kind of skills, uh, uh, in order that they may be able to, uh, play their role in this automated society.

And, uh, I, I know that the trade union people, uh, don't want to talk about, uh, uh, too much of a tracking program with respect to [unintelligible] heavy steel and, and so forth, because, uh, uh, the old, uh, doctrine of, uh, a long term period for the acquisition of steel still obtains in the, in the, in the autonomous unions today. Uh, I don't know, uh, how, uh, sound it is, but I ought to question, uh, a policy which requires, uh, a boy to spend 5 years to become a brother [In this usage, "brother" means union member], when it only takes 4 years to become a doctor. Uh, this is a situation that, uh, seems incredible, but nonetheless, that's the procedure and, uh, it's going to be difficult to change the position of the, of the, the powerful trade crafts senior [word]. But, uh, this is one that we, we, uh, need to meet and, uh, I, uh, I, I hope that it may be possible for, uh, for, uh, these youngsters to be brought into some vast national, uh, training program, uh, to, uh, compel them to, uh, to, uh, go through the courses, and, uh, acquire skills. Now in New York, uh, Local 3 of the Electrical Workers Union, we, we have the first, uh, extensive and comprehensive program for, uh, the training of teenagers in a trade that derived, as a matter of fact, I've never known two Negro machinists to be given a pension. In any case, before the, uh, the program was initiated by Ben Arsdale, Ben Arsdale of the, uh, Electrical Workers Union, who is the president of the [word] body there in New York.

Now, I had the opportunity to talk with the, the Vice President, uh, Johnson, and the Secretary of Labor, uh, Wirtz [Willard Wirtz, Secretary of Labor, 1962–69], here with, Roy Wilkins and, uh, Whitney Young and a number of others, and I was amazed at the work that is being done here, and, uh, I want to say that progress is being made. There's no doubt about that. Of course, uh, from the point of view of the conscience that we are in, uh, [unintelligible] to, to step up the progress particularly on our nation's problem, and, uh, this is our most explosive question. Do you take the matter of, uh, accommodations, public accommodations, and this matter of jobs—they represent the, the power games, they represent the dynamite in our various communities. And, uh, I, know we, we, all we can do is to continue to repeat it, and, uh, uh, we, we certainly have, uh, the greatest appreciation in the world for the sympathetic attitude that, uh, the President has and the Vice President, also Secretary of Labor, uh, Wirtz.

If we had had this attitude, say, two years ago, we would be a long way forward, but, uh, this we didn't have; uh, but now, uh, I think we're on our way, but, uh, we need to find some kind of device, some kind of technique, some kind of tactic or strategy that will enable us to telescope, uh, certain, uh, areas, uh, uh, uh, of craft, uh, training and craft education, uh, so that we may be able to, uh, make a, make a plumber, make an electrician, uh, make a bricklayer, and, and make a carpenter, in much less time than, is now required to, uh, to produce these, and

President John F. Kennedy: I like the way you are all discussing the legislation that, I understand, Walter gets.

Walter Reuther: I'd like to say just two things. [Clears throat] First of all, I think, Mr. President, that we all are very appreciative of the recent seriousness that you have demonstrated in submitting the most comprehensive Civil Rights bill any President has ever recommended. We fully appreciate that. We feel very strongly that the FEPC thing is a very critical element of the whole through effort because it, it ties in with the kind of a house a Negro family can have, the kind of a *house* they have, the kind of neighborhood, and therefore, the kind of school. A job is really basic and this is why we think FEPC. On the Title III, [The old Title III section removed from the 1957 act, which would give the Attorney General the power to initiate lawsuits to correct the denial of civil rights] I don't, uh, we believe that, that, uh, we can get that through the subcommittee; we've been work—working very forcefully with Manny Celler [Emanuel Celler, D/Lib.-NY-10, Chairman, House Judiciary Committee] and his committee, and, uh, John McCormick indicates that he believes, and we didn't have to twist this out of him, he says this quite cleanly and openly: he believes that a bill that contains both FEPC and is your original proposal but plus FEPC and plus Title III, would clear the House. And obviously if we could get that kind of legislation through we'd be in the strongest possible position to start from, from the *strongest* point to earn the [word] of the Senate.

Now we have put together, this, this March on Washington, if it had just been a march, uh, then I think some people might have said, "Well, this effort, and, uh, the money and the time and energy went into that, just a one-day proposition, would not, could not be justified." But in the process, we've put together the broadest working legislation, legislative coalition we've ever had. And we're going to *work* not only on the Hill, but we're not able to mobilize the, the grassroots support back home, in, in, critical congressional districts where a fella has to be persuaded. There's no use working on Phil Hart [Senator Philip A. Hart, D-MI; on Commerce and Judiciary Committees] or people like Paul Douglas [Senator Paul H. Douglas, D-IL]—we know where they are; we've got to work in the mid-West, where people, uh, where there, there, there are very few trade unions, and where there are practically no Negroes, and when there is no pressure and where there is no sense of urgency. They're working those areas, and we've put together, I think, the *best* and broadest coalition to do a legislative job.

The other thing that I think will come out of this is, as I said today in my speech: after we get the legislation, that only means we've got a set of tools to work with. It doesn't mean that automatically this problem is resolved. What we have to do is to, develop a broad coalition of men of goodwill in *every* community where we've got to implement this program. And I think that this is what this March has done. It, it, it brought into being an active functioning coalition around this central question of equality of opportunity and, and, and, uh, first-class citizenship. And I think if we led this by practical work in each community, we can mobilize the community, we can mobilize the, uh, men of goodwill, and a, we could search for answers in the light of reason, by rational, responsible action, because if we *fail*, then the vacuum that we create through our failure will be filled by the apostles of hatred, and reason is going to yield to riot. Brotherhood is going to yield to bitterness and bloodshed. So I think that *this* is really a more significant aspect of what we are doing. We *have* put together the kind of coalition that can be meaningful at the community level across this country after we get the legislation, and it could be especially effective in mobilizing support for the legislation.

President Kennedy: That's fine. Let me just say a word about legislation. There's one thing that I, uh, request an indication we presented [unintelligible] The Attorney General was out in Chicago the other day, was shocked by some of the, the size of the class, the reading of the schools, the fact that teachers aren't, uh, involved, and, uh, no visiting at, by the teachers at the home, and, uh, they don't study and children won't study, and that's what makes me know that we've got, regardless of what their color or their mental [word]. Now, isn't it possible for the Negro community, particularly its leaders, to place an emphasis on the responsibility of these families even if they're split and all the rest, probably they have, on educating their children. Now, the last thing in the Jewish community, which suffered a good deal of discrimination, or the great effort they made, I think, has made them more influential with an education; an education [unintelligible] on their children. Therefore, they, they've been able to establish a strong position for themselves. This has nothing to do with what you've been talking about. But, it seems to me with all the influence that all you gentlemen have with the Negro community, if we could [unintelligible].

Roy Wilkins: There's nothing [word] can do about this case, they [word], they really have, uh, uh, concentrate.

President Kennedy: But I think what the Jewish group has done is educating their children, making their children *study*, making them stay in school and all the rest.

Voice: An old message, and all the rest, it really makes that a major effort in the coming months.

Philip Randolph: What they have done that is still [Voices overlap] a young man.

Voice: The major concern is that, and, uh, you have to respond about [word] what ideas

Whitney Young: One of the real problems, of course, the connection to appropriate only small appropriations have to be faced, but. One of the big problems, as [name] said, has been almost predicted, is that when the Federal government has all its resources into the local community, excluding those two places in New York, almost exclusively money has gone to white [word] agencies or new corporations that were established for the purposes of receiving these funds and administering the program, and almost invariably the established Negro agencies, agencies concerned about the Negro and whether the Negro administration, has never gotten any of them. Now this means we still have to, have to scrap, with the little bit we get from community chest and from the Negroes to do this job. I think you could be a big help to us. Pass the word down that couldn't be worse. A lot of people, and a number of these programs, a conscious effort ought to be made to see if this cannot be followed through, apparently with the probable leadership of Negroes concerned.

Voice: What of [word]?

Whitney Young: Uh, to let them do this job. We really [unintelligible]. But, the problem is that if, uh, at this moment [unintelligible] hopelessly, and we need, a tangible difficult massive element. A mitzvah. [Literally, "mitzvah" means "commandment," but it can also refer to any Jewish religious obligation; in this instance, it is used in the more general sense to refer to any good deed.] A commitment, a commitment, a commitment of a massive element. We're going to retrain, we're going to work on [unintelligible] family life.

Philip Randolph: This is what I meant for the Black people about the plan, this is what I meant, for a period of history we *did* get no preferential treatment, but this, the disaster is, is this, if thirteen percent of the total population were unemployed like the Negroes, we could have a shooting revolution. Uh, this thing fits, and I think we have to develop the concept of the credit union, smaller that are faced [word] for our community.

Voice: At the same time, sir,

Walter Reuther: Mr. President, you've got, you were casting votes off while the existing institutions, particularly I think, it is ministers who have such a, an effect on [unintelligible].

President Kennedy: I think so, that uh, aside from all the things that we can do in the government, and, uh, if we can get the Negro community to regard, to communicate to their children that the [education] is really the best way out. I don't think it will solve the Southern problem or the discrimination, but just, they need an indication that anyway that's it in the Jewish community and, to a degree

Rev. Eugene Carson Blake: Mr. President, for ties in to the FEPC, uh, twenty years ago we had Negro college graduates driving garbage trucks in [place] California. We can't blame the younger brother [word], I mean he don't, he has no interest. Now this, you've got to move the openings, they always are telling each other they were written on the upbringing and they were telling us there weren't any one qualified and so long, and, uh. Two things just seem to be how this works, I think. This will be done if you can get the opening, the assured opening, because, uh, I think that the Negro community will push as hard as anybody else to get education and get ahead if, uh, if it isn't that built-in, uh, discouragement.

President Kennedy: Well, let's talk a little about these, uh, [unintelligible].

Floyd McKissick: Well, may I tell you something on this same thing, we are very greatly familiar with this program that links the North and South. This program is

Voice: Its not the same. [Unintelligible]

Floyd McKissick: But we have a program similar to this, uh, in North Carolina sponsored by the NAACP and CORE.[6] Suitably at which time we had [word] get them trained on our horse [?], uh, for a number of years we have placed some 200 of them in [word] job positions; but, uh, we will still have a great amount of difficulty because this is not an isolated problem, this is part of the *total* problem in that, uh, uh, you can send children to school but if their parents have not been educated, the child, by the time it reaches the 6th grade, can't communicate with his parents most of the time because the parents only finished the fourth. Uh, you have an additional problem in that the parents are not able to stay home, uh, to work, I mean, they have to work, get out and do some kind of work, and there is a lack of pare, uh, uh, lack of parental control in many of the homes. Um, we've also had model care programs in training children to just be equipped to transfer to an integrated school, uh, which is, which is a tremendous problem in draining the resources of Caring for Students [the program] for 26 months. Uh, over a period time, 26 months to get kids ready to go an integrated school because they're going to move so fast. We've been engaged in this, uh, child, uh, in this problem, and this, uh, program of education. We just concluded a workshop, sponsored by, in [place] North Carolina, sponsored by NAACP, uh, CORE, uh, SNCC, the Student Non-violent Coordinating Committee, together, just completed a *direct-action workshop.*

But in the direct-action workshop, mind you, and that's one of the advantages of a civil rights organization, uh, in a direct-action much emphasis was put on training. And vocational training, and, uh, getting the training school to accept the qualifications. But nevertheless, uh, public accommodation fit *entirely* into this because without the Public Accommodation Acts in the South, you have killed the Negro child's chance to aspire, he doesn't *aspire* to do anything; he believes he is not. Uh, these problems are interrelated and interlocked.

President Kennedy: [unintelligible]

Rev. Eugene Carson Blake: Mr. President, I wanted to comment on your point. I think we'd agree with Whitney Young and, that there need to be more resources going into those factors that you mentioned that're so important in terms of the religious groups having sources which have never been at their disposal which may now come. But I'd like to reiterate one of the two main, that is, city after city the, for example, the public school system, if your schools in the ghetto are getting the worst teachers, basically, the budgets allocated for those schools, on a library basis, on a teacher basis, right down the line are [unintelligible] diminished [word].

President Kennedy: Well, let me just say a word about this, uh, our problem about FEPC, and uh. In fact our problem is legislation. Because uh, we're, we have a very, uh, [unintelligible] difficulty. We just need a count of how our votes look. [President Kennedy begins a lengthy analysis of the vote breakdowns in Congress for a civil rights bill, showing that in the Senate, especially, there will be problems passing the bill.] Now if you get sixty Republicans for the FEPC, I'm for it. One million percent. [Voices overlap] Anyway, we might as well have FEPC in there and get more of a chance to get the whole thing.

Voice: We get our fellas together [Voices overlap].

President Kennedy: Jimmy Roosevelt's [eldest son of President Franklin D. Roosevelt] been talking to us, Kastenmeier of Wisconsin [Rep. Robert W. Kastenmeier, D-WI] loves it, but I think, I've seen all those fellas, the vice president's seen them a lot longer than I have. To get it all in the Senate, [names], we finally end up with eighteen to twenty votes in the Senate. [unintelligible] And it may be that we can get fifty Republicans. Now we, let's all start off with that assumption. You have to get fifty Republicans to get *this* bill by. If we can get [word] Republicans to go ahead and put FEPC, I'm for it. On the other hand, I don't want to have the whole thing voted down in the House.

Voice: We understand that.

President Kennedy: It may not be. It may be that what, if anybody votes Republican nowadays, and would vote with FEPC, I don't know. We have to find out whether they would. Obviously we'd be better off if we had FEPC in there, if we're going to have to peel something off in the Senate. Now [word] me when I'm getting into the Senate if we can't get cloture and that's a pretty tough count. You'd be better off if you had more in the bill, you'd be able to make some adjustments and probably pick up some votes. So I would just, I would rather have FEPC in [unintelligible] Next year, the year after, than to do it now. So it's really just a question, I think we've got to try to get the bill by, and if we can get 60 Republicans or close to it for FEPC then I'm for that. And if that's cold, then we'll be glad to stay in touch with you. It's a head count, really, John, and we now

Voice: I think we

Rev. Martin Luther King: Would the same thing apply to (clears throat) Title III of the old bill, they're extending the powers of the Attorney General? Is there as much, uh, [Voices overlap] opposition to that as FEPC?

President Kennedy: Well, ah, they concentrated their attention to, uh, I don't know that, uh, Reverend; I'd have to find out about that. And they, they concentrated their attention on public accommodations, they concentrated their attention to settling Title III now. I think that we, that that's why I'm very anxious to get public accommodations by, because if they amend it or modify public accommodation in the House, they'll then go to work trying to take out even a lot of limited [word]. But I think if we can just stay in touch, this thing isn't gonna be decided now, at least till the beginning of next week. We ought to come down on a final count sooner or later on what the Republicans will do.

Voice: Yeah.

Voice: I, wouldn't you say that Mr. Halleck [R-IN, the House Minority Leader from 1956 to 1965] more or less committed himself this afternoon.

[Many voices overlap]

Walter Reuther: Clearly the problem is the financial problem. Is there anything you could do, I mean, and another

President Kennedy: That's right. That's what, uh, this fella

Walter Reuther: They don't get enough credit for what they did. I mean, and all they lost, is all. This was momental [?]. Well, and, uh, I, I, I mean, I'm not interfering in [Voices overlap]. Is there any way you could, you could transcend this thing at this point, or this kind of a thing, why I think that there would be more votes available, but how, I

President Kennedy: One thing at that, I've had some experience with the, one of the gentlemen's questions, uh, is uh, there's always some reason why a guy didn't vote, maybe they did not get enough credit, or maybe [Senator] Walter Judd is defeated. Whatever it is, it's always, but I completely agree the maximum ability, uh, I think when we call it—in fact, he said the same thing: let's make this as non-partisan as we can and from the beginning try to get President Eisenhower to get involved. We've had three meetings here at this table before we put our bill in. In fact, it's a good position, as much for the end as for the beginning, so I think we ought to keep that up. Now we will have a meeting, and at your suggestion we will ask him all to come down here before this bill comes [word].

Walter Reuther: And he'll have his picture taken with you and [word], why, uh, he'll vote for it.

President Kennedy: No. [Much laughter, overlapping voices] We have that, I think I completely agree with your [unintelligible].

Voice: Non-partisan.

Walter Reuther: Mr. President, uh, we, some of us hesitated in making this [word] which wouldn't sound well with it, but it fits in a backhand way with giving them, giving them some credit in the sense that it, it gives an inverse, uh, power to their veto by saying that, that there once was a time when civil rights legislation had to pass the deep Southern Dixiecrat [states' rights Democrat, member of a right-wing Democratic splinter group in the 1948 U.S. presidential election organized by Southerners who objected to the civil rights program of the Democratic Party] opposition, and had, but now it has to pass the Republican approval. Well, this is a back-hand way of, of irritating Mr. Halleck and all the rest of them; but actually, it comes at a place where we have to consider, uh, whether Republicans will go for this or go for that or vote for this or vote for that. And I wish there were some way, Reverend Blake, that we could find out, how to, to please them and yet not surrender our own, uh, honest feeling on this matter. They, they need to have credit for what they, they did introduce a package of bills as we told them this morning, and thanked them for doing it. What, uh, they didn't urge those bills, and so on and so forth.

Voice: But he mentioned on two of the occasions there [Voices overlap] we have to talk about

Rev. Eugene Carson Blake: People never think they're appreciated. The very thing for me about separating the, uh, the package is I bet there are people who will vote for the package as it now is and then say we're on record for civil rights and reasonable against FEPC and before we get something else. Are the means reverted? And all these are at this moment in time, so [Voices, including Kennedy's, overlap] so basic ethics. I just, I'd rather rise or fall on something that can be meaningful because most of the package, except for the train cars, we're, in effect, going into the cellar. And then, the big problem with the [word] we've got to give *these* people something to hold on to, just going up the stairs.

President Kennedy: Well, I wish they would pick up the FEPC, the Republicans, if they really want to get something you can see, it would be useful to make that their contribution to it and their issue.

Rev. Eugene Carson Blake: Well, this is the problem of the, let's just say in this crowd that I represent, we ought to be able to do more with those mid-West Senators, than anybody else here.

Walter Reuther: They're your people! [Laughter]

Rev. Eugene Carson Blake: And I know I'm not experienced in this, except that I'm hoping that in your list of a hundred and so [words] not only willing to sign their names but they also pick up the phone and call their Senator that we're trying to get, people that, non-partisan groups from church and labor and industry, behind the package.

President Kennedy: One of your distinguished lay leaders could be a big help in, uh, Mr. Luce.

Rev. Eugene Carson Blake: I know.

President Kennedy: A member of the organ.

Rev. Eugene Carson Blake: Yes.

President Kennedy: An active one. That could help a lot with the, the Republicans.

Philip Randolph: Well, Mr. President, uh, from the description you've made of the state of affairs in the House and the Senate, it's obvious that, uh, it is going to take nothing less than a crusade to, uh, win approval for civil rights measures.

Voice: I think it would be helpful.

Philip Randolph: For there to be a crusade, and I think that nobody can lead this crusade but you. I, I, uh, I think that, uh, that, uh, uh, the people above have got to be appealed to over the heads of the Congressmen and the Senators.

President Kennedy: Well with, uh, doing the, uh, we're, uh, I think it would be helpful if you gentlemen indicated as you leave here that this is a matter that, uh, that, uh, involves, uh, both parties, that uh, I'm confident, which I said at the press conference, that I'm confident that the Republican Party is for the [words] for this, we ought to say it's confident, and go forward now with this great heritage of Lincoln and all the rest, and just treat it as if you *anticipated* their support. Then I know you won't [word] more difficult for them. [Voices indicate assent]

Walter Reuther: Don't you think, Mr. President, the remarks made any impression upon the hardcore politicians?

President Kennedy: I'm sure it will. What it is in essence, uh. A lot of those fellas think that the, uh, Negroes are, since Roosevelt, they're more inclined to be Democrats. And that, uh, what they're trying to do is play to the South and, uh, with some success, these days, and uh, that, uh. What we have to do is have them understand in view of the fact that it goes much, this issue goes much beyond the Negro community. So, I, I think that it would be helpful to indicate that you expect the Republicans to find a way to do it; you've got too great a commitment in there, the whole party's history, not to support a [word] progressive [word].

Voice: Right!

President Kennedy: Let's just take it for granted for a while. It makes it more difficult for them to vote no.

Whitney Young: In the confines of this vote I, I was amazed to find that Goldwater [Senator Barry Goldwater, R-AZ] had financed, subsidized the Negro [word], come to this meeting and try to talk to all of us as much as possible to let us know that the Senator was not going to go and fight the Republican Party, that he was for civil rights legislation. He voted for it. Uh, the thing is that he still feels, I think, that he doesn't want yet to give up completely on the possibility of what Negro votes the Republicans have got. I, to me it was [word] just to hear this, uh, I think we ought to give him a chance.

President Kennedy: That's right. I agree with that. I would think, I think we ought to go on the assumption you're going to get them, and therefore so many Republicans involved, church groups [words] with them, and I think we ought to go on the assumption we're going to get sixty votes. And I, I'll leave it this way, if, and we can maintain an, contact with Walter, perhaps as liaison on this legislation, if we think that, uh, we can get, uh, votes [words].

Voice: I'm all for it.

President Kennedy: I think it would be easier, then, we can get them. On the other hand, someday [name] will come down tell us what he *will* vote for. [Voices overlap] Those are the hard figures. Maybe the Vice President would like to say something.

Vice President Lyndon B. Johnson: I think that you, uh, outlined the problem with men themselves, how many and [words]. Having said this, meeting here you wouldn't be for FEPC. Now we have to go, as I said to you last time we were here, to be about the states. He's read, read off the list, and you see right where they are. The president's issued the strongest executive orders on housing, employment, armed services, that any administration's ever issued. He's made the strongest recommendations to Congress, so far, and earns his $4 of pay. Uh, now, he's had more conferences in this room over here, where [name] used to hang out in Washington and he's has [word] and he's had women, and he's had lawyers, and he's had the business advisory council, all of them, the Attorney General, the Vice President who says the feeling [is it is] time to get behind this legislation.

Uh, we, uh, I think he's demonstrated [in] his television appearance and other public statements that he's champion of called human rights. There's a moral commitment because that's what's right, regardless of what political thinking I have. Now, there's one thing that a President can do, he can plead and lead and persuade and, uh, even threaten Congress, but he can't run the Congress. Franklin Roosevelt died, his popularity in '37, lost his court plan overwhelmingly, and he only lost two states in the end, in the '36 election. I came here during that period.

And this President can't get those 60 votes, if he turned this White House upside down, if he preached on the television an hour every day. It'd just drive some of those men stronger [word]. Now may be that men at this table can do it. Uh, but, uh, they gonna be pretty hard because, uh, those men have, uh, agreements, working relationships — [voices overlap] knows and there's, uh, uh, Roy knows, they have working arrangements with him and they have for years.

And we just got to get in there somewhere over there and see what, uh, I think Dirksen's much more pliable and much more likely to go along with it ultimately than, I think, Halleck and [name]. The President, uh, talked about getting credit, he called him down here and said, now we want you in on the take-off, we want to know what kind of bill you'll support, we want your suggestions, and therefore I can go and recommend. What would you be for? And before he left, I wrote him a note, said be sure to ask Halleck just what he will support. But, uh, he wanted to go back and study and study and study. Now we studied since May. So it all gets down to how many of those, uh, people can we get out of the others.

Rev. Eugene Carson Blake: I think the key is what the Protestant Church can do, because in the whole mid-West, I mean there are no labor unions. The

Protestant Church, and I think that what we can get them do, I think we can get the key businessmen. Now, I

[Voices overlap]

President Kennedy: . . . national advisory business council and that was the biggest, that was the *worst* meeting we had all summer. They sat on their tails, and, uh, they walked out, said the President says there'll be more demonstrations this summer; that's all we could get out of them. We had all the golden names of American business at that meeting. I was dismayed. So I

Walter Reuther: We gotta get a small group, small nucleus of fellas, who are prepared, really, to shake com—the business community up, or otherwise

President Kennedy: Sure, show me.

[Voices overlap]

Walter Reuther: In Detroit, I've worked with these fellas. I went to the president of General Motors Corporation, I brought the [name] report. I talked to Lynn Townsend, president of Chrysler, I talked to all of them. And I said: "Look, you can't escape this problem. Now there are two ways of resolving it. Either by reason or by, by riots. Now, at the civil war that this is gonna trigger is not gonna be fought in Gettysburg, it's gonna be in your back yard, in your plant, where your kids are growing up." I told 'em all. I get, the president of General Motors, Ford, Chrysler, American Motors, all deserve our local civil rights committee. Now, we gotta do that in the whole nation. We gotta get fellas like Tom Watson [Thomas A. Watson Jr., CEO of IBM Corporation since 1956], Joe Locke, who's on the board, [name]. You'd better sit down with your fellas and tell 'em: Look, this country's in trouble and you have to help meet this challenge. We, we gotta get this, this problem behind us. American democracy and just to resolve this basic internal problem. And they've gotta help do it. And I think that, that we can get half a dozen or a dozen of these fellas, and, you know, kick it up as though they had a, they had a chore to do, then you can make an impact. If you call a big meeting, and you haven't got a little group organized, at best they'll try give it a sense of direction or a little push. Nothing'll happen. The same thing is true of the labor movement. I mean, we couldn't, Phil Randolph and I couldn't line up every A, AF of L-CIO [AFL-CIO, the American Federation of Labor-Congress of Industrial Organizations, is a voluntary federation of American unions formed in 1955] executive council member. But we're not gonna quit.

Philip Randolph: I don't support this idea of thinking that some of the businessmen that [unintelligible] I walk in [unintelligible] and we take this [unintelligible]

[Voices overlap]

Walter Reuther: Increasingly, one of the top alternatives [Voices overlap]

Rev. Eugene Carson Blake: I support this, too. I think the executive community will change its mind about the FEPC thing, when it hasn't gotten through the Congress yet. I think their reaction to FEPC is completely different from the reaction to these other things that we were talking to them about. I think they would love to settle for making this one advance, as far as civil rights are concerned. I'm glad to say that I, I said, quite fully, I mean, that if I was running at this thing right now, I would go ahead on the assumption that this part of Illinois last year, that looks dead [unintelligible]. I *think* the business community has changed its mind, and I'd go ahead to Congress, do the business community all right. And I rather think that it could be brought out on this point more easily than on almost any other program.

Whitney Young: Except there's one new technique.

Rev. Eugene Carson Blake: And only some reasons for what I've said.

Whitney Young: Yeah. But there's one new technique. I mean, you call them together. It would be [word] to have one, two, or three responsible civil rights leaders in the room. They, this makes all the difference in the world. And they'll say to you when, you know, when nobody else is around. But you have one, two of them there, and that'll tell them. The mood of the people.

Voice: I think it makes a big difference.

Whitney Young: But don't undertake . . .

Voice: It seems to me we don't want to undertake [words]. This is *very, very* important.

Rev. Martin Luther King: Mr. President, do you think if we just appeal to the moral conscience of President Eisenhower on this issue and seek to get him active. Do you think this will influence Mr. Halleck?

President Kennedy: That won't. That won't take.

Rev. Martin Luther King: It seems to me we need to do more

Voice: Tom Rupp should really work

Rev. Martin Luther King: and he happens to be in another denomination [Laughter, voices overlap][7]

President Kennedy: I'll see him. Well,

Voice: I think this would be good.

Voice: This would be good.

Rev. Eugene Carson Blake: It has got to be done. I think we could be stronger if we had a few people like this together, maybe with your, your invitation, with, we, we need, we need somebody from their own Catholic Church, will, will emphasize, influence Eisenhower as much as, as I can. I mean that this is a moral issue. That he can be got at on that ground. And of the, and of the, but, if he thinks I'm trying to, uh, push him, uh, but if we can, we can get this inter-religious thing that we're, that we're doing, and, uh, it would seem to me, maybe a group of the tough Senators and Eisenhower *and* some religious leaders *and* some of your civil rights leaders together and just say we've *got* to get this thing out, and how can we do it?

President Kennedy: Now, what about your going up to see him with, I think you've brought attention on this group. A very successful meeting. There'll be more. What about you going to see him in the next few days? Of asking if he can come with this group? Or you could add, get some Catholic or some one or two other people who you think would be useful, and see what was to call the President, ask if he will support the team. Now, I don't know what if, I, I think maybe you get ambiguous answer, but on the other hand, it's *possible* it may have come up [Voices overlap] What about your going up to see him and have it publicized? Then everybody'd know you gone to see him. Then he'd have to say yes or no, using this meeting as a take-off.

[Voices overlap].

Voice: Right.

Rev. Eugene Carson Blake: I wouldn't dream of it.

Voice: Me having to do

President Kennedy: [words] It's just, uh, separate from us.

Vice President Lyndon Johnson: It would be a mistake to indicate you'd ever talked to us. The President pled with him in this room, and I sat there before we sent the message, and urged him to make suggestions, asked him to go along and join us.

President Kennedy: I think you people, uh, would keep Walter in the background [laughter all around].

Walter Reuther: Well, I, I vote, I'm wide enough to go with my chin here [more laughter all around].

President Kennedy: [speaking over the laughter] get one or two other, you could get a Catholic, uh, one of these Bishops, uh, and, or, uh, an alternate, you know a businessman or two, and, uh,

Rev. Eugene Carson Blake: Yeah, I think it would be very useful like that.

[Voices overlap]

President Kennedy: I just want to point out when you leave the press will be asking you, and, uh, I wondered whether you had, uh, do you have a spokesman, uh, should

[Voices overlap]

Rev. Eugene Carson Blake: It's Randolph, because he's booked.

President Kennedy: Well, I, uh, you'll follow me if not, *I* have a statement which I'm going to put out, you know, very briefly, and say:

"We have witnessed today in Washington tens of thousands of Americans—both Negro and white—exercising their right to assemble peaceably and direct the widest possible attention to a great national issue. Efforts to secure equal treatment and equal opportunity for all without regard to race, color, creed or nationality are neither novel nor difficult to understand. What is different today is the intensified and widespread public awareness of the need to move forward in achieving these objectives—objectives which *are* older than this Nation.

Although this summer has seen remarkable progress in transmuting civil rights from principles into practice, we have a very long way yet to travel. One not, one cannot help but be impressed with the deep fervor and quiet dignity that characterizes the thousands who have gathered in the nation's capital from across the country to demonstrate their faith and confidence in our democratic forms of government. History has seen many demonstrations of widely varying character, for a whole host of reasons. As our thoughts travel to other demonstrations that have occurred in different parts of the world, this nation can properly be proud of the demonstration that occurred here today. The leaders of the organizations sponsoring the March and all who participated in it deserve our appreciation for the detailed preparations that made it possible and for the orderly manner in which it was conducted.

The Executive Branch of the Federal government will continue its efforts to obtain increased employment and to eliminate discrimination in employment practices, two of the primary goals of the March. In addition, our efforts to secure enactment of the legislative proposals made to Congress will be maintained, including not only the Civil Rights Bill but also proposals to broaden and strengthen the Manpower Development and Training Program, the Youth Employment Bill, amendments to Vocational Education Program, establishment of a work-study program for high school age youth, strengthening of the adult basic education provisions in the administration's education program, and the amendments proposed to Public Welfare Work-Relief and Training Program. This nation *can* afford to achieve the goals of a full employment policy; it cannot afford to permit the potential skills and educational capacity of its citizens to be unrealized.

The cause of 20 million Negroes has been advanced by the program conducted so appropriately before the nation's shrine to the Great Emancipator, but even more significant is the contribution to all mankind."

We will put that out as you leave. [This statement was released at 6:15 P.M., after the meeting with the leaders of the March on Washington for Jobs and Freedom.]

[Voices overlap]

Floyd McKissick: There is something that we should call your attention to that is partly, uh, that's partly more particular, two organizations here. That is the matter of segregation in our armed services. In particular, in the state of North Carolina, we have given it to the contact Mr. McNamara [Secretary of Defense Robert S. McNamara] and requested them to go. Now, we realize that time is of the essence, particularly in the military towns, where these soldiers are located. The soldiers have been denied the right to demonstrate. Now, sooner or later, uh, I'm afraid, that the soldiers *will* demonstrate. Uh, this is a problem and I'm fixing especially today to [words]. I think that, uh, I don't know how to shame a command runner like [word] Commander in Chief of the Armed Services [words] wrong.

Voice: I think that problem is their problem. [Voices overlap]

President Kennedy: I think [unintelligible] to give you the floor, and, as you know there've been some statements made, and Secretary McNamara made a note. I'm concerned about troops demonstrating. It is always hard to, to control a demonstration, uh, possibly, and then there's the ever rest of troops, and so on, that we, I think this, if we

Rev. Eugene Carson Blake: It might help us right now.

President Kennedy: I, I think the, maybe, I, I, I want to get clear why and our judgment was that troops demonstrating this summer would not help us here in, in our efforts. That's why the order was put out, to put the strengthened troops was made with my approval. It's now, right about that judgment

Rev. Eugene Carson Blake: But there is an alternative [unintelligible] armed forces.

President Kennedy: No, we're looking into North Carolina as one of the states is, uh, uh, the evidence is of discrimination against those men. This always be — beginning of what this, what's going to come in that matter in the future, I mean, to say to you

Voice: But they declared the town was off-limits [unintelligible].

President Kennedy: Well, we got a, we got a lot of, uh, interesting things that we got to sign those orders. The requested troops happens, that, that really [word] gets right now.

I want to express thanks to you for coming, and to tell you I think you did a great job, it was very helpful to all of us. We will stay in touch with, uh, you through Walter and, uh, particularly on this question of the head counts. I think when you go out it would be a good time to indicate, Mr. Randolph, your strong message that both parties, would be supporting the right thing, and I think if you could start that theme it would be very useful. And get this thing some bipartisan [unintelligible].

[Burst of laughter from the participants.]

OCTOBER 29, 1963: PRESIDENT KENNEDY MEETS WITH HIS NATIONAL SECURITY COUNCIL ON THE QUESTION OF SUPPORTING A COUP IN SOUTH VIETNAM

Even as efforts to attain racial equality continued throughout America, as they would for many years, the nation was becoming embroiled in a vicious war in Vietnam. It began in the 1950s as a program of support for a French war in Indochina, and progressed through U.S. encouragement of a nascent South Vietnamese government. The South Vietnamese government, headed by Ngo Dinh Diem, defied an agreement designed to unify Vietnam (the 1954 Geneva agreement) through nationwide elections. Diem's government pursued Vietnamese communist rebels long after the French war had ended. The Vietnamese communists began active resistance against Diem in 1959. Diem's repressive political measures also alienated many other Vietnamese. By John Kennedy's time, a vicious conflict existed between South Vietnamese forces and antigovernment guerrillas backed by communist North Vietnam. Kennedy took office viewing South Vietnam as a laboratory in which new tactics of counterinsurgency could be tested, and the Saigon government as having good chances in this conflict.

Actually, within days of Kennedy's 1960 electoral victory, the growing unpopularity of the Saigon government headed by President Ngo Dinh Diem was revealed when dissident army officers joined with frustrated nationalist politicians to launch a coup (which failed). American observers on the scene frequently reported on the need for Diem to institute political reforms in the Saigon government, and in more than one of the bilateral accords that he reached to increase aid to Saigon, President Kennedy thought he had secured Diem's agreement to reform measures. Instead the Saigon mandarin became increasingly unapproachable, and no government reforms were made. Growing Vietnamese frustration with Diem was evident in constant talk of coups in Saigon and in a February 1962 incident in which South Vietnamese air force pilots bombed the presidential palace. Diem escaped harm on that occasion, and his sole response was to watch the South Vietnamese military even more closely.

The United States, for all its aid, continued to be unable to influence Diem to move in the direction of reform. In the meantime the antigovernment guerrillas became stronger, and North Vietnam began supplying them with major quantities of weapons along with cadres to form new forces. By 1963 the situation in South Vietnam appeared so serious that President Kennedy found himself in a quandary about what to do, and was sending out teams of senior officials to conduct special surveys almost every other month.

In May 1963 a brother of Diem's, Ngo Dinh Canh, in charge in the old Vietnamese imperial capital, Hue, ignited what became known as the "Buddhist crisis" by ordering the suppression of a religious procession celebrating the Buddha's birthday. Displaying Buddhist symbols and flags in violation of government decrees led to deaths and injuries among the parading Buddhists, who were fired upon by security forces. Buddhists throughout South Vietnam were outraged, and Saigon became a center for increasingly intense Buddhist protests, including ones at which monks and nuns immolated themselves to protest Diem's government and his favoritism toward Catholics. Diem made promises to negotiate a settlement with the Buddhists but again dragged his feet. Instead, late in August, Diem's police and military Special Forces made a major raid on key Buddhist centers in Saigon. To help spread the political heat that flowed from the "pagoda raids," as they were called, Diem took steps to make it seem that the South Vietnamese army, rather than the president himself, was responsible for the raids. This further soured relations between Diem and his military establishment.

A Central Intelligence Agency operative at the U.S. embassy in Saigon had been approached as early as the July 4 holiday regarding military doubts about Diem, and especially about his brother Ngo Dinh Nhu (a different brother from the one in Hue), who effectively ran key parts of the Saigon government. But the incipient hatred of the Ngo family rose to new heights following the pagoda raids. Within days two different South Vietnamese army senior officers had talked to the CIA or to their U.S. counterparts in an attempt to assess the potential American response to a coup against Diem. This led to a series of high-level meetings in Washington during the late summer and fall of 1963. A cable sent in President Kennedy's name, but quickly rescinded, expressed support for measures that got the Saigon war effort back on track. Then the new line of keeping hands off Saigon politics melted under the pressure of knowing just how bad conditions actually were. More Kennedy-ordered inspection trips brought back widely divergent views as to whether the military situation was improving, but there was nearly unanimous agreement that with Diem at the helm deterioration of the situation was inevitable. In addition, the United States stood in danger of being associated with Diem and Nhu's pagoda raids because the CIA supported the South Vietnamese Special Forces that had been the backbone of the strike.

Kennedy tried in several ways to convince the Saigon leader to institute reforms and dismiss Ngo Dinh Nhu, including halting some ·economic aid, withdrawing certain American troops from South Vietnam, threatening to halt CIA aid to the South Vietnamese Special Forces, and making public statements calling the war a Vietnamese affair. Diem made no open response. Nhu actually sponsored a Saigon street protest during which his agents were supposed to invade the U.S. embassy and kill Ambassador Henry Cabot Lodge. A newspaper Nhu owned also blew the cover of the CIA station chief, forcing his return from Saigon.

By early October 1963, the South Vietnamese generals had determined to reactivate the coup plans they had held in abeyance for more than a month. Again CIA officers were brought in, this time to ask for information they could use in planning. The South Vietnamese generals again sounded out the Americans on their attitude toward a coup. The CIA opposed the initiative, but other Washington officials wrestled with finding a way to force Diem to get rid of his brother. Meanwhile the Vietnamese generals moved ahead and soon were giving their CIA contacts very frequent reports on the status of their plot, from which the agency was able to identify which South Vietnamese troops might remain loyal to Diem in the event of a coup, as well as those who would be controlled by the plotters. On October 21, CIA Director John McCone told President Kennedy that Saigon was about to explode.

American historians agree that U.S. support for the military coup against

Diem cast the nation over the precipice into the Vietnam War. There is no similar consensus on what might have been the effect of the opposite action, but many observers treasure this possibility. That is, even at this late date, if the United States had told the South Vietnamese military that Washington was dead set against any move to overthrow the civilian leadership in Saigon, a coup might have been averted. The CIA's channels could have been trusted to deliver the message. The last opportunity to change the course of America's policy occurred on October 29, at the meeting included here, when a group of top officials saw Kennedy and reviewed the situation in Saigon. Some doubts were expressed, but much of the conversation focused upon possibilities for the coup and its aftermath, and how U.S. diplomats, military men, and CIA officers in Saigon should act in the context of the coup. William E. Colby, chief of the Far East Division of the CIA's operations directorate, opened the meeting with a briefing on the forces that could be expected to align with the different sides in the coup, after which other participants began their discussion.

In addition to President Kennedy, those present at the meeting of October 29 included Vice President Lyndon B. Johnson, Secretary of State Dean Rusk, Secretary of Defense Robert S. McNamara, Attorney General Robert F. Kennedy, Director of Central Intelligence John McCone, Joint Chiefs of Staff Chairman General Maxwell D. Taylor, National Security Adviser McGeorge Bundy, Undersecretary of State W. Averell Harriman, and an assortment of lesser officials from the State Department, the Department of Defense, the CIA, and the National Security Council staff. The group discussed a cable that would be sent to the U.S. embassy in Saigon and made changes in its wording. The original drafts of the cable appear at the end of the transcript.

Part of the issue was that the U.S. ambassador in Saigon, Henry Cabot Lodge, had been scheduled to return to Washington, D.C., for consultations. Kennedy and his advisers mull over whether to permit the Lodge trip to occur, change its timing, or cancel it, and what consequences any of those courses might have on the impending coup. Unaware of the South Vietnamese generals' exact plans or their timing, JFK bristled with questions about how strongly the United States would be implicated in the coup action. Kennedy also saw a political angle, commenting about Lodge at one point in the latter portion of this meeting that it "looks to be his ass, he's for a coup" (as if U.S. support might be chalked up to Republicans, for whom Lodge was a standard-bearer, not to the United States as a whole). Bobby Kennedy, Dean Rusk, General Maxwell Taylor, and CIA Director John McCone also express certain reservations. What is remarkable about the discussion on October 29, 1963, is that a broad array of top officials voiced doubts about the coup, including JFK himself, without any effect on the actual course of events. President Kennedy does not announce a clear decision, but the group proceeds as if the United States does support the coup.

Another major theme in Kennedy's White House meeting is what instructions to give Lieutenant Colonel Lucien Conein, an Army officer detached to work with the CIA. Conein was an old Vietnam hand and knew many of the senior South Vietnamese military officers. For that reason he had been sent back to Saigon for one more tour of duty, and while there had become the principal American contact with the South Vietnamese generals. One of them Conein used to meet at his dentist's office. President Kennedy and his colleagues discuss Conein's orders repeatedly and at length.

A second meeting at 6:00 P.M. following a short break and desultory discussion of other foreign policy matters included a slightly different set of officials. The latter meeting reviewed in detail the language of and changes to the cable and gave final approval for sending it. One key issue would be the information to be given to Ambassador Lodge versus that for the commander of the U.S. military advisory group in South Vietnam, General Paul D. Harkins. Some days earlier Harkins had declared himself completely opposed to any coup action. And there were worries in some quarters that if he knew about a coup, Harkins might warn Diem. The South Vietnamese generals, who knew of Harkins's stance, used it to justify excluding the Americans from detailed knowledge of their plans. The final cable in question is also included with this selection to make clear the implications of what was at stake in the Oval Office that day. It appears at the end of the transcript.

Almost all historians of the American war in Vietnam have pointed to the coup against Ngo Dinh Diem that took place on November 1, 1963, as a key event in that tragedy. The consensus view is that American support for the coup froze the United States into a position that made extricating the nation from the Vietnam conflict almost impossible. The words of the various officials at the White House meetings of October 29 clearly show that none of them had such long-term effects in mind as they made their decision that day. President Kennedy and his cohorts also demonstrate a can-do attitude toward changing the behavior of the Saigon government, even while Bobby Kennedy, the president's brother, and several other top officials shared their doubts. But the objections were not sustained, and several of the doubters went on to suggest language for the cable of instructions to be sent to Saigon. In any case, the depth of South Vietnamese resentment toward Diem is what drove the coup plotters, who were not turned aside by what Washington said. Meanwhile the United States was so heavily implicated in the opposition to Diem that even opposing the coup did not save Kennedy from charges of complicity. Revelation of this formerly secret conversation makes the events in Saigon even more tragic than they have previously seemed.

On November 1, 1963, South Vietnamese leader Ngo Dinh Diem was overthrown by his generals and their troops. Diem escaped with his brother Nhu, but both were captured by the plotters the next morning. Both men were murdered. Supporting the coup made the United States responsible in South Vietnam in exactly the fashion Bobby Kennedy had feared.

John F. Kennedy
October 29, 1963, 4:20 P.M.
Meeting in the White House with National Security Council on the Question of Supporting a Military Coup in South Vietnam
Present: Lyndon B. Johnson, Vice President; Robert McNamara, Secretary of Defense; Robert F. Kennedy, Attorney General; John McCone, Director of the CIA; General Maxwell Taylor, Chairman of the Joint Chiefs of Staff; Major General Victor J. Krulak, Special Assistant for Counterinsurgency and Special Activities of the Joint Staff; Governor W. Averell Harriman, Undersecretary of State; U. Alexis Johnson, Deputy Undersecretary of State; William Bundy, Assistant Secretary of State; Richard Helms, Deputy Director of the CIA; Joseph A. Mendenhall, Bureau of Far Eastern Affairs, Department of State; William E. Colby, Chief of Far Eastern Division of the CIA; McGeorge Bundy, National Security Adviser; Michael V. Forrestal; Bromley Smith

William Colby: We believed that the, uh, the pro-GVN [Government of Vietnam; i.e., the Diem regime] forces were, were about 5,000 stronger than the anti-GVN forces. Today we carry them as about the same, with a larger more, unit carried in the neutral or uncommitted area. In other words, these would go out

President John F. Kennedy: by the numbers on each side of the program

Male Voice: Oh, yeah.

William Colby: The pro and, the pro is 9000, the 9800, the anti is also 9800.

President Kennedy: And then the big

William Colby: The, the, uh, neutral areas cutting from the task.

President Kennedy: And then the

William Colby: Now

President Kennedy: The, you would have those as, what, the Marines or the, Tuan. What is his name, that colonel? At the, the pro-ARVN groups

William Colby: Pro-GVN

Male Voice: Uh, the, the pro, pro the palace

President Kennedy: And what groups are those? That's, that's

William Colby: Well, they're the, uh, th-this moves over into an analysis of the specific units involved and here we consider that the critical point is which are the key units, not, uh, how many soldiers from Saigon feel one way or the other. But which are the, the really strong units. And of these, you can identify about 4 or 5 such units. You have the Presidential Guard, you have the, um, the Special Forces, you have the Airborne, you have the Marines, you have the Air Force. Uh, and you have an armored unit just on the outside of Saigon, here. Uh, of those units, you carry, we carry the Presidential Guard, except for one element about which there is some question now, as pro palace. Because Special Forces, obviously, is pro the palace. Because armored unit outside of Saigon is pro the palace. Anti the palace, we carry the Airborne units, which is the paratroop units and some parts of the Marines, although this is a little vague, also, as to just how anti they are. These are the main forces. Plus the Air Force, which is pretty much solid anti palace. The, the sum total result of it, if you skip all the rest of the, uh, the incidental units, the, the key units come out about even, even match. There's enough, in other words, to have a good fight. On both sides.

President Kennedy: [Chuckling] Thank you for your decisive [Laughter and comments from others]

William Colby: Now we also have done a little homework on the, uh, precise

President Kennedy: Uh, in other words, change it's orders is really what?

William Colby: Well, change [Voices overlap] There are certain units which have moved over. Of, there were a couple of, of Marine units that we did carry as pro palace and we now carry as

President Kennedy: And these names were given in that Lodge cable of, uh, Jack, Ambassador Lodge's is the one before. Did you give any change in the

William Colby: There were certain of them, yes. The Marine, I think, was the main one. That's one of the main ones, [unintelligible]. Ah, we also have done some homework on what we're talking about when we're talking about coup groups. And we have identified out of the *welter* of intelligence on this thing, essentially two critical groups. These are what we call the generals' coup and another group which is a combination of a couple of elements working, but I think in the best of times is the Can Lao [the political party of Ngo Dinh Diem] dissidents. These are people who *were* associated with the government one time or another who've moved into dissidence. They're fairly, they're politically fairly sophisticated. Uh, and younger elements, most of them. Outside of these two groups, there are other people *in* Saigon who would join a coup, or who talk about coups but who really don't have that degree of interest in it. Some of these are the old oppositions, the, uh, the, uh, the Dai Viet [a traditional Vietnamese nationalist movement outlawed by Diem], uh some of the key military personnel, and so forth. But, as definable coup groups, you have these two elements. Now, there is very little contact between the two, although the generals have indicated a realization that they must move toward a government of civilians afterwards, and have talked, in some general terms, about who would be in it. Diem, the, the Can Lao group has realized that they need military force in order to come, bring it over. And they have made a few minor contacts with the generals and considerably more contacts with junior military officers with the idea of getting the junior officers to move and then dragging the rest of the generals and so forth on. But there's not much contact between the two. Then the GVN [Government of Vietnam, the name Washington used to refer to the Saigon government] reaction and activities that they have taken to defend themselves and to, to, to meet this threat [unintelligible].

Undersecretary of State Averell Harriman [?]: On that list, how, what, what about the disposition of forces there?

William Colby: This is the irony. There has not been much substantial variation in the forces to the, uh, we have not had, had, uh, reassignments or, or, uh, changes of commanders. The only substantial, uh, force movement was the Ninth Division movement down to the province. But the units in the Saigon area are not terribly different from what they used to be.

[Pause, faint voice in the background, Colby answers briefly but his words are garbled]

Male Voice: Can I ask a question?

William Colby: Uh

Attorney General Robert Kennedy: Uh, you have to assume that Diem felt that there's gonna be a coup against him for, probably, the last couple of months. Uh, are there any hints, so, therefore, he's made his own arrangements, intelligence-wise, forces, to protect himself, are there any, uh, units on which he relies, or which he feels are going to support him, and that he put in key divisions to put down a coup which, in fact, are, uh, now in these groups that are planning a coup?

William Colby: I think the only that I can identify of that nature was the reference to one or two units in the, in the Presidential Guard.

Male Voice: Four Things? [possibly a codename]

William Colby: Yes, Four Things.

Robert Kennedy: Well, now, is that sufficient, uh, to make a material difference?

William Colby: It could make an initial difference, but, uh, in the balance of, of, uh, units, if you move back again, take the tanks, for instance, uh, if they are met by this tank unit, why they can be met rather handily. I don't think there's enough to say that the balance is tipped in the, in the key forces.

Robert Kennedy: Well, then, he's there, what he has is, without exception, he has six forces to, uh, protect himself he should get he could use against a coup any time soon.

William Colby: I bet, I think he has, he has the same forces he's always maintained, for his own protection, his personal protection. He also is leaving in place the units that he knows are somewhat unfriendly, uh, disaffected, which he's known for many, many a moon. In other words, the Airborne for instance.

McGeorge Bundy: Notice this, uh, report, following up on the, in this morning's intelligence, the effect that there may be a general shake-up. I may have something that is

William Colby: There has been a story around for about a week or so. If there would be certain claims. May have the come up over, over, actually over national day, there was some talk of, we just don't have any more specific on this.

President Kennedy: Based on, uh, other troops, of South Korea or Pakistan, and these, uh, Iraq, are these forces, uh, our Asian forces could be significant. Or do you have a disposition,

Voice: That a coup move could be forestalled?

President Kennedy: I think if you'd done the same study of South Korea, you would have shown they didn't have it at all, would you?

William Colby: Well, I, uh

President Kennedy: And you were only up to 4,000 troops. There'll be others, will do.

William Colby: Yes. Well, I think, uh, it, the coup in Saigon in 1960, of course, showed exactly that. That the, the paratroopers seized the city and held the city for a whole day; they did not get the Palace. But then the troops from outside moved in and supported the Palace. Relieved the city.

President Kennedy: What does the '60 experience tell us about this?

William Colby: Oh, I think the '60 experience on this one showed that by maintaining its security in the palace area, something to keep the palace going, and I think it's taught Diem a lot of lessons, too, in terms of, of communications with his outside units. He, uh, has a much better radio system than he did then. He has arrangements made for this type of reaction. He has, for instance, uh, there is a story that, that when an Airborne unit is given trucks, there, the Armored unit is alerted, just as an order, an, a matter, matter of normal practice.

But, uh, when they get that degree of mobility, why then counter forces is alerted, and the, the increase by bringing the Special Forces in, I think he has reacted to the increased coup talk in the air, so he has increased his immediate defenses.

General Maxwell Taylor: If I understood your earlier briefing you suggested that this stuff that might turn up in the first 24 hours is on the whole unfriendly.

William Colby: To Diem?

General Maxwell Taylor: Yeah.

William Colby: Well, I think the first 24 hours would be a, a fight between . . .

[Voices overlap]

General Maxwell Taylor: Being an out-of-town outfit [referring to coup troops coming from outside Saigon]?

William Colby [showing units plotted on a map]: Well, the one unit up here, we just don't know too much about. The one down here we would guess is unfriendly.

President Kennedy: Unfriendly?

William Colby: To Diem.

Voice: Track a good

Secretary of State Dean Rusk: May I ask how much of a—our intervention in '60 had to do with the final outcome?

William Colby: Very little I think, sir. We took, uh, uh, a line at that time, I mean, I was in the Embassy at the time, of urging negotiation on both sides. And urging that, uh, that both sides not commit forces to a pitched battle [loud coughs] they negotiate out their differences. I think the, the critical thing that happened in 1960 was that the, the units out in the outskirts did prove to be loyal to Diem, to the Palace. Did move in

President Kennedy: How much fighting was there in '60?

William Colby: Quite a lot. There were a couple of hundred wou—what, a hundred people killed, killed? [Other voices in background] About a hundred, two hundred people killed. The fighting continued very sharply until about noontime.

Joseph Mendenhall: I would say that if the coup forces had pushed their initial advantage that morning and hadn't stopped to negotiate. They could have had the, had the victory because they had the advantage at the outset, after a few hours, fighting, but then the forces outside the city rallied to Diem's support and saved the day for him.

[Silence; paper rustling, voices in distance, pause thirty-six seconds]

President Kennedy: To me, that, uh, based on what you just told us, which is why I wanted you over in more detail about the units based on our analysis here

McGeorge Bundy: It seems to me, Mr.

President Kennedy: the following units

McGeorge Bundy: Mr. President, that might be a separate message essentially an assessment message, addressed to both Lodge, Harkins, and the CAS [CIA, Saigon Station], asking how they would feel. What you might do is summarize what Colby has told us and ask them if they concur or differ, and on what grounds, because . . .

Dean Rusk: I think that would be a good way to point that out. You could get them specifics as to these particular units, their orientation

President Kennedy: That should go all at the same time

[Voices overlap]

McGeorge Bundy: It should be referred to in their message but not spelled out in it, would be my suggestion.

President Kennedy: Why should it be separate?

McGeorge Bundy: Uh, simply because it's a technical assessment problem, it's, and if we can make two separate messages [unintelligible] may be wrong. The drafting problem I don't think needs to come back here. This one I think we ought to sign.

President Kennedy: OK, well I think your point is

Director of Central Intelligence John McCone [?]: Mr., Mr. President, may I suggest that we set the detail for sep, separating, and I think there's some merit in that, and I suggest we at least put in this paragraph where we ask for their assessments, a summary and two or three sentences of the assessment we've just heard, which is more of the fear of imbalance in the firefight than undoubtedly exists.

[Voices overlap]

McGeorge Bundy: We are giving separately our idea of estimates . . .

[Voices overlap]

McGeorge Bundy: . . . And comments thereon.

President Kennedy: Exactly.

McGeorge Bundy: Mr. President, the, uh, truthful immediate question oddly enough is whether Lodge should come back because if, if he, if we don't change his schedule, we have to get a lot more into this message than if we do. Uh, we're inclined, I think, uh, those of us [in] a preliminary way, subject to comment from the Secretary of State, I don't think he's had a chance to comment on this one. I think that there's some advantage with keeping him there, as the second paragraph of this draft message suggests. Uh, with the proper craft, military aircraft, we can get him back at the same time we otherwise would. We have the advantage that if something crucial happens, we can put him down in Hawaii and wait till we get more light on it, get him back in, or anything else rather than confining him to the rather rigid and in-infrequent schedules of Pan American [an airline].

Dean Rusk: Mr. President [clears his throat], it seems to me that, um, we all certainly have to assume that Diem and Nhu are pretty well informed about all this stuff that's going on. There have been, uh, two or three other discussions other than the one that Conein [Lt. Col. Lucien Conein, a covert intelligence officer with the CIA who had Indochina experience since 1945, and was now serving as the CIA's intermediary with the coup plotters] has had with, uh, Don [Major General Tran Van Don, Commander of the Army of the Republic of Viet Nam], um, that indicate that coup talk is pretty rampant there. When you look at Roger's [Roger Hilsman, assistant secretary of state, Far East] report of his talk with Diem, on his day with Diem, well this is entirely consistent with Diem's knowing a good deal about this coup talk prospects, action there, both the spirit and the things that were said. Um, I think that our big questions are first, um, uh, do we think that, uh, there's enough in this for us to exercise our responsibility by being silent? Uh, do we, or should we make it clear through whatever contact we have, that we are not interested in a civil war, that if there is a, uh, change of government, that can be, uh, carried out, uh, quickly and with minimum loss of life, that's one thing. But, by, uh, protracted civil war is something quite different. And that we are not, uh, we are not disposed to, uh, even by silence, to, to encourage that kind of a situation. Then we're not convinced that the, that, uh, these are changes that would be brought out without severe fighting which would be equally disruptive to the country. Now this is one of the assessments we have to make. I was putting the problem at the moment. Um, the, um, if there is to be the kind of fighting that could go on for, say, two days here, at least, um, without at the moment knowing how it could come out, both sides are almost certain to ask us for help. What do we do there? We say we, we're not going to give either side any help, then, uh, this already, uh, makes a big difference to Diem. If we say that we will give the insurgents some help, we've got to guarantee they're successful. Now, if we say that we, if we give Diem help at that point, if we think that [the] jig is up and it doesn't do to support the government, then I think we've, uh, really disrupted the chances of getting on with the war in a very fundamental fashion. Because the, the morale of the armed forces, the leadership and the civil service, all the rest of them, will be so shaken, as far as the United States is concerned, that this is a, um, this is a tough one. I-I'm inclined to think that, uh, since Gen. Don himself indicated to Cabot Lodge that he ought to go ahead with his plans, uh, and since we want to minimize, uh, our involvement at this stage, that we ought to consider letting, um, Lodge pass the word to Don, uh, that, uh, uh, we, uh, we are concerned about, uh, about any action that would result in prolonged fighting among significant elements of the armed forces. And that Don, that Lodge would, um, would, uh, continue on his present, uh, present schedule. Meanwhile briefing Harkins into the picture, er,

Harkins [General Paul D. Harkins, head of the U.S. Military Assistance Command–Vietnam] may know some things, like what movement, what troops are doing what, that will add something to the knowledge that we have here. We are very much, we're working pretty much in the dark here in this present situation. And, uh, we, we're not gonna get much more light thrown on it unless these, uh, generals do give us a 48-hours on this instead of a 4-hours notice about what they have in mind. Um, I must say, I, I don't think we ought to, to put our faith in anybody on the Vietnamese side at this point, Don or anybody else in terms of who's saying what to whom behind our backs among the Vietnamese themselves. Now those who know Don may have a different view. But I, uh, I'm skeptical about, uh, the, uh, likelihood that the Vietnamese are gonna be playing completely honest with us, and completely dishonestly with each other. And I don't think they owe us that, or think they do, and they're not going to play with Westerners on that basis. So I think there are problems here are, are pretty far-reaching. I would, uh, I would think, uh, we ought to, uh, at least caution these generals that if they move or if they, uh, we, they ought to expect to have a situation well in hand immediately with minimum loss of life. If they want to tell us a little more about what they have in mind, that's, that's fine. But, uh, what we're not interested in is a prolonged civil war.

President Kennedy: What about if, uh, it seems to me if Lodge, if this coup is going to take place, there is the suggestion Friday that Lodge delays his departure, and it's complete, which would be admission that, uh, Lodge is aware of it. I don't see any reason why Lodge shouldn't leave and, uh, let Harkins be in charge, if there's any coup activities. Let the command of the area go to Harkins. He would be the, he'd be the responsible officer, and I think we've all got confidence in him. I don't, candidly, I think, I would say probably, odds are against the coup. If it happens, I think it's just as well that Lodge continue on his regular route, and, uh, in addition you've got a very good man, experienced man, there anyway, General Harkins, who knows he's at Lodge's back. The man's been working out of there anyway. It's certainly not an advantage to have him delay his departure three days. Good lord! I think let Lodge go, and put Harkins in charge. Any kind of miraculous [word] but useful, from Ch-Chargé to, uh, Harkins. Now [words] I've just covered Lodge, but now as far as the other things indicating our concern and all the rest, we have to write our cable. Part of it will be written into the cable at the end of the correlation of forces. The problem will be maybe you write with this thing, put more, you, you change . . . the business about leaving and, uh, and then we go ahead, uh,

I think the order of State is Secretary McNamara, at the bottom of page one, Bob, uh, forces look to us pretty well balanced. I just assume the difficulty is, I'm sure that's the way it is with every coup. It always looks balanced until somebody acts on it.

General Maxwell Taylor: I think it's unrealistic.

President Kennedy: The difficulty is this is one group of Special Forces.

Maxwell Taylor: I think it is unrealistic to line this up as if it were a football game. Because it all depends on a few key people.

[Voices overlap]

Maxwell Taylor: They're not afraid they're gonna draw.

Dean Rusk: It depends on who does what in the first three or four hours.

Maxwell Taylor: That's right. A few key people.

[Voices overlap]

President Kennedy: Well, we ought to be able to get from them the, what key individuals are, or who, maybe some of these others we can't tell about. But we are confident, are we not, about the, the Blue forces, we-we-were with this government, or some of those are questionable?

[William Colby answers, but indistinctly.]

President Kennedy: Special Forces, that Colonel's group, will move, and they have how much — [South Vietnamese Colonel Le Quang Tung, a Diem loyalist, had six companies of Special Forces troops that had been the main strike force in the Buddhist pagoda raids.]

William Colby: Yes.

President Kennedy: 5, 4 or 5 thousand?

William Colby: A couple of thousand.

President Kennedy: A couple of thousand. And we're confident of what, who else

William Colby: Presidential Guard

President Kennedy: What, how much?

William Colby: They're about two thousand.

President Kennedy: Ah, that's four thousand.

William Colby: Uh, the other unit is the tank battalion, and I wouldn't say that we're absolutely confident on that. That's all, the key point there is that you have 21 tanks.

President Kennedy: Um, what's

William Colby: One good question of the property [equipment?] they will have. And I don't think we can, you know, stay absolutely sure on that.

President Kennedy: [unintelligible] depends on the way they come about.

Voice: Three essentials

President Kennedy: Uh, say they [unintelligible]

Secretary of Defense Robert McNamara: I-I think above all, Mr. President, if Lodge is leaving there, you must, in this message, make clear who's to be in charge of coup planning. We have to re-write paragraph three, the top three paragraphs of page three, Mr. President

[Voices overlap]

Robert McNamara: I would recommend that, that, uh, Trueheart [William Trueheart, deputy chief of Mission in Saigon, Department of State] [Deleted, five seconds, no doubt a reference to Trueheart giving Kennedy's orders to the CIA] the instruction to Conein to receive this report, to give him new instructions so we have a clear understanding of who's running Conein and his contacts with Don, and we state in here, which you've just stated, is what Conein should tell Don as to our attitude, and those three stay on top of him hour by hour during this critical period. Any time they disagree, they immediately refer to this group back here. Up to this point, as far as I know, Harkins has not even been informed of the coup plan.

General Victor Krulak: He's been informed of various strategies. They should be

Robert McNamara: Well, not, not recently, and if had a, he doesn't, uh, we have one in case he hasn't been

Victor Krulak: and these must

Robert McNamara: What we're working on here today.

Multiple Voices: That's right!

President Kennedy: Big Minh? [General Duong Van Minh, South Vietnamese army commander and top coup plotter].

Voice: Exactly.

President Kennedy: He was a

Robert McNamara: I think this message must be very clear, and Lodge must do this before he leaves. Secondly, I think it's extremely important that before Lodge leaves he [Deleted, five seconds] Truehart, chief of the country team, until such time as a coup starts at that point; Harkins takes command, Trueheart becomes his political adviser.

Director John McCone: I don't think it's necessary to agree to [word] a three-man thing here [Deleted, nine seconds]

Averell Harriman: I think that, uh, if you're going to have two people get together, then Harkins and Trueheart could do it, and they could make the decisions. If they disagree [Deleted, three seconds] would be instructed to carry out the instructions of the two just as he's instructed to carry out Lodge's instructions. Uh, uh, I wouldn't think that

John McCone: a troika complicates the decision

Averell Harriman: a troika complicates it, but I don't think it's

John McCone: Well, I, I, accept that now

Averell Harriman: He thinks that's the way to do it [words, other voices]

[Deleted, five seconds]

Averell Harriman: And uh,

Robert Kennedy: Taking direction from Lodge would have

Averell Harriman: Taking direction from Lodge, that could go right on that way, with, with, with Harkins and Trueheart or with Fido [Unidentified code-name, probably a reference to one of the South Vietnamese generals] on [noise interferes]

[Voices overlap]

Robert Kennedy: Could I, I may be a minority, but I just don't see that this makes any sense on the face of it. Uh, I mean, it's different from a coup in the Iraq or [a] South American country; we are so intimately involved in this, and what we're doing, really, is, uh, what we talked about when we were sitting around the table talking about all this kind of thing we talked about four weeks ago. We're putting the whole future of the country and, really, Southeast Asia, in the hands of somebody that we don't know very well, that one official of the United States government has had contact with him, and he, in turn, says he's lined up some others. It's clear from the map and from the, from Diem who's a fighter, I mean, he's not somebody who's gonna balk, who's just gonna get out of there. He's a, he's a, determined figure, who's going to stick around and I should think go down fighting. And he's going to have some troops there that are gonna fight, too. That, if it's a si-, if it's a failure, that, uh, we risked such a hell of a lot, with the war, as I understood from Bob McNamara, was going reasonably well. And, uh, whether, uh, just based on these rather flimsy reports, uh, that a coup's gonna take place in two or three days, to risk the whole future of the United States in that area on these kind of reports, which are not extensive, and which don't go into any detail, which don't, uh, list, uh, recent that reports have come in from the ambassador don't really list our assets, or, or, and, or, or, show out or give a plan as to what's going to occur and how it's going to take place. I would think, we, we have some, we have some very large stakes to balance here, and we certainly, I think should be entitled to know what's gonna happen and how it's going to be effected. And not just hope that the coup's going to go through and they're going to be able to work it out satisfactorily. I would think unless we *knew* we're gonna be involved, everybody's gonna say that we did it, uh, then if we're gonna, if we think that's the right thing, I think that we should play a major role. I don't think we can go halfway on this, I mean, get the blame for it. If it's a failure, I would think Diem's gonna tell us to get the hell out of the country, and, see, he's gonna have enough with his intelligence to know that this, in these contacts and these conversations. And he's gonna capture these people, they're gonna say the United States is behind it. I would think that we're just going down the road to *disaster*. Now, maybe it's gonna be successful, but I don't think there's anybody, any reports that I've seen, indicate that anybody has a plan to show where, where this is going; and I think this cablegram, set out like it is, indicates that we are willing to go ahead with the coup but we think that we should then have a little bit more information.

Dean Rusk: Well, I, I think the cablegram ought to be, uh, changed in order to bring in some more of the feeling that was expressed early, and I, I have, I do share this concern of the Attorney General, the, uh, but if there is a, um, substantial part of the military leadership thinks they can't win the war without changing the government, then that would be the basis for the coup, or our interest in the coup. Then, I think that, um, we take a, equally heavy responsibility in saying to them we can't do this because then if, if, if that leadership, uh, becomes dissatisfied and disinterested then we got a, we got a valuable [?] situation.

Robert Kennedy: That's true. I didn't know if there's been any, any information that's been given to us that indicates that the same people, except for, uh, now it's 8400, 9400 against 9400; a month ago, it was 9400 against 8900. I think that's a hell of a slip.

Maxwell Taylor: I must say that I agree with the Attorney General at present. I found absolutely no suggestion the military didn't have their heart thoroughly in the war, and very little in politics in Saigon.[8] I would be willing to step farther in saying that even a successful coup, I would think that you'd help the

Viet [unintelligible] war. First because you'll have a completely inexperienced government, and secondly, because the provincial chiefs, who are so essential to the conduct of the field, will all be changed, and it's taken over a year now to develop any truly effective work in that area. For a while, uh, a most optimistic case, in the long terms it might be good, in the sh-short terms, then it's bad.

John McCone: I think our opinion, uh, is somewhat the same as General Taylor expressed. We think that, uh, even a successful coup; an unsuccessful coup would be disastrous. A successful coup, in our opinion, I feel very definitely that's right, would create a period of political confusion, interregnum [laughter in background, possibly in another room], uh, uh, uh, and would seriously affect the war for a period of time which is not possible to estimate. It might, uh, it might be disastrous.

President Kennedy: What would be necessary to change all these chiefs? I mean, after all, the personnel that, uh, this isn't a civil war, really, it's a, it's really a, uh, satisfaction comes most primarily with Nhu, only he's directly with them. Why is it necessary to have that kind of

Maxwell Taylor: I'm just assuming they would be replaced, but these are all Diem appointees, they're, they're hand-picked, they're

President Kennedy: This isn't, as I say, kind of class [word] why do we have that kind of major turnover in personnel? It doesn't necessary to be successful.

Maxwell Taylor: It would be necessary when you control it.

President Kennedy: Well,

Maxwell Taylor: In my opinion, Mr. President, the um, there is a relative chance of quick success, and that's the point that we do have a, do have a, an interest in finding out more about, uh, I have no doubt that the, that if the leadership, uh, uh, that we've been in touch with over the last several weeks, um, one way or another [clears throat], should, um, take on this situation, that there will be opportunities opening up with [clears throat] with the Vice President, others, playing a role that would, um, I think in the, in the relatively short time, greatly improve the situation as far as the war against the Viet Cong [Officially *Viet Nam Cong San* {Vietnamese Communists},

Saigon's pejorative name for the People's Liberation Armed Forces in South Vietnam] is concerned, but that's, it's a matter of judgment, and, uh, Governor, do you have a . . .

Averell Harriman: I feel that we're strong inside. I think that we're largely doing fine, but there'll be more v—less and less enthusiasm for this regime, and that, uh, I have no idea whether this coup could be pulled off or not, but if it can be, I'm, I'm not concerned. It will be ability to you, to, uh, to, to, to develop government, you know, blood and guts, of course the risk is, uh, whether they can do it rapidly or not, and pull it off. And I'm in no position to judge that. If we were satisfied with that, I would be, be con—really the basis for concern as much as I am today that we're gradually going down hill, and, um, at the end of the year, we'll, we'll, we'll, we'll find ourselves increasing difficulties unless something else has happened in the meantime. I don't think, uh, Diem's got the leadership to carry his county through to victory. [Pause]

Deputy Undersecretary of State U. Alexis Johnson: I think if Lodge were to have this hard question thrown at him, you talk about all the tragedies and, uh, you make clear to him that what we don't want is a, is a civil war, and that if the prospect is of prolonged fighting, rather than a quick political take-over with a minimum loss of life, uh, that, uh, he should caution these people to, um, hold their hand until they're ready to do it.

President Kennedy: But isn't it that our correlation of forces are, that, that, they're almost even in the immediate Saigon area. If that is true, then of course it doesn't make any sense to have a coup. Unless he has information or they can produce information which would indicate that the balance of forces quite easily is on the side of the, uh, rebels, then it seems to me that we should discourage him this time.

McGeorge Bundy: A balance of force, or *tactic* of surprise and of take-over, which is what a coup is, I think the basic thing is that we *do not want* a regimental combat means in a mish-mash of a three-day war in Saigon, because that

[Other voices, indistinct words]

President Kennedy: At most, I, I think we ought to name the in—, the units we think are either in doubt or belong to Diem, unless Lodge, unless they can indicate, uh, command support in those units, then the forces are equal, and, uh, we think that it doesn't make any sense to have a coup.

Voice: Then that doesn't give you much time.

President Kennedy: He [Lodge] can leave there tomorrow.

Robert McNamara: That's the disadvantage in having him pulled out, Mr. President, and that's one of the reasons for making in terms of delaying his return. We're all up against the gun now. If these people are correct as to when this thing is going to happen, we are now at 5 o'clock on the morning of the 30th out there, and it's gonna happen in, maybe 24 to 36 hours.

McGeorge Bundy: And we're not delaying his re, return to Washington, it is simply the time which he takes off for Saigon we're thinking of delaying.

Voice: He'll still be there Monday morning, trying to rest.

President Kennedy: If his announced departure is Wednesday, and let's say that the coup occurs Thursday or Friday, he has postponed, it is quite obvious then. He is,

Robert Kennedy: Do we, do we know, he's

Voice: How do we know? It's his ability

Voice: No, we haven't been able to get

McGeorge Bundy: But it must be known, because he must have made reservations

Voice: Yeah.

McGeorge Bundy: to go commercial, and, uh, Conein told Don that he was going but, in any event, his having made reservations to go commercial must be

Robert McNamara: Mr. President, could we perhaps leave this up to Lodge? I

Voice: Yeah.

Robert McNamara: I think he's gonna have, have a great difficulty with this message we send out to him. He's going to read this as a change in, in his instructions. Uh, we, we have, uh, rightly or wrongly, I think, led him to believe that we would support a coup, or at least that we would keep hands off. This is the way he interprets our policy.

McGeorge Bundy: I don't think we've said that to him, but I don't disagree that that's what he thinks.

Robert McNamara: And since October, since we returned, the message has gone out there and come back that would lead me to feel he thinks that. Furthermore, he's going to find it very difficult to leave in Harkins' hands the command of the station, in the event a coup takes place. He's going to have to talk to Harkins. This is gonna be a problem for him because I don't believe that they talk. And I think the message that came in yesterday or the day before clearly indicated that. I personally believe Harkins is not informed about any of this coup planning that has occurred in the last several days. It's gonna be very difficult, therefore, for Lodge to get Harkins in, and discuss this with him, and tell him that he, Harkins, is joined with Trueheart in being a 2-man team that will henceforth give instructions to Conein or see reports from Conein, send him back to see Don, and so on. And, further, it's gonna be difficult for Lodge to translate this message into a specific instruction to Conein and get Conein to see Don very quickly. Actually, Lodge is trying to leave, uh, Saigon about 12 hours from this moment. And if, for us to get the message drafted, get it out there, for him to do all these things, it's gonna be very difficult, I think. So I would strongly urge that we give him the option of delaying his departure if he chooses, and we can say, and I've already alerted the military plane to pick him up.

President Kennedy: It's Lodge that didn't want to know uh, what our message is, following the August message,[9] which we worked

McGeorge Bundy: Well that's already been superceded, Mr. President.

President Kennedy: Well, what is the sort of standing, uh,

Dean Rusk: Here, here are the basic, uh, instructions, here on October 9th.

President Kennedy: Is Mac, Secretary McNamara to back [?] about the coup

Dean Rusk: Yes, something to do about coup: "While we do not wish to stimulate a coup, we also do not wish to leave impression that U.S. would thwart a change of government or deny economic and military assistance to a new regime if it appeared capable of increasing effectiveness of military effort, ensuring popular support to win the war and improving working relations with the United States. We would like to [be, *sic*] informed on what is being contemplated but we should avoid being drawn into reviewing or advising on operation plans or any other act which may tend to identify U.S. too closely with change in government" [*Note*: Telegram through the CIA to Ambassador Lodge, October 9, 1963]. Um,

President Kennedy: Uh, this thing, uh, then, would be subject to his discretion; would you tell him that you sent the plane for him

Voices: Yes, that's right.

President Kennedy: If he decided to stay, go, he would have to, you ought to remind him that he would have to put in to the mix the fact that

McGeorge Bundy: I think this may blow his cover.

President Kennedy: I doubt, I doubt he'd wanted to see

McGeorge Bundy: Oh, Mr. President, you know, we do the working group here, revise this cable accordingly, and, uh

President Kennedy: Come back in

McGeorge Bundy: in just 10 minutes

Meeting reconvenes at 6:00 P.M.
Vice President Lyndon B. Johnson, Attorney General Robert F. Kennedy, General Maxwell Taylor, and Deputy Director of the CIA Richard Helms have not returned; Roger Hilsman, Assistant Secretary of State for Far Eastern Affairs attends this second meeting.

Voice: on our side

President Kennedy: Well, so let's say it here: Our reporting in Saigon indicates that, uh, the, they, it's important or almost im, my correlation of forces are almost equal, double feature, and that, therefore, there is a substantial possibility that there'll be a lot of fighting.

Voice: Or even defeat.

President Kennedy: Or even defeat. This being true, we think it would be disastrous to proceed unless they can give us evidence that, uh, indicates that the, uh, uh, majority strength is still in there.

Voice: Yeah.

McGeorge Bundy: It isn't so much majority strength, as it evidence of the, important evidence, of, uh, high prospect of rapid, successful action. It isn't really balance. Of course it's a question. What do you want to say to this council?

Voice: Let's say to the balance of forces

McGeorge Bundy: That does it.

President Kennedy: Uh, do we need to say to Lodge that if, uh, this thing takes place, if it does, he's so treating it as something we couldn't stop anyways, it's so, uh, downhill, even if that were so, we are *bound* to bear the responsibility for it, and that, uh, therefore, uh, I'd like to have him know ahead.

[Voices overlap]

McGeorge Bundy: But there's no harm in saying it again. You said it a couple of

President Kennedy: Therefore, could, uh, one blow defeat our whole effort in South Vietnam, so, we've got to do that.

Voice: Even large-scale aid.

President Kennedy: But now, to therefore, do you see a prospect of quick results? Uh, I'd like to have Conein have these force assessments? I think, when he sees them.

Assistant Secretary of State Roger Hilsman: Do you want to hear what, uh, Mr. Colby has, which is right on this point? Here, the cable last

Voice: Well, that short one, just like that.

[Voices overlap]

President Kennedy: We've got quickly that on again, I need to get some drafts.

[Voices overlap]

President Kennedy: OK. Well, why don't you say it is important to call attention to this Saigon, important, to call attention to the importance of Saigon with units. What about these words — important in there. They're ready to go where?

William Colby: This would be the leadoff of the second cables, uh, the second cable. It will be followed by a breakdown of the specific units.

President Kennedy: Well, then, I just, uh, wish — now, see what, with this conversation, you call attention to the important Saigon units still apparently loyal to GVN leadership. Oh, uh, raise serious issue as to what means coup group has to deal with them. That would be paragraph two?

Voice: Mm-hmm. Would. As to what means coup group has to deal with that.

[Silence for about fifteen seconds]

President Kennedy: And just change Harkins' [unintelligible — presumably instructions]

Voice: Yeah.

[Fifteen-second gap, with paper shuffling, other noises, and voices]

President Kennedy: I think we ought to close, uh, at this last time, we don't want to spend any time, time seems so important here, I think we ought to be more lost to the rocket [?], just the conclusion about the

Voice: Reiterating

President Kennedy: Proof ought to be on the coup people, otherwise it's even a mistake to proceed with [Noises]

McGeorge Bundy: They get a final paragraph

Voice: No, sir, I'll get you one.

Voice: [Unintelligible, whispering] takes us years to know [words]

Averell Harriman: Good, that's been beat up. [clears throat] Ye—the men, the President called him, security wants an indication that Lodge should tell him we don't think we ought to go ahead unless they, the coup feels that they should.

McGeorge Bundy: I didn't quite say that, [voices in background] what he says is, uh, I think this is very, this is likely to lead Lodge to come back and say again he doesn't think we could control [words] situation.

Voice: I bet you want to get

John McCone: Actually, we got Conein to pour in a little bit of cold water, and his, well the assessment isn't going to change much

[Voices overlap]

U. Alexis Johnson: Well, that ought to be in this first paragraph, what we said, serious, even prolonged fighting, or even defeat. Now does anyone get the

[Voices overlap]

Voice: I got a sense of it.

[Brief silence]

Victor Krulak: In their coup attempt, any one of these can be serious or even disastrous so we must have assurances.

Assistant Secretary William Bundy: Yeah, that's just right.

Robert McNamara: What I have before that is, Vietnam needs decisions. "We believe that what we say to coup group can produce delay of coup, and, uh, reporting coup plans to Diem is *not*, repeat, not our only way of stopping coup." There we may as well indicate where we have a divergence.

[Voices overlap]

Dean Rusk: I think that we [words], it is hard for us to see circumstances in which the [words] report [words]

Robert McNamara: Oh, I can fix that by making it not reporting to trail.

Voice: To trail could do that, yeah. [Noise, voices, silence]

Voice: Is it this?

Voice: Let's just keep Bill's [Bill Bundy's words in the cable] there [other voices overlap], much easier way to endorse this.

[Voices overlap, muted discussion among several participants]

William Bundy: On the next paragraph, if Don is not in good faith, then there is no real coup, is there?

Voice: That's right.

William Bundy: So this is, this is a double-barrel thing. If it, if Minh starts talking at all, he, he backs up the whole thing to good faith, and if he tells us it's a decent military plan, we then know a hell of a lot better

McGeorge Bundy: I must say, I, this is a rather ingenious scheme. I take it this is your broad theory of how, in fact, this'll be done.

[Noise obscures reply ending in "this idea"]

McGeorge Bundy: Bill said he'd better, Colby said he, he thought it was a feasible thing to do, to do, so

[Noise in background]

William Bundy: Given the changes on the aircraft [word — "probability"?] On Page 4, we reversed the Trueheart-Harkins

U. Alexis Johnson: May I suggest on Page 4, is a little clarification. Uh, in sum Trueheart acts, as far as they come to deem a normal situation. That's A.

Robert McNamara: I'd cut to act, I guess I didn't know who did it.

U. Alexis Johnson: Yeah, I'm sorry. To be char, uh, uh, chargé [overlapping voices agree] That's A.

Voice: Yeah.

U. Alexis Johnson: "The highest authority desires it clearly understood that Harkins should participate with Trueheart," uh,

[Voices overlap]

Robert McNamara: He really, I think, wants him to participate with Lodge too, you see

Voice: Yeah.

Robert McNamara: it's this sudden feeling we have in the last day or so that Lodge isn't telling Harkins about the coup.

U. Alexis Johnson: I know.

McGeorge Bundy: We're mixing up, we're mixing up several things here.

[Voices overlap]

Voice: At all times

Robert McNamara: Well, I think we *do* mean that if the coup begins after your departure,

[Voices overlap]

William Bundy: If Lodge is still there, he's, he's in charge, is the way I understood the president.

U. Alexis Johnson: That's right, that's right. The highest authority should participate in supervision of all content, in event coup begins after your departure, not, you know

Voice: Well, that's understood, because when we're talking about, oh, oh, that's right

[Voices overlap]

McGeorge Bundy: Suppose we put in, "With your departure, it's [word] the highest authority understands it clearly desires, clearly de—, clearly understood that with your de—," [President Kennedy re-enters the room] Mr. President, there's a little problem, I assume that if the coup begins while Lodge is still there, he's still in charge?

President Kennedy: Yeah.

Robert McNamara: If the coup begins after he leaves, but, then after your departure therefore would be, I think, just before Harkins and drop line 7.

U. Alexis Johnson: Well, that, that'll help it.

Voice: Yes.

Voice: [Unintelligible, followed by a short silence]

U. Alexis Johnson: Is it true Harkins reacted badly[10] [voices overlap]

McGeorge Bundy: We could say Trueheart in effect and

Robert McNamara: In effect, yes.

Voice: In effect.

Voice: Did Trueheart ever [words]

U. Alexis Johnson: And the next sentence is also after Lodge's departure, right?

McGeorge Bundy: Well, I think, uh, the other way of doing that, important to [word] in a session about Embassy . . . leaving out Trueheart.

[Voices overlapping chorus "Yes," one says "That'll do it."]

President Kennedy: Well, we got anoth —, [words] get to sex it up, Bob?

Robert McNamara: Yes, we have. I've got, uh, well, at the very end, we reiterate that "the burden of proof must be on, uh, the burden of proof must be on the coup [voices overlap] to show" that they can succeed. Uh,

McGeorge Bundy: Show that the probability of success is high

Robert McNamara: And the probability of success is high. Otherwise, it would be a *mistake*, it, to, to, uh, allow them to proceed because [words]

McGeorge Bundy: Otherwise we should discourage them.

President Kennedy: "Otherwise we should discourage them from proceeding."

Voice: That's right.

Robert McNamara: Mr. President, we have reviewed the revised language of this whole thing now.

President Kennedy: Because, uh, if, uh, we miscalculate we could lose overnight our position in Southeast Asia.

Voice: From the [word] sense

Robert McNamara: From the text that you have, if you [unintelligible]. The first paragraph remains the same. The second paragraph would read: "Believe our attitude toward coup group can still have decisive effect on its decisions. We believe that what we say to coup group can produce delay of coup, that betrayal of coup plans to Diem is not, repeat not, our only way of stopping coup. We therefore need urgently your assessment with Harkins and CAS, including their separate comments if they desire. We concerned that our lineup of forces in Saigon be cabled separately next message indicate approximately equ-, equal balance of forces with substantial possibility serious and even pro-longed fighting or even defeat."

[John McCone?]: Got to say "serious and prolonged fighting, or even defeat."

Robert McNamara: Uh, "either of these, any of these, could be serious or even disastrous for U.S. interests, so that we must have assurance balance of forces clearly favorable. With your assessment in hand, we might feel that we should convey message to [South Vietnamese General Tran Van] Don, whether or not he gives 24 hours notice that would" (a), (b) and (c) as it stands. On Page 2, there's no change except to make the sending of the plane *his* sending at the bottom.

Dean Rusk: Delay as far as [word]

Voice: Wait a second

Voice: [unintelligible except for "armed guard"]

McGeorge Bundy: The prospect of quick result

Voice: And important Saigon units

Voice: Important Saigon units

McGeorge Bundy: Yes.

Voice: Any objections?

[Voices overlap, the phrase "important means" is discernable]

Voice: Anything else, uh, to [words]?

Voice: Is sending.

McGeorge Bundy: [agrees] Is sending and will arrive.

U. Alexis Johnson: We're sending the plane out.

McGeorge Bundy: Yeah. Page 3, no change. Now, on Page 4

President Kennedy: You send the plane out now?

[Overlapping voices chorus "Yes," "Yep"]

Robert McNamara: Mr. President, what we've done is to rearrange that, the plane is an improvement no matter which account

President Kennedy: I see.

McGeorge Bundy: He comes as he pleases.

President Kennedy: I see.

McGeorge Bundy: Uh, it is clearly understood

Voice: That's an all ways [words]

McGeorge Bundy: How about a military plane having to be your decision?

President Kennedy: OK.

Robert McNamara: "It is clearly understood that after your departure Harkins should participate in supervision of all coup contacts and that in event a coup begins, he becomes head of country team and direct representative of President, with Trueheart in effect acting as POLAD."[11] We don't want to say Acting POLAD because that changes the formal

President Kennedy: POLAD?

Robert McNamara: Political Advisor. "Coup contacts we maintain continuous guidance and expect [word] divergences and assessments of Harkins[12] Uh, at the bottom I think we should say, "We are now examining post-coup contingencies."

McGeorge Bundy: I think that change was made already. [Voices overlap]

U. Alexis Johnson: I'd rather read that: "We reiterate that the burden of proof is on [clears throat] the coup, must be on the coup group to show a substantial possibility of quick success. Otherwise, we should discourage them from proceeding since a miscalculation could result in jeopardizing U.S. position in Southeast Asia."

Dean Rusk: Then you leave the contingency paragraph there?

Voice: Um-hmm.

McGeorge Bundy: Yeah. [Pause]

Robert McNamara: May I say again that, uh, we've got a very, obviously when you get this kind of tight situation you have two problems. One is the tightest kind of security, which really means that when people come to meetings and so on, they have to be careful about not coming in visible groups, especially people who are visible Vietnamese; that's one thing. The secretary of state [Rusk], Roger [Hilsman] is a very visible figure. We get the desk man [the State Department's full-time officer for Vietnamese affairs] for someone who can only be concerned with that. It's even more important to come quietly. The other is that, I think it will be helpful, subject to any concern anyone else may have, guidance telegrams that relate to policy, on any circuit, uh, if we could have one information copy over here, we can make sure that nothing is going sour in the next three or four days in terms of crossed wires. Is that agreeable? To keep one central file we would, I don't think we want to delay people's operational action by having everything cleared, but that way we would be in a quick position to tell if, well we've got a crossed signal anywhere.

Dean Rusk: Well, ac-, actually on this one, actually *they* are the policy, any involved with policy, uh, should be cleared. [Voices overlap] So that, uh, we have possibly four channels that we

Robert McNamara: Well, let's be sure then that the operational stuff [word] does come in here and sometimes has a shading effect on policy; no policy messages as such will be sent except on

President Kennedy: Well, we are not planning to send a sudden message to Gen. Harkins?

[Voices overlap]

McGeorge Bundy: The other question I have marked here is should this be outgoing to Lodge *and* Harkins or whether we should make it outgoing to Lodge and say on the military channel, this message now going to Lodge and you should know about it.

[Voices overlap]

Maxwell Taylor: There's one purely military and I just, uh,

McGeorge Bundy: You should inform, you should inform Harkins of the full contents of this message.

President Kennedy: Well, it's all out, uh, [word] accepted up by the [word]; that's what you say to Lodge and Har-, Harkins

McGeorge Bundy: Well that is a real problem in one sense, of who's in charge here.

President Kennedy: Yes.

McGeorge Bundy: Well may Lodge information Harkins?

Dean Rusk: No, I think there's a problem of distribution on the ground out there, in terms of how many people cut in. Would it be better to instruct Lodge to inform Harkins at once?

[Voices overlap]

Maxwell Taylor: Then I would recommend the possibility of a military message letting him know.

McGeorge Bundy: I don't like to send military messages [words] that say

William Bundy: They're hard to control.

Robert McNamara: They're hard to control and also indicate a division in control here. [Voice speaks in background] I'd strongly urge [sending the message to] Lodge and Harkins. I don't think there's any problem with distribution out there.

Dean Rusk: Well if, I don'—, I.

U. Alexis Johnson: If it went by Harkins would this go to the military headquarters for distribution [words]?

Voice: No, sir.

McGeorge Bundy: A fast channel.

William Bundy: A fast channel, eyes only for Lodge and Harkins.

McGeorge Bundy: That's actually what we would say.

William Bundy: Action Ambassador, eyes only Lodge and Harkins.[13] We've mo-, got to be clear the Ambassador's chops.[14]

McGeorge Bundy: That's the way to put it.

President Kennedy: Let's put it that way. Say to Lodge, you'll get it first. Because if he wants a referral copy, [words] to Harkins, it, uh, expressed immediately that, uh [voices overlap] Harkins be brought in completely, right away.

William Colby: If the [word] are only Lodge and Harkins, sir, it *will* be delivered to General Harkins.

President Kennedy: Then we want Lodge to bring Harkins over right then to stop this train of discussion.

U. Alexis Johnson: I would put that at the bottom.

Voice: Before you say that

U. Alexis Johnson: This message goes to Harkins also. Lodge, you and Harkins only, sug-, You should at once coordinate with him.

President Kennedy: [Words] being interviewed. This now [words]

U. Alexis Johnson: Lodge is going to get quite upset about that. If we put this message in for Harkins, it's, and Harkins has already had the other message, then, we shouldn't say *this* message. This is an associated message to be discussed with you.

Voice: Shouldn't it be it's a discussion [words]

U. Alexis Johnson: Absolutely.

McGeorge Bundy: I don't mind. Eyes only for Ambassador and then just say, um, uh, this and associated messages should be promptly passed to and discussed with Harkins.

Voice: Discussed with, uh

President Kennedy: Harkins, so that he's fully informed.

Voice: Discussed with

President Kennedy: And his, uh, views are obtained.

McGeorge Bundy: All right. At the end, or at the beginning?

President Kennedy: Well, if he's going to be in charge of it? Let's say, if you're care of this mes—why don't you put it all in the second sentence?

McGeorge Bundy: This is our answer, and it should be discussed with

President Kennedy: Immediately.

McGeorge Bundy: Together with associated messages.

President Kennedy: General Harkins, and, uh,

McGeorge Bundy: Who will be in, who will have

President Kennedy: Military responsibility.

McGeorge Bundy: Military responsibility.

President Kennedy: In this area.

McGeorge Bundy: Eyes only, therefore, Ambassador. And then I have to get, instruct him in the first sentence to discuss it at once with

President Kennedy: Yeah.

McGeorge Bundy: Is that fair with you, Bob?

Robert McNamara: Sure.

President Kennedy: Now, your, your message will be ready within a hour or so?

William Colby: Within an hour.

McGeorge Bundy: OK. Do you need to see that?

President Kennedy: [unintelligible]

McGeorge Bundy: Good.

[Meeting Resumes]

Robert McNamara: Now, we're trying to tell him not to put out quite so thick as that, to hold himself in a little more flexible position *if he can*, uh, without getting too much, uh, fuss, and then say that we do want him to stay until Saturday, at least. Uh, our second problem is the contact and assessment problem. We're trying to pick up the last sentence of his message, which, uh, uh, [Noise] that stopper about Harkins, and modify that, say that it isn't, that isn't what *we* mean. We think if he has substantial doubt about the coup, he should communicate those doubts.

Voice: About the success

Robert McNamara: About the success.

Voice: Where does success

Robert McNamara: In other words,

President Kennedy: If he has doubts about the success, even though it's substantial, let's see if he does not feel the coup

Robert McNamara: We don't believe we can ask for a *sure thing*.

President Kennedy: That's right, and I understand that. But, I mean, we ought to have it that he is more convinced than *not* that's it's going to

Robert McNamara: That's right.

President Kennedy: Then he's certainly going to stop it.

McGeorge Bundy: You want to say unless chances are substantially better than even, you should express your concern forcefully?

President Kennedy: Substantially [unintelligible]. It's possible, but I don't think we can meet his deal with the substantial. In addition, you ought to say that Harkins is, uh; this is his [Lodge's] fault for not bringing Harkins in. If he'd had Harkins in the last few weeks, I don't think he suddenly [Voice overlaps]

Robert McNamara: We have to say, Mr. President, one of our outgoings could be the basis for his not putting Harkins in.

President Kennedy: All right.

Robert McNamara: We, whoa, a couple of them. [Voices overlap]

McGeorge Bundy: We said keep Harkins out of contact, but why he didn't consult us

Roger Hilsman: Mac, I agree that the outgoing could have been read that way; but that isn't why Harkins is not in this plan.

McGeorge Bundy: No, that's why [Voices overlap]

Robert McNamara: He would be quite concerned, Mr. President, that Harkins and Lodge weren't communicating. Two days ago I sent out a message to find out what was going on. We got a reply this morning. I don't want you to take time to read it all, but if you just read his reference in the margin. It points, I think, you'll see there's been a failure of communication on many subjects.

McGeorge Bundy: Is that when Lodge took over the press office? [Words, followed by a brief pause]

Voice: I will say [unintelligible]

President Kennedy: [unintelligible, except for "Conein"]

Robert McNamara: Well, I must say, I interpret it as their not feeling comfortable with our military, on coup planning.

Voice: I think that [words].

Averell Harriman: Well, shouldn't this message indicate that, uh, the President expects him from now on to keep, uh, Harkins fully informed?

Robert McNamara: Well, that was in yesterday's message, but it can be said again.

Averell Harriman: That was, that was the problem with, uh, that particular message.

Robert McNamara: Yeah, I think you're right.

President Kennedy: You see, Ambassador feels that 74228 [Identification number for a cable] does change 63560, it's a change the governments desire.

Robert McNamara: We read those to ourselves, Mr. President, while you weren't here, and we just don't see it. But they look to us like.

McGeorge Bundy: They look to us like—I, I'm sure the Ambassador thinks they've changed, but, they didn't change with these instructions.

President Kennedy: I said Lodge couldn't think that and he knows that we've a lot of information about coup, but as far as, hm, looks to be his ass, he's *for a coup*. [Voices overlap] He's for it for what he thinks are very good reasons. I say he's much stronger for it than we are here, but well I admire his, his nerve if not his, his prudence, uh, but at least he *is* for, uh, isn't for it, just as much a gut way. So therefore he's got a good many reasons why he can't help us.

Voice: That's right.

Robert McNamara: We've written a [words] we've written a series of [words] which Harkins reads, meaning that we would hope both, uh, Lodge [Voices overlap]

Voice: Meaning we hope they get in touch.

Voice: [Laughter] That's exactly right.

President Kennedy: "I'm not opposed to a gov't change, no indeed." That, that's a colloquial aside, "I'm not opposed to change, no indeed, but I am inclined to feel that at this time the change should be in methods of governing rather than complete change of personnel. I have seen no batting order proposed by any of the coup groups. I think we should take a hard look at any proposed list before we make any decisions. In my contacts here I have seen no one with the strength of character of Diem, at least in fighting communists."[15]

Voice: He's regarded as a personal [words—friend of President Diem?] and he doesn't realize the conflicts underneath [words].

Voice: Sir,

President Kennedy: [continues reading Gen. Harkins' telegram] "I am not a Diem man per se. I certainly see the faults in his character. I am here to back 14 million SVN people in their fight against communism and it just happens that Diem is their leader at this time. Most of the Generals I have talked to agree they can go along with Diem, all say it's the Nhu family they are opposed to. Perhaps the pressures we have begun to apply will cause Diem and Nhu to change their ways. This is apparently not evident as yet. I'm sure the pressures we have begun to apply if continued will affect the war effort. To date they have not. I am watching this closely and will report when I think they have." I'm way ahead, one, two. . . . [Pause]

Roger Hilsman: How many governments do you want in Saigon, Mr. President?

Averell Harriman: Do you, uh, do you want to, uh

Robert McNamara: Yeah, on this command thing, we would, we, you suggest we'll have to look at the exact language, and I'm not sure we've got it right yet on the control-and-assessment problem. I think we should feed in here that on all this we want Harkins fully informed. Then there's the help of the command arrangements for the coup, and during the coup, which we think he's misunderstood. We think before the coup we intend no change, that Trueheart will be the chargé, although we do believe that, uh, in contact with Conein and both in instruction to him as to what he ought to be finding out and in debriefing, both Harkins [tape excised for two seconds]

Voice: With Trueheart?

Robert McNamara: So there ought to be a troika feeding the content. During the coup, Harkins takes charge. We are not talking about anything visible to the Saigon government, but something visible to us. And, uh, finally, we need contingency instructions for the case of a coup. Lodge obviously fears that Harkins might put a coup down, if he were put in charge while Lodge is away. We intend, uh, a hands-off attitude as far as possible. I think his own telegram is not too bad on that.

President Kennedy: But, uh, don't we have us back a little more before we get into [words]. What did we get into last night about the armed forces

McGeorge Bundy: I, I covered that briefly

President Kennedy: We're not satisfied with his answer, the attitude

Robert McNamara: No, you wanted the other way to do this thing: [words] personal tone of this sentence may help, and that is I think make it Eyes Only for Lodge from you. Let's write an "I." So that he can get a direct [Voices overlap]

Voice: . . . Mr. President, is Lodge's: "Do not claim we have the power to delay or discourage a coup." I mean, if we make a judgment. [Voices overlap] Of course we control.

President Kennedy: Let's write our thing of last night — just to say to him, uh, we cannot agree with that, number one, and we cannot accept being in a *passive* role unless you get more information from Don.

McGeorge Bundy: He doesn't even accept it himself, as he said, that if he thought the thing weren't going to work, he'd do everything he could

President Kennedy: Lodge says he doesn't give us anything to think it's going to work. Do you want to get out a wire?

Robert McNamara: Yup, I will, Mr. President. Now, uh, and I will check it, if I may, at the staff level around, or send it direct to principals, whichever you prefer.

Dean Rusk: I think the latter is better.

McGeorge Bundy: All right.

President Kennedy: If we don't actually, uh, he can't get it till tomorrow morning now.

McGeorge Bundy: Well, it's midnight there.

President Kennedy: He won't get it until tomorrow; he won't get this tomorrow morning.

McGeorge Bundy: Well, we get it out, no there's nothing, there's nothing that he can do anything about at 2:00 A.M. in any event unless

President Kennedy: But I think the earlier he gets it in the morning

McGeorge Bundy: Well, I think we ought to get it, I don't see any differently about your seeing before you take off, which is, uh, mid-afternoon.

President Kennedy: Yeah, I just think he ought to be, uh, backing much harder on our asking for dispositions, uh, must have that wire from, uh,

McGeorge Bundy: You think he's using [Voices overlap]

President Kennedy: I thought your fellow did a good job yesterday, John.

John McCone: Uh, Colby?

President Kennedy: Yes.

John McCone: He's very [words]

President Kennedy: But, I, uh, thought that, uh, must be, somewhat impressed by Colby's, uh, intelligence.

Robert McNamara: We've been supporting Colby messages out and not answering, Mr. President. Uh, and [words] cut order of battle.

John McCone: We have uh a, a report here that the [Voice overlaps: "I think this message"], from our station chief as to what happened being worked on with MACV, the 5th Division forces,[16] and so forth. Take that.

Voice: Now you'd like to spring that as from you to him?

Voice: I think that's a little more positive.

John McCone: Mr. President, uh, on our collection let me say this: I think we're on a down slope at the present time. And the question is, there is a chance that we really, uh, we should all [words] when it goes fast if there's a coup it doesn't work. I still think that, uh, that chances are very high that, uh, there's no outcome of this unless there's a real chance of failure. It's serious it seems to me.

Robert McNamara: We have as evidence on a number of different circuits, and I think I would associate this [Voices overlap]

John McCone: What about [Voices overlap]

President Kennedy: Harkins doesn't agree. What is the

Voice: I would do that too, sir.

President Kennedy: What?

Voice: I would do that too.

President Kennedy: Explain this again. [Voices overlap]

Voice: John [McCone] has a new handle—

Averell Harriman: There is a CAS [CIA Saigon station] assessment here that, uh, let's see, uh, "the standing of the Diem regime is attriting away, that we can no longer be confident that we achieve victory over the Viet Cong in the foreseeable future. Starting with the Hue incident on 8th May there has been increasing disaffection of the articulate segments of population, principally in the urban areas, a gradual constriction of political following advising Diem and Nhu, leaving only those individuals who advocated a hard line from the outset. Rejection by Diem and Nhu of measures to redress the situation, so even most superficial reforms are heightening confrontation of the GVN and the United States government. The loss of confidence in the situation within the economic sector, a hardening in determination on the part of significant elements of the military for safety, situation in hand. These are all" [Voices overlap]

Voice: Who furnished that? [tape excised for three seconds]

Averell Harriman: I had to say this in the surest, clearest sense 'cause I don't think we attach too much importance to a single report, that's a, that's an authorized serial report on the possibility of defection among South Vietnamese [word]. This is [words]. And it's not evaluated, here. [Pause] At the moment all the [word] seem to be following the same direction.

John McCone: This one is the top labor leader, who Colby thinks is himself important.

Dean Rusk: Who is to be a close associate of Diem, period.

[Voices overlap]

Voice: . . . held here in the United States [words] be allowed to [words].

Voice: Who is [name]?

McGeorge Bundy: . . . Can, if I may [words]

President Kennedy: You have any thoughts?

Robert McNamara: No, I, I'm sorry if there are cables which suggest what I say is [word]. Well I, I, we just *have* to strengthen that country team out there. Must get a man of Colby's type in there as fast as you, because, I mean, *none of us* has a feeling that Conein has been instructed by anyone other than Lodge and we know, there're bound [word] instructions to Conein to carry out the daily contacts. I personally doubt Trueheart is strong enough under this situation.

McGeorge Bundy: I, I myself, Mr. President, that the second national [words], the whole country team, it'll be healthy when they're not there.

President Kennedy: [unintelligible, except "Good"]

Dean Rusk: Is Colby, any way Colby available to run a station?

John McCone: Yes.

President Kennedy: Colby, and then what, somebody to assist Lodge, Trueheart.

U. Alexis Johnson: I really think that this is about the best we can do. I don't think we can run the day-to-day contacts on these coup

[Voices overlap]

Dean Rusk: . . . and Trueheart was in charge, and Nolting's not there, I thought he handled the situation extraordinarily well during a very tough period, when he saw Diem almost every day, said the right things and thought of the right things. This was during the, uh, the Buddhist, uh, uprising.

John McCone: I told you, I, I'm, I think there are reasons why I might, as they come out of the gory [words], I'll be wearing a rose, and you'll be wearing a [words].

Dean Rusk: I agree with that.

[Voices overlap]

President Kennedy: That might have been the way that we heard about [words].

Voice: But, but the problem Dean [answering Rusk] is, that, that there is not, uh, exchange of views there between Lodge [voices overlap] and Harkins, uh, uh, and, and, it's not a tightly run organization. We're in a very difficult situation here.

Voice: I agree this is true primarily, almost, almost so heavy on the, on the coup planning part.

Voice: Also on the military appraisal.

McGeorge Bundy: [Words] They're not sharing assessments of the day-to-day life now. This is serious. [Voices overlap]

Voice: I suppose it's

McGeorge Bundy: Maybe both sides.

President Kennedy: [Words] I should think probably a riot, we're back where we were. Had it shown itself at the beginning [noise] is all we [words].

Voice: Deterioration.

Voice: Oh, I think we can get through it.

Voice: I think [word], Mr. President.

President Kennedy: I think, probably without you, we had contributed to a weaker [word — "development"?]

Dean Rusk: I hope this cable is ready; we'll make it very clear to the Ambassador that, uh, our failure to intervene at this time is based upon his assessment this will succeed, rather this will not fail.

President Kennedy: I think we take, as I say, Joe [Mendenhall] [words], Joe's judgment's always right, he's, I'd say, the most loyal young man I've ever met, he came back, knew it was hopeless, it was endless. I, uh, I mean, I really say it's an awful lot of these boys, but however that is the only one I've ever [words].

Let's put it all [to] Cabot. Then you're talking an end to this thing [Voice speaks over the president] What?

Averell Harriman: There's just one thing that troubles me a little bit. Cabot is totally inexperienced out there. He's been there just over 60 days. I don't think he'd ever been there before, and

President Kennedy: Been there as a young reporter once?

Averell Harriman: Maybe. As a young reporter.

Dean Rusk: He once was there on some trip.

[End of tape]

~~TOP SECRET EYES ONLY~~ 10/30/63

EYES ONLY FOR AMBASSADOR LODGE

FROM: BUNDY

1 Your 2063 shows important difference in our views and we must repeat that we cannot accept conclusion that we have no power to delay or discourage a coup. In your paragraph 12 you say that if you were convinced that the coup was going to fail you would of course do everything you could to stop it. We believe that on this basis you should do everything you can to stop or delay any operation which, in your best judgment, does not give better than even prospect of quick success.

We recognize the danger of appearing hostile to generals, but we do not share implication in your message that only conviction of ~~imminent~~ certain failure justifies intervention. We believe that your standard for intervention should be that stated above.

2. If then you should conclude that there is not a better than even chance of quick success, you should communicate this doubt to generals in a way calculated to persuade them to desist at least until chances are better. In this communication you should use the weight of your best advice and explicitly reject any implication that we oppose the effort of the generals because of preference for present reg

~~TOP SECRET EYES ONLY~~

Draft of cable to Ambassador Lodge.

TOP SECRET EYES ONLY　　　　　　-2-

We recognize need to bear in mind generals' interpretation of
U. S. role in 1960 coup attempt and you should maintain clear
distinction between strong advice given as a friend and choice of
sides by USG.

3. We ~~xx~~ continue to be deeply interested in up-to-the-minute
assessment of prospects and are sending this before reply to
our ▓▓79126. We hope for continuous exchange latest
assessments on this topic.

4. ~~On command arrangements outlined paragraph~~ To clarify
our intent, paragraph 7 of our 79109 is rescinded and we restate
(a)
our desires as follows: While you are in Saigon you will be chief
of country team in all circumstances and our only instruction is
that we are sure it will help to have Harkins fully informed at all
stages and to use advice from ▓▓ him ▓▓▓▓ in framing guidance
for coup contacts and assessment. We continue to be concerned
that neither ▓▓▓ nor any other reporting source is getting the
clarity we would like with respect to alignments of forces and
levels of determination.

(b) When you leave Saigon and before there is a coup,
Truehart will be chief of the country team, and our only modification
of existing procedures is that in this circumstance we believe that
all instruction and debriefing of ▓▓▓ should be conducted in immediate

TOP SECRET EYES ONLY

TOP SECRET EYES ONLY   -3-

consultation with Harkins ▓▓▓▓ so that all three know what

✓ is said ▓▓▓▓ and what he reports at all stages.

            military situation develops

    (c) If you have left and a coup occurs, we believe that ~~the~~

situation

~~satisfaction~~ requires final local U. S. authority to be vested in

most experienced officer/with appropriate background and that

officer in our view is Harkins.   We do not repeat not intend that

this internal switch in final responsibility should be publicized in

any way, and Harkins will of course be guided in basic posture by

our instructions, which follow in paragraph 5.   Thus we do not

believe that this switch can have the effect suggested in your paragraph 8

  5. This paragraph contains our present standing instructions

for U. S. posture in the event of a coup.

    (a) U. S. authorities will reject appeals for direct

intervention from either side, and U. S. -controlled aircraft and

other resources will not be committed between the battle lines or in

support of either side, without authorization from Washington.

    (b) In event of indecisive contest, U. S. authorities

may in their discretion agree to perform any acts agreeable to both side:

such as removal of key personalities or relay of information.   In

such actions, however, U. S. authorities will strenuously avoid

appearance of pressure on either side. It is not in the interest of USG

~~TOP SECRET EYES ONLY~~   -4-

to be or appear to be instrument of existing government or instrument of coup.

6.   We have your message about return to Washington and if announcement has not already been made, we suggest that it be kept as low-key and quiet as possible, and we also urge that if possible you keep open the exact time of your departure.   We are strongly sensitive to great disadvantage of having you out of Saigon if this should turn out to be a week of decision and if it can be avoided we would prefer not to see you pinned to a fixed hour of departure now.

which ~~unless~~ produces a ~~real~~ military confrontation Saigon

This is the draft cable (the notations are McGeorge Bundy's

~~TOP SECRET~~

DRAFT OUTGOING TO LODGE

Your 2023, 2040, 2041, and 2043 examined with care at highest levels here. They give much clearer picture groups alleged plans and also indicate chances of action with or without our approval now so significant that we should urgently consider our attitude and contingency plans.

Concur you and other US elements should take no action that could indicate US awareness coup possibility. However, believe you could defer your departure until Saturday if we send berth-equipped military aircraft to take you out Saturday afternoon, arriving Washington Sunday morning. You could explain this being done as convenience and would still permit your arrival Washington on same or even earlier schedule. A further advantage such aircraft is that it would permit your prompt return from any point en route if necessary.

B$_e$ lieve our attitude to coup group could still have decisive importance and we therefore need urgently your assessment with Harkins of chances of success as well as your estimate group's capacity to govern. Although cables indicate some civilian contacts on periphery, they do not give any clear picture group's intentions for

SANITIZED ~~TOP SECRET~~

NLK-82-230

BY _____ NARS. DATE 11/1/84

Draft of cable with notations by McGeorge Bundy.

TOP SECRET - 2 -

civilian association or leadership. While notice as little as four hours would greatly complicate expression of US position, we still may have alternatives of continued explicit hands-off policy, positive encouragemen or discouragement. ████████████████████████████ ██ ██████████████████████████ Agree that disclosure to GVN, while more decisive, would raise manifold problems and would have to be considered in more serious light.

From operational standpoint, ████████████ ██ ██████████ We badly need some corroborative evidence whether Minh and others directly and completely involved. ████████████ ██ we need better military picture and that Big Minh could communicate this most naturally and easily to Stillwell? We recognize desirability involving MACV to minimum, but believe Stillwell far more desirable this purpose ████████████████████████████

If coup should start, question of protecting US nationals at once arises. We can move Marine BLT into Saigon by air from Okinawa within 24 hours if Tan Son Nhut available. Independently, orders being issued today to seaborne Marine BLT from Subic Bay to

TOP SECRET

TOP SECRET   - 3 -

Cap St. Jacques area, in position to close Saigon within two to three

hours. Although this action might become known, past history of

short notice exercise is such that we do not believe it would tip our hand.

In event of coup starting, you, or in your absence DCM,

would of course still be senior American. However Harkins would

promptly have to take broad measures for security US forces and safety

US nationals, and in so doing would have to exercise extensive emergency

functions under you or DCM's political guidance. This further under-

scores importance keeping him fully and currently informed of all

developments.

We must also consider contingencies. If after start of coup

attempt, coup group or GVN should ask for US help one against the other,

our present thinking is that we should adopt firm hands-off policy at that

point and make this clear and public. However, if ascendancy were not

quickly established one way or other, our military measures for safety US

forces and nations might involve confrontation with one side or other.

If coup should succeed promptly, we would have to consider

position at once, with our present best guess that we would affirm support

subject to conditions such as present guidance. Tougher case would be if

coup failed and we were confronted with charges US complicity, request

TOP SECRET

TOP SECRET : - 4 -

to withdraw, or even sharp switch GVN policy such as opening serious negotiations with North Vietnam. These questions unlikely to arise p your return here, but for guidance of DCM and others our present thinking is that we should rebut charges and seek to restore nearest to status quo ante possible. One contingency action should certainly be preparation basic draft disavowal statement, and amendments to meet any specifics adduced on basis actual ▨▨▨ contacts or any others GV might drag out.

TOP SECRET

Telegram from the President's Special Assistant for National Security Affairs (Bundy) to the Ambassador in Vietnam (Lodge)

Washington, October 29, 1963 — 7:22 P.M.

Eyes only for Ambassador Lodge from McGeorge Bundy.

1. Your 2023, [*document number not declassified*], 2041 and [*document number not declassified*] examined with care at highest levels here. You should promptly discuss this reply and associated messages with Harkins whose responsibilities toward any coup are very heavy especially after you leave (see paragraph 7 below). They give much clearer picture group's alleged plans and also indicate chances of action with or without our approval now so significant that we should urgently consider our attitude and contingency plans. We note particularly Don's curiosity your departure and his insistence Conein be available from Wednesday night on, which suggests date might be as early as Thursday.

2. Believe our attitude to coup group can still have decisive effect on its decisions. We believe that what we say to coup group can produce delay of coup and that betrayal of coup plans to Diem is not our only way of stopping coup. We therefore need urgently your combined assessment with Harkins and CAS (including their separate comments if they desire). We concerned that our line-up of forces in Saigon (being cabled in next message) indicates approximately equal balance of forces, with substantial possibility serious and prolonged fighting or even defeat. Either of these could be serious or even disastrous for U.S. interests, so that we must have assurance balance of forces clearly favorable.

3. With your assessment in hand, we might feel that we should convey message to Don, whether or not he gives 4 or 48 hours notice that would (a) continue explicit hands-off policy, (b) positively encourage coup, or (c) discourage.

4. In any case, believe Conein should find earliest opportunity express to Don that we do not find presently revealed plans give clear prospect of quick results. This conversation should call attention important Saigon units still apparently loyal to Diem and raise serious issue as to what means coup group has to deal with them.

5. From operational standpoint, we also deeply concerned Don only spokesman for group and possibility cannot be discounted he may not be in good faith. We badly need some corroborative evidence whether Minh and others directly and completely involved. In view Don's claim he doesn't handle "military planning" could not Conein tell Don that we need better military picture and that Big Minh could communicate this most naturally and easily to Stilwell? We recognize desirability involving MACV to minimum, but believe Stilwell far more desirable this purpose than using Conein both ways.

6. Complexity above actions raises question whether you should adhere to

present Thursday schedule. Concur you and other US elements should take no action that could indicate US awareness coup possibility. However, DOD is sending berth-equipped military aircraft that will arrive Saigon Thursday and could take you out thereafter as late as Saturday afternoon in time to meet your presently proposed arrival Washington Sunday. You could explain this being done as convenience and that your Washington arrival is same. A further advantage such aircraft is that it would permit your prompt return from any point en route if necessary. To reduce time in transit, you should use this plane, but we recognize delaying your departure may involve greater risk that you personally would appear involved if any action took place. However, advantages your having extra two days in Saigon may outweigh this and we leave timing of flight to your judgment.

7. Whether you leave Thursday or later, believe it essential that prior your departure there be fullest consultation Harkins and CAS and that there be clear arrangements for handling (a) normal activity, (b) continued coup contacts, (c) action in event a coup starts. We assume you will wish Trueheart as chargé to be head of country team in normal situation, but highest authority desires it clearly understood that after your departure Harkins should participate in supervision of all coup contacts and that in event coup begins, he become head of country team and direct representative of President, with Trueheart in effect acting as POLAD. On coup contacts we will maintain continuous guidance and will expect equally continuous reporting with prompt account of any important divergences in assessments of Harkins and [*less than 1 line not declassified*].

8. If coup should start, question of protecting U.S. nationals at once arises. We can move Marine btl into Saigon by air from Okinawa within 24 hours if Tan Son Nhut available. We are sending instructions to CINCPAC to arrange orderly movement of seaborne Marine btl to waters adjacent to South Vietnam in position to close Saigon within approximately 24 hours.

9. We are now examining post-coup contingencies here and request your immediate recommendations on position to be adopted after coup begins, especially with respect to requests for assistance of different sorts from one side or the other. Also request you forward contingency recommendations for action if coup (a) succeeds, (b) fails, (c) is indecisive.

10. We reiterate burden of proof must be on coup group to show a substantial possibility of quick success; otherwise, we should discourage them from proceeding since a miscalculation could result in jeopardizing U.S. position in Southeast Asia.

Lyndon B. Johnson

MARCH 2, 1964: PRESIDENT JOHNSON DISCUSSES VIETNAM WITH
DEFENSE SECRETARY ROBERT S. McNAMARA

President Johnson and Robert McNamara have a late-morning phone conversation that reviews the issues currently at play in the public and Pentagon arenas. One is policy regarding strategic nuclear forces. The bulk of their talk, however, concerns Vietnam. By now Diem has been overthrown and murdered, the American effort in South Vietnam is growing rapidly, and the United States is carrying out covert attacks on North Vietnam. As he liked to do, in this talk with Secretary McNamara, LBJ referred to the views on these subjects of various senators and congressmen, along with newspaper editors, which he quotes to McNamara at several points in the conversation. The White House press office, at this time still headed by Kennedy Press Secretary Pierre Salinger (the "Pierre" referred to at one point in the telephone call), assembled a media report for the president early every day, with summaries of news articles and broadcasts plus editorial opinions. President Johnson was an avid consumer of this information and used it frequently in his phone calls as this conversation shows.

It was Robert McNamara who placed this call, and his first issue had to do with defense policy. Senator Barry Goldwater, then emerging as the leading Republican candidate for the nomination to run for president in the 1964 elections, had been charging that U.S. nuclear missiles were unreliable. In fact there was a problem with the solid fuel propellant used in the earliest versions of the Minuteman intercontinental ballistic missile that was being deployed at that time. McNamara tells LBJ that Air Force officers have been feeding secret information to Goldwater to buttress their case for a new manned bomber program. But it is equally likely that the Republican senator, who was a reserve general in the Air Force as well as a member of the Senate Armed Services Committee, had come by the information in his regular briefings. To respond to the charges, McNamara suggests that the Navy should put out a report stating that their ballistic missile submarines by themselves are capable of fulfilling all the attack requirements planned for a nuclear situation. President Johnson rightly questions whether such a measure would lead to a dispute between the Navy and Air Force. Interestingly and candidly, Secretary McNamara actually replies that such bureaucratic infighting might be desirable. Debates over the proper mix of nuclear forces and various weapons programs went on through all the presidencies featured here and others as well. For example, the manned bomber program referred to here was eventually concretized by an Air Force study of and request for what it called the "advanced manned strategic aircraft." That study would be passed along to the Nixon administration, which approved development of what became the B-1 bomber. The B-1 was actually canceled by President Jimmy Carter, who was looking ahead to the B-2 stealth bomber, and then was reinstated by Ronald Reagan in the 1980s.

Once they dispose of the general defense issues, LBJ and McNamara turn to Vietnam. The president has been asked repeatedly in recent weeks about proper U.S. courses of action in Vietnam, and Johnson tells his secretary of defense he wants a summary of alternatives that he can pull out and read when the question comes up again. What is especially important about this conversation in early 1964 is that it takes place before President Johnson has made any of his major decisions on opening a bombing campaign against North Vietnam or committing troops to combat in South Vietnam. LBJ's comments imply his lack of enthusiasm for a troop deployment, and he more directly states his distaste for either a withdrawal from Vietnam or an international agreement formalizing neutrality for Vietnam. The last comment is significant because France was at this time pressing a diplomatic campaign to solve the Vietnam problem by means of neutralization along the lines of Cambodia and Laos, originally put in place by the Geneva agreements of 1954. Talking to McNamara, Johnson cites the views of a number of congressional leaders and newspaper editorial writers on the Vietnam problem. In a 1997 retrospective conference in Hanoi on missed opportunities in the war (at which, incidentally,

McNamara was present), former North Vietnamese officials conceded that the possibility of such a neutralization formula applied to South Vietnam was one opportunity they missed during the conflict. Very likely both sides missed this chance for peace for the same reason—it would have prevented each of the sides from ending the war in victory. President Johnson also disliked the idea of responding to a French diplomatic initiative and, as historians have only begun to understand, had built loyalties of his own to the Saigon government.

Instead Lyndon Johnson had given a speech in Los Angeles that warned North Vietnam against continuing to support the National Liberation Front insurgency against the Saigon leadership. The president had told Hanoi that by providing such support it was playing a "deeply dangerous game." The speech proved far more controversial in the United States than LBJ had anticipated. Political commentators and leading figures feared the war in Southeast Asia that was threatened, however vaguely, in the president's speech. The words were not Johnson's own but had come to him in a speech draft that he thought unobjectionable before his Los Angeles appearance. On the phone with McNamara now, President Johnson sought to find out whether the Pentagon had been the source for the text, and whether his secretary of defense had seen the phrase or objected to it. McNamara had not. The president also conceded that one of his own staff, Press Secretary Pierre Salinger, had told others that that phrase in Johnson's speech was especially important, in effect giving it greater importance than Johnson might have. LBJ would pursue this matter elsewhere (see his conversations on March 4)—he had been told by officials in Saigon that the phrase might have come from the State Department's chief policy planner, Walt W. Rostow. McNamara essentially advised LBJ to say as little as possible about Vietnam.

Finally the conversation turns to concrete action in South Vietnam. Ambassador Henry Cabot Lodge, at this time a possible presidential contender in the 1964 elections, had been sending cables to Washington recommending measures that were possible. On February 19, Lodge had pronounced U.S. economic assistance sufficient, with the exception of money to increase South Vietnamese military pay. The next day Lodge had said that pressures could and should be applied against North Vietnam. McNamara tells the president that the money for pay had already been approved. As for the "pretty offensive steps" that LBJ mentions here, both he and McNamara were aware that a covert program of graduated military pressures against the North had been in progress since January 1964. That program would eventually lead directly to the Gulf of Tonkin incident (see conversations of August 4, 1964). In any case, President Johnson's political interests are on display in this conversation where he states a concern not to have it appear that the one thing Lodge asked for has been denied, and demands that a record be made on the matter of what action had been taken on the ambassador's recommendations.

Lyndon B. Johnson
March 2, 1964, 11:00 A.M.
Telephone Conversation with Secretary of Defense Robert S. McNamara
Regarding Vietnam

President Lyndon B. Johnson: Yes?

Woman's Voice: Secretary of Defense Robert McNamara on Nine Oh.

President Johnson: Bob, how're we doing?

Secretary of Defense Robert McNamara: Oh, fine, I think, Mr. President. I thought your press conference was terrific on Saturday.

President Johnson: Well

Secretary McNamara: Came over damn well.

President Johnson: We got another one on Wednesday. One of these quickie ones, so you find us some stuff over there.

Secretary McNamara: I'll do everything I can. I thought I'd hold one Thursday before I leave. I'm going to have to do it either then or at the plane site. I might as well control it over here.

President Johnson: Um, what's new? Anything?

Secretary McNamara: No, I think we're coming along reasonably well. We've had really quite an underground battle here on missile dependability, Goldwater's charge. And the Air Force has been, I think I mentioned to you briefly, feeding it, I think, surreptitiously, both because it supports their, their desire for a manned bomber and also because I think there's a substantial number up there that are pro-Goldwater. But, uh, I, I think we've got it reasonably well under control; and I'm having issued today a very strong statement. Paul Nitze,

Secretary of the Navy, concurred in by Admiral McDonald, saying in effect that it doesn't make any difference whether the Air Force's bombers or missiles are reliable, that the Navy can win the war alone. And uh documenting it. It doesn't say quite that language, but the theme of it is that. And, and I think

President Johnson: Won't that start a fight between them?

Secretary McNamara: Well [laughs], that's what I'd rather like to do. I think divide and conquer is a pretty good rule in this situation. And as, and uh, to be quite frank, I've tried to do that in the last couple of weeks and it's coming along pretty well. And I think we've got Goldwater dampened down for the minute on, on attacking us.

President Johnson: Uh, I want you to dictate to me uh, a memorandum, a couple of pages. Uh, four-letter words and short sentences and several paragraphs so I can read it and study it and commit to memory. Not for the purpose of using it now. I'm not going to give out your figures on 20,000 killed last year compared to 5,000. But on the situation in Vietnam, the Vietnam picture. If you had to put in, 600 words, or maybe a thousand words, if you have to go that long. But, uh, just like you talk. Uh, I'd like for you to say that there are several courses that could be followed. We could send our own divisions in there and our own Marines in there, and they could start attacking the Vee, Viet Cong, and the results that would likely flow from that.

Secretary McNamara: Mm-hmm.

President Johnson: Uh, We could come out of there and say we're willing to neutralize, let 'em neutralize South Vietnam and let the commies take North Vietnam. And as soon as we get out, they could uh swallow up South Vietnam. And that would go. Or we could pull out and say the hell with you, we're going to have Fortress America, we're going home. And that would mean that here's what'd happen in Thailand, and here's what'd happen in the Philippines, and come on back and get us back to Honolulu. Or we can say this is the Vietnamese War, and they've got 200,000 men, and they're untrained; and we've got to bring their morale up. And they have nothing really to fight for because of the type of government they've had. We can put in socially conscious people and try to get 'em to improve their, their own government, and then what the people get out their own government, we can train 'em how to fight. And 200,000 of them ultimately will be able to take care of these 25,000. And that uh after considering all of these, it seems that uh the latter offers the best alternative for America to follow. Now if the latter has failed, uh, then, uh, we have to make another decision. But at this point it has not failed. And, uh, in the, last month, X number of Viet Cong were killed, and X number of South Vietnamese. Last year, 20,000 killed; 5,000; while we have lost a total of 100 people. In one day in Korea we lost a thousand, or whatever it is. And that, uh, after all, this is it.

Now I'm talking to people every day that are asking this question. And I've got to have some kind of a summarized, logical, factual, analysis of it. And I believe that you could give it to me better than anybody else because you've been out there three times, or four, whatever it's been. And uh I assume that you think that the course we're following is the, is the one that's less, least, dangerous, and least expensive at the moment; or will you be advocating another one pretty strong? You may advocate that after you come back. If you don't, why maybe we're wasting money on your going out there. But, I would like to have for this period, when everybody is asking me, something in my own words I can say—well, here are, here are the alternative[s]. And here's our theory. And here's what we're basing it on. Now we don't say that, that we win; we don't know; we're doing the best we can. We think we ought to have to train them. Why did you say you'd send a thousand home? I'd put a sentence in that uh because they'd complete their mission. An illustration is that several hundred of them were working as military police and they trained military police, so we didn't need to keep them there. Why did Secretary McNamara say they they were coming back in '65? Because uh when you say you're going to give a man a high school education and he's in the 10th grade and you've got two years to do it, you can train him in two years; that doesn't mean that everybody comes back. But that means your training ought to be in pretty good shape by that time. Now there may be other problems, but that's what's said. Not anything inconsistent, except the people who know nothing about it.

But now this morning uh, well, now here's a summary. Senator Scott said eh about the war in Vietnam yesterday, said "the war which we can neither win, lose nor drop is evidence of an instability of ideas, a floating series of judgments, our policy of nervous conciliation which is extremely disturbing." There's one of a hundred Senators that says that, and that's front page of the *Baltimore Sun*. Senator Javits, called on the State Department to issue a white paper documenting the necessity for the U.S. to stay in South Vietnam, *Detroit Press*. Senator Case says, "We can hardly be worse than we have been doing lately, hoping we find other alternatives than the two mentioned either going in and fighting the American troops, or pulling out entirely," *Washington Post*.

Erwin Canhan, editor of the *Christian Science Monitor*, said, "The President's press conference was placid and calm and not informative. Answers did not suggest that he was preparing the American people for the worst." And warned that public opinion is not prepared for a big Vietnam commitment, such as the '62 Cuban showdown on Korea. Alexander Kendrick, ABC, says, "the answer cannot be delayed much longer," and he warned, "psychologically we're approaching the Yalu River again, where Chinese and possibly Russian intervention must be expected." Uh, now, they're all saying, that following our speech in Los Angeles, where we said that this is very, very dangerous business

Secretary McNamara: Mr. President, may I interrupt you? Who put the line in, I'm curious as to that?

President Johnson: I don't know. I don't know. I don't know. I would assume Bundy. "Deeply dangerous game," but I don't see anything wrong with it, even yet. I think it is deeply dangerous when anybody starts aggression. Now, that was not where it started at all. I blew my top here for a whole damn week. I jumped on you and jumped on Rusk both, why you were saying out in Saigon that you're invading North Vietnam, even if you were going to invade it. Now I know what Rostow, how he feels, and I know how we all feel, but they came back a week before we said it's a deeply dangerous game; this stuff was pouring out by reams, and the first story said military officials in Saigon, it came from Saigon. I talked to you about it, and you said that that wasn't correct, so I jumped on Rusk about it; and Rusk comes back and points out the story itself, military officials, and that's where it came from. Now the story came from Saigon that we're getting ready to do this. A lot of people in Saigon they tell me said that they got it from the State Department here, that Rostow had a propaganda move on to really invade North Vietnam and always had had it. Now I don't know enough about the inner workings of these two departments, but I know that this thing has gone on ten days or a week before we got it, and I can get the clippings and show them where they were full of it. But now they want to hang it on a little higher person and say that I indicated that we're going to invade uh Vietnam or that we're going to hit the Chinese, or that we're going to bomb Moscow. Now I didn't do any such thing. I said that this is deeply dangerous, and it *is* deeply dangerous. It's dangerous for any, any nation to start aggression and start enveloping uh neutral, uh freedom-loving people. And I uh think it was dangerous to 5,000 of them, 20,000 of them that got killed there last year. I think you could, uh, I think maybe Pierre, did get into an argument with somebody and say this is an important sentence out in

California because they were writin' about the sentence that said the communists—what was it Phil Potter—communist civil war; and they wanted to know what we meant by civil war and we were talking about the fight that was going on between the Chinese and the Russians, calling each other ugly names and things like that, and we say that is civil war. But uh, they're trying to transfer this stuff, that's been coming out of Saigon, onto this deeply dangerous statement, and uh the, the, we're just not doing it. They say that the administration is putting out all this propaganda itself. Now I'd just give anything in the world if we could stop everybody from talking except the Secretary of State and Secretary of Defense and the President, and that we could clear those things. Was not this Los Angeles speech cleared with your department?

Secretary McNamara: No, I didn't see it. I

President Johnson: [Interrupts] Well, it was given to Bundy to clear with everybody?

Secretary McNamara: Well . . .

President Johnson: It should have been.

Secretary McNamara: There wasn't anything in it I would change, or have made a difference.

President Johnson: Well, it ought to be. Now is there anything in the press conference you'd change?

Secretary McNamara: No [chuckles], I thought it was excellent.

President Johnson: Do you think it's a mistake to explain what I'm saying now about Vietnam and what we're faced with?

Secretary McNamara: Well I, I do think, Mr. President, that would be wise for you to say as little as possible. The frank answer is we don't know what's going on out there. The signs I see coming through the cables are disturbing signs— poor morale in, in Vietnamese forces, poor morale in the armed forces, disunity, tremendous amount of coup planning against Khanh. About what you'd expect in the situation.

President Johnson: Then why don't we take some, why don't we take some pretty offensive steps pretty quickly, then? Why don't we uh commend Khanh on his operation and try to, try to prop him up? Why don't we raise the salary of the soldiers to improve that morale instead of waiting a long time? Uh, why don't we uh do some of these, do some of these things uh that uh inclined to, to, bolster them?

Secretary McNamara: Well, I'm not sure that uh they'd hear or

President Johnson: I sure as hell don't want to get in the position Lodge recommended to me, the one thing he recommended is please, give us a little more pay for our soldiers, and we turned him down.

Secretary McNamara: Oh, no. We've done that?

President Johnson: We haven't acted; we said we're gong to wait until you go out there.

Secretary McNamara: Well, no, he knows that there's money for that, there's no problem on that issue.

President Johnson: Well, then why don't we clear it up so we get him answered. Now I think that politically, I'm not a military strategist, but I think that as long as we've got him there and he makes recommendations, and we act on them, particularly if we act favorably, we're not in too bad a condition politically. But I think that when he wires us and says the only damn thing I want you to do is give them an increase in pay because the morale is terrible, and we say, well wait; then if something happens in between, I think we are caught with our britches down. And I would, I would give some uh

Secretary McNamara: Well that, that raise has gone through

President Johnson: No, we told them that we'd wait.

Secretary McNamara: No, I think that the raise has gone through to the soldiers. The Vietnamese people are getting the pay, I think it was the first pay increase I think was to be the latter part of February. The question is—and the only question if there is any waiting at all—is whether AID should increase the payment to South Vietnamese government, to offset the increase.

President Johnson: Well, then, we ought to decide that because you ought to read that wire that he sent us, that's the best wire we got, and I replied back

Secretary McNamara: I remember it.

President Johnson: And we ought to, we ought to take the wire that you sent Khanh as soon as he took over, for me, and then got his reply back, and then let's check on it again, and see what he's doing.

Secretary McNamara: I'll do that.

President Johnson: Let's make a record on this thing, Bob, so that

Secretary McNamara: I agree with you on that, as a matter of fact, I'm

President Johnson: I'd like to have a wire out there to him nearly every day or so on something. Either approving what Lodge is recommending, or either trying to goose them up to do a little something extra. Now I've been rather impressed from the news reports of this fellow's social consciousness, his [General Nguyen Khanh's] getting out in the . . . villages and talkin' to people and offerin' them something that they claim that uh, that uh the Nhus and Diems never gave them, and that uh this other outfit that took over [a reference to the military junta that overthrew Diem on November 1, 1963, and was itself ousted by Khanh in January 1964] didn't have time to give them. And I was rather encouraged by Lodge's cable of yesterday in which he said that he showed more efficiency than either one of them.

Secretary McNamara: That's right. And I agree with

President Johnson: I don't know why his 200,000 are not showing some results and why we keep saying that everything is bad, looks blue.

Secretary McNamara: Well, I think this is the question, Mr. President. We've not seen the results yet. And maybe they'll come, but it's a very uncertain period. He is behaving properly, there's no doubt of that.

President Johnson: Why don't we send Lodge a wire back in reply to the one he sent yesterday that we hardly agree with him—they ought to clear out an area and show some results. And to please tell Khanh that we think this is absolutely essential to our continued uh uh morale here, or our continued support, or something.

Secretary McNamara: Sure we'll do that.

[Tape gets fuzzy and clicks off.]

MARCH 4, 1964: PRESIDENT JOHNSON DISCUSSES VIETNAM WITH STATE DEPARTMENT POLICY PLANNER WALT W. ROSTOW

President Johnson's desire to steer away from public statements on Vietnam after his Los Angeles speech had effectively been quashed by his press spokesmen telling reporters the warning to Hanoi on its deeply dangerous game had been significant. Having explored the source of the language in his Los Angeles speech, and the leaks that had made more of it than LBJ perhaps wanted, the president zeroed in on Walt W. Rostow, a former National Security Council official who by 1964 was at the State Department as chairman of the Policy Planning Council. At this time Rostow was vacationing in Aspen, Colorado. Walt had spent the afternoon skiing and was relaxing in the bathtub when, at 5:05 P.M. local time, the telephone rang. It was President Johnson calling from Washington. LBJ did not mince words, and his anger is quite audible on the tape—one illustration of the way these audiotapes may be the most definitive sources on the actions of presidents.

Lyndon Johnson was concerned about three particular reporters and what they had written and said. Chalmers Roberts and Carroll Kirkpatrick worked for the *Washington Post*. The other reporter was Elie Abel of ABC News. Roberts, the diplomatic correspondent for the paper, had reported on the Los Angeles speech and its deeply dangerous rhetoric. He had linked that text to Rostow and given that official's interpretation of the speech as saying that this meant the United States would trigger a war in North Vietnam. Johnson asked Rostow if he knew anything about this.

Rostow denies knowing anything about the report, though he admits having spoken to a stream of journalists, implicitly including Chalmers Roberts. Rostow speaks in generalities about U.S. concern over blocking frontiers to the infiltration of enemies and insists he had been talking about a planning process, not a specific project. Almost two months before his conversation with Lyndon Johnson, Rostow had written a memorandum to Secretary of State Dean Rusk warning of an impending setback in Southeast Asia that could be avoided by "a direct political-military showdown with Hanoi."[1] The discussion of "Plan Six" in their conversation is a reference to a Southeast Asia Treaty Organization (SEATO) contingency plan—in 1961 SEATO had completed its Plan 5, which provided for intervention in lower Laos. At that time Walt Rostow had been in the Kennedy White House as deputy national security adviser and had pressed hard for something more, envisioning the insertion of a military force to block the narrow neck of Indochina by occupying positions across Vietnam and lower Laos. That concept was not a formal plan but had often been referred to as Plan 5+ or Plan 6. In his own recounting of this episode in a 1972 book, Walt Rostow does not refer to Chalmers Roberts at all, but only to Elie Abel, and says that he, Rostow, had explained to the president the origins in 1961 of Plan 6—an untruth as listening to this tape will confirm.[2] LBJ shows no familiarity with such a plan in this conversation. Instead Lyndon Johnson makes no bones about telling Rostow that since *he* does not yet know what U.S. policy is in Southeast Asia, the State Department planner cannot know either, and instructs Rostow not to speak to the press.

Lyndon B. Johnson
March 4, 1964, 6:05 P.M.
Telephone Conversation with Walt W. Rostow, Director, State Department
Policy Planning Staff
Regarding Discussing Vietnam with Reporters

President Lyndon B. Johnson: What line? Line One?

Unidentified Male Voice: Yes, sir.

President Johnson: Walt, Walt. We've got a little discussion that uh Mr. Rostow has been speaking for the administration and raising hell about uh uh having a little war up in North Vietnam, and some of the reporters are quoting around here that Chalmers Roberts got a speech on my California speech in which you pointed out that uh this meant uh uh uh, was going to trigger uh an offensive in North Vietnam. Do you know anything about that?

Walt Rostow: No, sir.

President Johnson: Have you had any talks with Chalmers Roberts about North Vietnam?

Walt Rostow: Uh, Chalmers Roberts. There have been a, a set of fellows coming in, sir, uh to see me uh over the last three weeks, and I've told them all exactly the same story. One, the uh position of the administration is that we are going to hold Southeast Asia. Two, that uh we are now proceeding on instructions to make the most of the situation within present terms of reference. Three, in accordance with the President's reference in the State of the Union message, uh of a reference to Hanoi and Havana, and other remarks, we're obviously thinking about uh the problem of the crossing of frontiers. But I've taken that, one, two . . . but that's a planning process that will await the return of McNamara.

President Johnson: [Irritated] Number one, I wouldn't talk to them about it at all. Number two, the president doesn't know the position of the administration so *you* can't know it. And, number three, they're using it to say that uh you call a man and you give him this pitch, and they come to me and I unload on them and tell them they've got no right to be writing it because I tell them I don't have any knowledge of any plans this administration has to do that. And if I don't have any, the administration oughten to have any. So uh, I told Rusk that. And I've told uh McNamara that. And I want to tell you that. And when we get a plan, if we want it worked out with the, with the, Chalmers Roberts, then we'll talk to him. Until we do, let's don't make ourselves subject to the charge that we have an administration spokesman [from the] State Department saying one thing, and the President saying the other. Elie Abel, night before last, went on television, NBC, over the nation and he says that the administration's very cruel to the poor, unassuming reporter because the administration calls him in and tells him we're going to war in North Vietnam, then Johnson says, "I didn't say any such thing." Which I haven't said.

Walt Rostow: Well, sir, one thing you can be assured of is that I have told no one anything of that kind.

President Johnson: Well you just be careful about talking to them because they, they are quoting you as, as advocating Plan Six or Plan Somethin' else that I don't know anything about, and uh whatever you advocate, you advocate with me and don't advocate with the press unless all agree

Walt Rostow: Oh, I.

President Johnson: on what we're going to do before we do, and uh uh, I don't want any more of this Abel stuff based on anything that somebody says over there to them. Now they're, when I check them, they come back and say, "Well, Chalmers Roberts wrote this story the same day that Carroll Kilpatrick reported Johnson's speech, and Johnson said this is a very dangerous game and Rostow says what he means by dangerous game is, that by God, we're going to knock them off ourselves."

Walt Rostow: No, sir. I've never pretended to to speak for you. What I've, what I have said is that we, we are

President Johnson: They don't say me, they say the administration, so you gotta be careful about talking to 'em. Unless you just have to talk to those reporters, go into it uh, I'd just go on and do my planning and uh let let us handle the press.

Walt Rostow: That'd be grand with me, sir.

President Johnson: OK.

Walt Rostow: Right.

President Johnson: Bye.

MARCH 4, 1964: PRESIDENT JOHNSON DISCUSSES VIETNAM AND HIS ROSTOW CONVERSATION WITH NATIONAL SECURITY ADVISER McGEORGE BUNDY

Following his conversation with Walt Rostow, President Johnson went immediately to the Cabinet Room of the White House, where he met with the Joint Chiefs of Staff for a little over an hour, beginning just five minutes after his phone call. Senior among the group was General Maxwell D. Taylor, the chairman of the Joint Chiefs, who was slated to leave shortly for Saigon on an inspection visit to South Vietnam. Having just castigated Walt Rostow for talking about taking the war to North Vietnam, here Johnson heard Max Taylor advocate intense counterinsurgency in the South coupled with "a progressive program of selective air and naval attacks against North Vietnam using means beyond those employed in the past."[3] Taylor, perhaps America's most intellectual general of that era, had given this response in answer to LBJ's asking what course the general was inclined to recommend at that moment. The other Joint Chiefs expressed themselves similarly, including Army General Earle Wheeler; Admiral David McDonald, the chief of naval operations; General Curtis E. LeMay of the Air Force; and Marine Corps commandant General Wallace Greene. Taylor's notes of this meeting say "the President accepted the need for punishing Hanoi without debate." The Army officer went on to write that Johnson made more practical objections, "particularly the political ones with which he is faced." White House records of the same discussion indicate Marine Commandant General Greene enumerated four possible options for Vietnam, including the Taylor preference, but also continuing the present course, withdrawing, and agreeing to the neutralization of either South Vietnam or both the South and the North. Neither of the last two possibilities appears to have been explored in detail. President Johnson orders General Taylor to conduct an investigation of the sources for the newspaper articles that had upset him. The meeting also included a presidential demand to find more women to be employed in highly visible positions at the Pentagon, consideration of nuclear weapons release directives, and talk of options to use against Fidel Castro in Cuba. Returning to Vietnam, Johnson further instructed the generals on a subject with political implications in the 1964 election—the question of whether Ambassador Henry Cabot Lodge's recommendations had been fully dealt with in Washington. A Republican, Lodge was a possible candidate in the campaign. In fact, LBJ instructed the generals to compile a record of the response to each Lodge request and pass it on to the State Department.

Johnson's meeting with the Joint Chiefs broke up at 7:25 P.M. Exactly one minute later, the president telephoned his national security adviser McGeorge Bundy. Listening to this tape affords a very good test for Johnson's opinion, which he gives Bundy as they agree to meet in the morning for a more extended review of the president's séance with the Joint Chiefs of Staff. At the moment we can let General Taylor have the final word. Of Johnson, Taylor writes, "It is quite apparent that he does not want to lose South Vietnam before next November [the presidential election] nor does he want to get the country into war."

The timing of Johnson's telephone call to McGeorge Bundy indicates that LBJ could not wait to recount the meeting with the Chiefs. In the portion of their conversation related to Vietnam [the portion included here],[4] Bundy, familiarly known as "Mac," brings up the name of the reporter, Elie Abel. We have seen LBJ thoroughly disgusted about what had happened in public with the "deeply dangerous game" rhetoric in his Los Angeles speech. Here Bundy reveals his role, for he himself had had an interview with the journalist. Mac tells the president that he has procured a transcript of his own encounter with Abel, and it proved he had merely told the reporter that he would not add to what Johnson had said in the speech. Clearly Bob McNamara, the Joint Chiefs, and Walt Rostow were not the only ones whom LBJ had sought out for explanations of items that were appearing in the media.

President Johnson himself turns the conversation to his talk with Walt Rostow who, for much of the initial year of John Kennedy's presidency, had been Bundy's deputy in the White House. LBJ gives a fair description of his talk with Rostow, including Johnson's great line, "I said how in the hell do you know if I don't know?"

Johnson also brings up the meeting he had just left with the Chiefs. Making it clear the generals had favored attacking North Vietnam, Johnson recalls the objections he had made. The listener will hear the president refer to Congress, mothers worried about their sons, and his own status as a so-far unelected president (LBJ would win election in November 1964). Lyndon Johnson wanted to get through the months until the election and *then* make his Vietnam decision.

Lyndon B. Johnson
March 4, 1964, 7:26 P.M.
Telephone Conversation with McGeorge Bundy, National Security Adviser
Regarding Vietnam

National Security Adviser McGeorge Bundy: [Chuckles] Well, uh, Mr. President, I've got the goods on Elie Abel, but I'm passing that through Pierre.

President Lyndon B. Johnson: All right. What are the goods?

McGeorge Bundy: Well, I got the p—[pet?] transcript of what I said and what I said was the, it's essential that I not add anything further to the uh subject. The President said what he wanted to say, and he does not want further comment. And so I won't comment further.

President Johnson: All right. Now I called Walt Rostow, and

McGeorge Bundy: Ah-yup.

President Johnson: He's been talking to a good many of them. And I just said that now uh, if he said, well, I'm just telling them what the administration's plans are.

McGeorge Bundy: [Incredulous] He said that to you?

President Johnson: I said, "How in the hell do you know if *I* don't know?" Well, he said, "I'm talking about our planning, I'm not talking about what we're going to do." And I said, "Well uh, you put me in position where I might near got to do it, if you go talking about our planning. Now I want you to talk to me about the planning, not to newspapers."

McGeorge Bundy: Yeah.

President Johnson: And he said, well, if that's the way you feel about it, that's the way I'll do it. I said that's the way I feel about it.

McGeorge Bundy: Yeah.

President Johnson: I'm not sure I want to. Now they came in, Elie Abel says that uh the speech that carried *my*, Kilpatrick's report from California, also carried uh an adjoining column uh, Chalmers Roberts interview with Rostow. Well, they don't say that.

McGeorge Bundy: Yeah.

President Johnson: But, they're saying in effect that we're gonna hit North Vietnam. Now I spent a lot of time with the Joint Chiefs, you ought to have been up here; I didn't think of it, but I

McGeorge Bundy: Well, I was over at the Pentagon. They love to be private, Mr. President.

President Johnson: All right. Well, anyway, remind me in the morning to go over all that with you

McGeorge Bundy: I'd like to catch up with you, yes sir.

President Johnson: The, the net of it is, though, that uh they say get in or get out.

McGeorge Bundy: Yup.

President Johnson: And I told 'em uh let's try to find an amendment that will s—, uh we haven't got any Congress that'll go with us, and we haven't got any p—, mothers that'll go with us in the war. And in nine months I'm just an inherited, I'm a trustee, I got to win an election, or Nixon or somebody else has. And then uh, uh you can make a decision. But in the meantime, let's see if we can't find enough things to do to keep them off base and to stop this shipments that are coming in uh from Laos and pick a few selected targets to upset them a little bit without getting another Korean operation started. Taylor doesn't think they'll ever be a Korean operation. The Marine man does; uh the Navy man uh is in-between the Marine and Taylor; the Air Force thinks it will be a Korean-type operation; the Army eh, didn't say much. But uh, uh Taylor thinks that you've got to pick some specific targets

McGeorge Bundy: Yeah

President Johnson: And offset 'em, and so I told him to make up that list of everything and come back and see if his trip did him any good. He got his ideas now, and let's see what he does after his trip.

McGeorge Bundy: Right.

President Johnson: Then I think he ought to meet with us, he and McNamara before they go tomorrow.

McGeorge Bundy: Well, you've got an NSC meeting and it's on this subject, Mr. President. They are coming in then

President Johnson: Well we ought to meet with them before

McGeorge Bundy: Do you want to meet with them a minute beforehand? Because I think it's going to be very important to, I'm going to have a draft letter to Lodge for you in the morning.

President Johnson: Right.

McGeorge Bundy: And I think also it's important to have a letter of instruction to McNamara because one thing that they are particularly wary on, they don't want anybody on this trip coming back with two different plans, 'cause you don't

President Johnson: Right.

McGeorge Bundy: want people, John McCone especially has a way of saving his skin.

President Johnson: [sighs] Oh, God!

McGeorge Bundy: to be blunt about it.

President Johnson: Yeah, that's good.

JUNE 9, 1964: PRESIDENT JOHNSON DISCUSSES VIETNAM WITH DEFENSE SECRETARY ROBERT S. McNAMARA

With the United States still at a relatively early stage of involvement in South Vietnam, President Johnson has a telephone conversation with Robert McNamara that eerily prefigures the tragedy of the Vietnam War. The occasion is McNamara reporting to the president on testimony he had just given before the Senate Armed Services Committee. Lyndon Johnson and McNamara go over the main issues raised, along with relevant political matters. The conversation shows that as early as 1964, before he ever sent U.S. troops into combat in Vietnam, LBJ was aware the American people harbored serious doubts about getting into a war there, and that both Johnson and McNamara agreed that the U.S. government had not built a consensus for its policy. The news McNamara was bringing to the president in private, he says explicitly here, was much more pessimistic than what officials, including McNamara, were giving the public. McNamara tells the president that both South Vietnamese military strongman General Nguyen Khanh and American Ambassador Henry Cabot Lodge would agree with this negative assessment. In secret cables Lodge had been pressing Washington to increase military pressures against North Vietnam — an action already underway in the form of covert commando raids called 34-A operations — but both political and military factors impinged on this activity.

Much of America's Vietnam experience is epitomized in microcosm in this 1964 conversation. President Johnson again expresses doubt about where the nation was headed, but also recalls his April 1961 visit to Saigon. At that time Johnson, as vice president, delivered a message of support from John F. Kennedy and permitted himself to become so impressed with South Vietnamese leader Ngo Dinh Diem that for a long time he refused to question the American purpose in Vietnam. Officials such as McNamara and Lodge were aware the war was going badly but their answer was greater application of force, even while top leaders (here explicitly including both McNamara and the president) were aware the administration had failed to build a consensus for the course it was taking. McNamara also offers great hope for a special pacification program in South Vietnam, a hope that was to be raised any number of times during the course of the war. Rather than face the large question of whether to break off U.S. involvement, LBJ and McNamara focus on managing short-term political issues in Congress and on public information.

In 1964 Lyndon Johnson was about to stand for election as president of the United States in his own right. Henry Cabot Lodge, his ambassador in Saigon, was a prominent Republican and a possible opposing candidate (Lodge would in fact be the vice presidential candidate on a Republican ticket headed by Senator Barry Goldwater). Here Johnson and McNamara devote much of their conversation to ways of handling Lodge. The reference to "seven divisions" in the talk is to the concept of sending a large army to South Vietnam (at this time the United States had only military advisers and some aviation units, about 16,000 persons all told, in that country), which Lodge opposed even while he demanded stronger action against Hanoi. The seven divisions represented an effort the size of the Korean War, and was the specific force level envisioned by U.S. military planners for an intervention in Vietnam in 1954 at the time of the battle of Dien Bien Phu. Lodge's notion that the United States could escalate in Vietnam without getting into the war was common among government officials at the time. Founded upon the concept that a diplomacy of coercion could employ precise amounts of force without descending into war, this notion was mistaken.

Much of their phone call involved President Johnson and McNamara considering how to handle Congress. LBJ reads McNamara a long letter he had received from Mike Mansfield, the Democratic majority leader in the Senate. In that letter Mansfield assures Johnson of support for whatever decision the president may make, but also declares his opinion that U.S. national interests would not be served by a war in Vietnam. President Johnson takes the point that in Mansfield's view the United States should get out of Vietnam and Johnson declares he will not make such a decision. Secretary McNamara takes the point that the Johnson administration must do more to educate the American people to convince them of the need for a war. On that President Johnson agreed, and it was at this time that LBJ approved a presidential directive to create an interagency group headed by Robert Manning to manage public information on Vietnam. Manning is referred to in this telephone conversation.

Of great interest to the president is what McNamara could report about his meetings with Congress. Massachusetts Republican Senator Leverett Saltonstall, the top Republican on the Armed Services Committee, is another figure who tells the administration he does not think Americans understand the need to be in Vietnam. Also referred to are Committee Chairman Senator Richard Russell, Senator George Mahon, and Representative Leslie Arends. The major matter of Johnson's concern about the congresspersons is their reaction to events in Laos, where LBJ had ordered a series of reconnaissance flights nicknamed "Yankee Team" and then, when one of the planes was shot at, ordered armed escorts and retaliatory bombing.

Finally, and this would also become a continuing feature of the Vietnam experience, Secretary McNamara refers to the Central Intelligence Agency (CIA) and its analysts led by Sherman Kent. McNamara cites them as having a more pessimistic opinion on progress in Vietnam than some others. This would continue to be the case through most of the Vietnam War.

Lyndon B. Johnson
June 9, 1964, 6:20 P.M.
Telephone Conversation with Secretary of Defense Robert S. McNamara
Regarding Reporting Air Strikes in Vietnam to Congress

President Lyndon B. Johnson: Hello?

Secretary Robert McNamara: Yes, Mr. President?

President Johnson: How did you get along . . . the Congress today?

Secretary McNamara: The uh, uh, Senator Russell didn't want to meet with us because he said that you'd talked to him. Saltonstall is concerned uh as to where we're going. He doesn't think that the American people know why we're in Vietnam. He wasn't particularly concerned about the reconnaissance flights. Uh, Vinson uh and uh Arends I reported to you.

President Johnson: What do you answer Saltonstall? Why don't you tell him that Dulles got us in there.

Secretary McNamara: Well, Saltonstall says that he knows why we got in. And he's generally in favor of being there, but he doesn't think the people understand. And uh they ask him questions indicating that they don't understand. What he says is we ought to tell the American people why we're there and explain to them why Southeast Asia is important to us as many of his constituents think it is not.

President Johnson: Um-hmm.

Secretary McNamara: Uh, I think that he's, he's right, in a sense. We are going to have to do more work on making it clear to the American people why this is important to us. No question in my mind about it.

President Johnson: I do too, I do too.

Secretary McNamara. There's no question in my mind about it, that's the kind of thing that Bob Manning has got to emphasize, and all of us have to spend more time on it. Uh, uh, George Mahon is is a little timid; he's just uh, uh, uncertain about the whole situation. He's not concerned about the reconnaissance flights per se, he's just uh worried about the situation in Southeast Asia, and the criticism that he thinks is going to be directed to the government because of it.

President Johnson: Uh-huh.

Secretary McNamara: I think that in that respect, he reflects uh a substantial body of public opinion. He's a rather timid person anyhow, and he's simply reflecting the fears of many of his own constituents.

President Johnson: Uh-huh. Anything else?

Secretary McNamara: No, sir, that's all.

President Johnson: Uh-huh. I've been trying to evaluate this thing. We haven't taken any real serious losses, and we can't put our finger on anything that's uh, really justifies this acceleration of and escalation of public sentiment that it's going to hell in a hack since you were out there in March. Uh, is that a build-up of our critics largely? Have we fed that? Where did it come from we're losing? Is that the Lucas stories coming out of there? Uh—

Secretary McNamara: No, I think it's uh, I think it's the appraisal. If you, if you went to

President Johnson: You take this country, now. It's all concerned that that we've lost Southeast Asia. And that we're in a hell of a shape. Now where did that come from?

Secretary McNamara: All right, well, I think that it came from two things. Uh, if you went to Sherman Kent and the estimators in the CIA and said, how's the situation today in South Vietnam versus three months ago or four months ago, I think they'd say it's worse. And, and therefore

President Johnson: That's not what Lodge and Khanh think, is it? They think it's a little better, don't they?

Secretary McNamara: Well, uh, I don't think they really believe that, Mr. President. No, sir, I, I think that they both would indicate that it is a very weak situation. I think they think that it's better in the sense that it's better to have Khanh there than it was four or five months ago to have that Committee [the Military Revolutionary Council of South Vietnamese generals] running it. But I think Lodge is personally very much concerned about it. The very fact that he's constantly pushing for pressure on the North, military pressure on the North; and of course, that letter that he sent in today, that we read at lunch was, the primary purpose of that was to tell you that he thinks that you ought to go ahead and apply military pressure on the North. What he was saying is don't be scared away from my plan to apply military pressure on the North by the thought of putting in seven divisions. We should never think of putting in seven divisions. It isn't necessary. You ought to apply military pressure anyhow. And this is Lodge's way of saying that things are in pretty bad shape. Now, my point is that the CIA estimators, Lodge, many of the rest of us in private, would say that things are not good, they've gotten worse. And you see it in the desertion rate, you see it in the morale, you see it in the difficulty to recruit people, you see it in the gradual loss of population control. Now, while we say this in private and not in public, there are facts available in the public domain over there that find their way in the press. And I think that this is one way that uh our people get this feeling of, of uh, the fact that we're not moving ahead. The second way is the clear the case of Laos where the Pathet Lao just advanced on the ground within the last three weeks and have kept their gains. And I think it's these two events that lead the people to feel a sense of pessim—pessimism about Southeast Asia.

President Johnson: While I was talking to you uh, a note from Mansfield which is interesting:

"What follows is in the context of my full support. . . . What follows is in the context of my full support of whatever decisions you may have to take and the awesome responsibilities of your office. You alone have all the facts and considerations. You alone make the decisions. The Senate, we can give you only in the last analysis our trust, our support, such independent thoughts as may occur to us from time to time in the hope that they may be constructive. You know far better than I how delicate a maneuver was first, the reconnaissance flights, second, the bombing of anti-aircraft sites in Laos. These two steps have opened up the immediate possibility of a far more direct U.S. military involvement in Laos than we now have in Vietnam. I presume these reconnaissance flights were designed primarily as a show of U.S. determination as an aid of some sort for the government of Laos. Nevertheless, they did lead to the shooting down of U.S. planes and the U.S. bombing of anti-aircraft centers. Clearly this process of action and reaction can continue and grow deeper. It may be that circumstances require that the process continue and deepen. Only you are in the position to make that determination in the light of the whole of the interests of the nation, but I gather from our conversation that a deepening involvement is not what you believe desirable or necessary in terms of the nation's interests. You indicated to me that the bombing [of] sites was not to be repeated but you cannot count on the absence of the need for repetition of the bombing so long as reconnaissance flights continue over Laos. What happens if other U.S. recon planes are shot down. Having once taken out anti-aircraft sites for bombing, are we not to repeat the operation; and if we cannot stop the attrition by air, must we not do it by land force or suffer the consequences?

"I think it is most dangerous to assume that if reconnaissance flights continue additional planes will not be shot at and if they fly low enough that some will not be brought down. But the basic reality remains—if it is not in the national interest to become deeply involved from the military sense on the Laotian front, we will avoid those actions which compel us even against our inclination or expectation to become more deeply involved. We will avoid further unilateral commitments and actions and take every possible initiative to bring about a peaceful settlement. But if our interests justify and in the last analysis become fully involved in Southeast Asian mainland, then there is no issue. What must be done will be done.

"My own views are well known. On the basis of my limited knowledge, I do not conclude that our national interests are served by deep military involvement in Southeast Asia. But in this situation what I or any other Senator may conclude is secondary. The responsibility rests with you, and we can only give you our support in whatever decisions you make. If the decision must be for continuance of the course which is leading to deeper involvement, however, I would most respectfully suggest that the bases for these decisions must be made much clearer and more persuasive to the people of this nation than has heretofore been the case. My judgment and public attitudes are far from understanding, much less accepting, even the limited degree of our present involvement in Southeast Asia."

So, what he comes out and says, he thinks we ought to get out of there, which we can't and not going to; and if we don't, then we got to educate the people as to why we are in there.

Secretary McNamara: Well, I think he is absolutely right. If we're going to stay in there, we're going to go strictly up the escalating chain, we're going to *have* to educate the people, Mr. President. We haven't done so yet. I am not sure now is exactly the right time.

President Johnson: No and I think if you start doing it they are going to be hollering, "You're a warmonger."

Secretary McNamara: That's right; I completely agree with you.

President Johnson: I think that's the horn that the Republicans would like to get us on. Now if we could do something in the way of uh social work, in the way of our hospitals, in the way of our province program and the way of our fertilizer and the way of remaking that area out there and given them some hope and something to fight for, and put some of our own people into their units and do a little better job of fighting without material escalation, for the next few months, that is what we ought to do.

Secretary McNamara: Mr. President, this is what I call my Eight Critical Province Program, and that is what we laid out. We finally sent it out to Lodge by cable three nights ago. Friday, I guess it was. And it was that to which he replied this morning. Step H and I on there, that involves the use of 580 additional U.S. personnel in these critical provinces. And it was that step that he objected to—or at least he said he wanted to make it perfectly clear that he had not agreed to it. He's going to comment further in a later cable, so we just got to push like hell on this.

President Johnson: Well I wonder why we don't come right back to uh, a cable to him. Why don't you draft one and send it over to State from uh, State to him or from me to him, saying that we have felt since '61 that uh one of the great problems there was giving those people something to fight for, and we recommended that to Diem in '61 when I was out there and got his agreement he would do more of it, and he didn't do enough of it soon enough. That's one of the big problems we have. We deeply believe in it and feel it's got to be done, and urge him to uh carry out what we want uh done.

Secretary McNamara: He said in this cable he'd respond uh more fully when he had gone over the detailed plan. I think it might be wise, in view of our relations with him, to give him a day or so to do that.

President Johnson: All right, maybe. I have got a report. I don't know what it says, but I know it goes into that a good deal. It was made in '61, and I could hang it on that and say I personally recommended this in '61 and I want to reiterate what I would like to see done and hope I can have your cooperation in doing it.

Secretary McNamara: Well, it gets you on the line, though, of putting more Americans in Vietnam; and this is one of the issues he could charge against you or the Administration—we've got too many Americans there trying to run the country, take over and causing resentment among the Vietnamese. He has already had a kickback from Khanh and Deputy Prime Minister Hoan on the four men he put in the government, and I am sure this is in his mind here on this five hundred. I think it would be better if you kept out of it and let us handle it

President Johnson: [breathily] All right.

Secretary McNamara: [continuing] and I will make a note on my pad two days from now if we don't get a favorable reply, to go back to him on this.

President Johnson: OK. Bye.

JUNE 23, 1964: PRESIDENT JOHNSON DISCUSSES THE INVESTIGATION OF DEATHS OF THREE CIVIL RIGHTS WORKERS IN MISSISSIPPI WITH FBI DIRECTOR J. EDGAR HOOVER (IN TWO CONVERSATIONS)

An important catalyst in the struggle for civil rights in America in the 1960s was the violence of Mississippi segregationists. In June 1963, Medgar Evers, the field secretary for the state for the National Association for the Advancement of Colored People (NAACP), had been assassinated as he walked from his car to his home in the city of Jackson. Just over a year later, a hugely troubling episode of segregationist savagery occurred in Neshoba County. In the space of a few days, the Mount Zion Church in Longdale was burned, then three civil rights volunteers disappeared. The three were James Chaney, an African American NAACP worker from Meridian, Mississippi; Mickey Schwerner, a Congress on Racial Equality (CORE) volunteer, also based in Meridian; and Andrew Goodman, a college student who had arrived just the previous day to take part in the civil rights work of Freedom Summer. The men disappeared on June 21. It would later be established that they had been arrested on trumped-up charges of speeding or suspicion in the Mount Zion church blaze by a sheriff's deputy in Philadelphia, Mississippi. Held until the middle of the night, they had been released into a trap on Highway 19, the road back to Meridian. Supremacists of the Ku Klux Klan and the affiliated White Citizens Council killed the civil rights workers after they had been stopped again, according to the trial evidence by the same deputy. At first the murders were unknown; the only information was that Chaney, Schwerner, and Goodman had disappeared.

The news broke on the morning of Tuesday, June 23, when the *New York Times* headlined "3 IN RIGHTS DRIVE REPORTED MISSING." There began a flurry of activity in Washington. President Lyndon Johnson, working toward passage of the same civil rights bill that Jack Kennedy discussed with African American leaders in a previous segment of this collection, was instantly on the phone rallying officials for action. As LBJ explained to White House lawyer Lee White shortly after noon, he had already asked the Federal Bureau of Investigation

(FBI), two weeks earlier, to flood Mississippi with its special agents. Now he wanted the missing men found, but already Johnson and others suspected murder. He expected a visit from Mickey Schwerner's mother and Andrew Goodman's parents as well, and asked White to take care of them (later the president would plan a "drop by" while the family members were in White's office). In later phone calls that afternoon, President Johnson spoke of the missing civil rights workers with both Attorney General Robert F. Kennedy and his deputy, Nicolas deB. Katzenbach, along with Mississippi senator James Eastland.

Meanwhile, in Philadelphia, Mississippi, the first evidence in the case was emerging. FBI Special Agent John Proctor had arrived in the town that morning, quickly followed by ten more men, Supervisor Harry Maynor, and then Chief Agent Joseph Sullivan. About midmorning Proctor received a phone call from Lonnie Hardin, the superintendent of a nearby Choctaw reservation, who asked Proctor to come see something the Indians had found. Proctor and two FBI men drove to Bogue Chitto, the reservation on Highway 21, where they discovered the burned-out car the civil rights workers had driven. The car, a 1963 Ford station wagon owned by CORE, had been driven away to disguise the crime. The car had been burned to conceal the evidence—so badly its blue color was hardly discernible. Choctaws had seen it on an abandoned logging trail overgrown by brush, about eighty feet away from the road. Proctor did not want to use his own radio net to report the discovery—it used the same frequency as the local sheriff's department—so he went to local citizens' homes and asked to use their telephones. This considerably slowed the arrival of the report in Washington. Thus a discovery made in Alabama an hour or so before President Johnson had his first conversation on the matter this day (12:35 P.M.) was not reported to LBJ until after 4:00 P.M. J. Edgar Hoover, the FBI director, called with the news. It is noteworthy that Hoover already expresses the opinion that the civil rights workers have been killed.

Lyndon B. Johnson

June 23, 1964, 4:05 P.M.

Telephone Conversation with J. Edgar Hoover, Director, Federal Bureau of Investigation, Regarding Finding the Car Belonging to Mickey Schwerner, James Chaney, and Andrew Goodman, Three Missing Civil Rights Workers

Director J. Edgar Hoover: Uh, Mr. President?

President Lyndon B. Johnson: Yeah.

Director Hoover: I wanted to let you know we have found the car.

President Johnson: Yeah.

Director Hoover: Now, this is not known, nobody knows this at all. But the car was burned and we do not know yet whether any bodies are inside of the car because of the intense heat that uh still is in the area of the car. The license plates on the car are the same that was on the car that was in uh Philadelphia, Mississippi, yesterday. And apparently this is off to the side of the road. It wasn't going toward Meridian, but is going in the opposite direction. Now whether there're any bodies in the car, we won't know until we can get into the car ourselves. We've got agents of course on the ground and as soon as we get definite word, I'll of course get word to you. But I did want you to know that apparently what's happened, these men *have* been killed. Although as I say, we can't tell whether anybody's in there in view of the intense heat.

President Johnson: Now what would make you think they've been killed?

Director Hoover: Because of the fact that it it, it is the same car that they were in in Philadelphia, Mississippi. And the same license number is on the outside of the car. Now, as I say, the heat is so intense you can't tell on the inside, everything's been burned, whether there are any charred bodies or not. It is merely an assumption that probably they were burned in the car. On the other hand, they may have been taken out and killed on the outside.

President Johnson: Or maybe kidnapped and locked up.

Director Hoover: How's that?

President Johnson: Or maybe kidnapped and locked up.

Director Hoover: Well, I would doubt whether those people down there would, would even give 'em that much of a break. But of course we're going to go into that very thoroughly. Not only as to the fact as to whether they're still alive, if they're not yet, if they're not in the car, then they maybe have been killed and their bodies buried in one of those swamps down there.

President Johnson: Where did you find the car? How far from Philadelphia?

Director Hoover: The car was ab . . . was about, I'd say, eight miles from Philadelphia, but not in the direction of Meridian. It was in the opposite direction. Now they had left Philadelphia, according to the reports that we had earlier, to go to Meridian, which is about twenty miles. This, however, was on State Highway 21, and the car was off to the side of the highway, uh although it could be seen from the highway. And a, an Indian agent, uh there's an Indian reservation down in that area, although the car is not on the reservation, an Indian agent saw the car and immediately notified us, and we went there, and there we found this condition.

President Johnson: How long had the car been burned, you reckon, six or eight hours?

Director Hoover: Well, we, we, we, we frankly don't know. The intense heat would have indicated that the car probably had been burning, uh, for maybe six hours, or five or six hours.

President Johnson: What would you indicate that it was filled with, gasoline?

Director Hoover: I would think so, yes. There wasn't any indication of any explosion like dynamite or anything of that kind. And a, of course, dynamite wouldn't have caused the intense heat and fire that kerosene or gasoline would have.

President Johnson: It looks like those fellas jumped out of the car that was burning.

Director Hoover: Well, you would think they would unless they'd been bound and were locked in that car and then the car set afire.

President Johnson: Well, why wouldn't an agent be able to look a car and see if there's any bones in it?

Director Hoover: See whether there are any bodies in it?

President Johnson: Any bones, yeah.

Director Hoover: Well, the the reason for that is is the car is so burned and charred with heat that you can't get close to it. Except that we did get the license number, which is on the outside of the car.

President Johnson: You mean it's still burning?

Director Hoover: Well the car is still burning, yes.

President Johnson: You mean you think this happened in the last few minutes, then?

Director Hoover: No, I don't think it's the last few minutes. I think it's happened within the last, uh, maybe five or six hours. You see, they didn't leave there until uh sometime yesterday, I think it was.

President Johnson: OK. You call me as soon as you can. Now this group's coming down here to see Lee White, my assistant.

Director Hoover: Yes.

President Johnson: Uh, do you think, in the light of this, that this Congressman [name unintelligible] raisin' hell for me to see them. Do think I ought to step in, just tell them I talked to you, and you're doing everything you can?

Director Hoover: I think it would be all right. I, I, I don't like to have you having to see these people because we're going to have more cases like this down South. And every time that it occurs, they're going to have these families come on here to Washington, and of course, the Congressmen being politically minded, they'll want you to see them. Now, they've seen Katzenbach, as I understand, over here.

President Johnson: Yeah.

Director Hoover: And, uh, politically it might be wise for you to just step in and say that you've been in communication with the Bureau, somewhat along the statement that you issued this morning. I, I wouldn't give the details of a number of agents that we've got; you said it was substantially augmented. And

I think, that's a, that's entirely sufficient. And that you're being kept a, advised of any progress that is being made.

President Johnson: That's good. OK, thank you a lot. Bye.

Director Hoover: Bye.

President Johnson: You'll let us know as soon as you hear anything.

Director Hoover: Oh, yes, I'll call you, Mr. President.

President Johnson: OK.

Lyndon B. Johnson
June 23, 1964, 4:21 P.M.
Telephone Conversation with J. Edgar Hoover, Director, Federal Bureau of Investigation, Regarding Finding the Car Belonging to Mickey Schwerner, James Chaney, and Andrew Goodman, Three Missing Civil Rights Workers

President Lyndon B. Johnson: Yes, Edgar.

Director J. Edgar Hoover: Yeah, M, uh, Mr. President?

President Johnson: Yeah.

Director Hoover: I, I think this can be done when you see these people. I think it's proper that you can now say that the car has been found. And has, eh, the car was burning, has been found, and that agents are endeavoring now to get inside of the car. What I find now, and the last word I just got, was that the inside of the car, from the intense heat, has melted and burned everything into ashes. Now we've got to, therefore, pry the doors open, which we are doing, and getting in to the inside, to examine to see whether there's any human bones inside the car. If they are, we know the bodies then were in the car. But everything has been consumed in the car, even to the metal inside the car being melted. Now this Indian agent that first flashed this information to us said that he saw this car yesterday burning. And then he reported it to us today. So, therefore, the car has been extremely hot and it's uh, the agents now are able to have gotten the tools ah, they are able to ah pry open the doors of the car to examine the inside. Whether we find any human bones or ashes of human bones that can be examined from that point of view, we won't know 'til we can have the uh experts in the laboratory examine that down there.

President Johnson: Fine, Edgar. Much obliged.

Director Hoover: Fine.

President Johnson: Yup. Keep me informed.

Director Hoover: OK.

AUGUST 3, 1964: PRESIDENT JOHNSON DISCUSSES AN INCIDENT IN THE GULF OF TONKIN WITH DEFENSE SECRETARY ROBERT S. McNAMARA (IN TWO CONVERSATIONS)

On August 2, 1964, the American destroyer *Maddox*, on patrol off the coast of the Democratic Republic of Vietnam, was attacked by several North Vietnamese torpedo boats. The attack happened hours after South Vietnamese raiders struck at two targets on the North Vietnamese coast as part of a U.S. program of graduated covert pressure against the North that was known as Operations Plan (OPLAN)-34A. This marked the beginning of a series of events that has come to be called the Tonkin Gulf incident.

The *Maddox* was actually on an intelligence mission off the northern coast, carrying with a van of extra communications and electronics gear along with a complement of specialists from the Naval Security Group, a naval complement to the National Security Agency. Their task was to intercept North Vietnamese communications. The ship was in international waters when attacked, but had been inside territorial waters claimed by North Vietnam when Hanoi's torpedo boats were sent to sea. Vietnamese authorities have disclosed that the response was ordered by local commanders without reference to Hanoi. The *Maddox* did not expect any attack—the mission commander had been briefed in Taiwan previously that there would be none—but she was also completely unaware of the provocation to North Vietnam that had occurred simultaneously in the form of the OPLAN-34A strikes. There was no real surprise, however. The North Vietnamese torpedo boats' communications were intercepted, as well as the orders sending them out, and the craft were detected as they approached the U.S. warship. In the ensuing battle two of the three boats were sunk and the third badly damaged, with no losses to the *Maddox*. The action in the Tonkin Gulf took place in the afternoon local time, which was before dawn in Washington, and by early morning in the capital there was a scramble to decide what to do about the situation.

This telephone call represents the first conversation between President Johnson and defense secretary Robert McNamara on the incident. Johnson had already had some conversations with political advisers, and it is noteworthy that his talk with McNamara centers on handling political aspects of the incident. It is also notable that McNamara in this conversation clearly favors explaining to Congress the link between the incident and the OPLAN-34A activities. McNamara would take the position in later public hearings that he was unaware of any such link and as a result would be the target of intense criticism. LBJ himself was well aware of the connection and had explained it to an adviser in a different conversation less than an hour earlier. The president here tells McNamara to limit discussion to key congressional figures, including Speaker of the House John McCormick, Senate Majority Leader Mike Mansfield, and Minority Leader Everett Dirksen. From this telephone call it appears that McNamara's later public comments were made under instruction from Lyndon Johnson.

Lyndon B. Johnson
Monday, August 3, 1964, 10:30 A.M.
Telephone Conversation with Robert McNamara, Secretary of Defense,
Regarding the Gulf of Tonkin Incident(s) Involving the Destroyer
U.S.S. *Maddox*

President Lyndon B. Johnson: Now I wonder if you don't think it'd be wise for you and Rusk to get Mac, uh, the Speaker and Mansfield to call a group of fifteen to twenty people together eh from the Armed Services and Foreign Relations to tell them what happened. A good many of them are saying to me

Secretary Robert McNamara: Right. I've been thinking about this myself, and I thought that uh

President Johnson: They're going to start an investigation

Secretary McNamara: Yeah.

President Johnson: if you don't.

Secretary McNamara: Yeah.

President Johnson: And you got Dirksen up there

Secretary McNamara: Yeah

President Johnson: and he's saying you've got to study it further, and say to Mansfield, "Now the President wants us, you, to get the proper people." And we come in and you say, "They fired at us. We responded immediately. And we took out one of their boats and put the other two running. And we kept our . . . , we're puttin' our boats right there, and we're not running on in."

Secretary McNamara: And it's hard to destroy.

President Johnson: That's right

Secretary McNamara: Right. And we're going to, and I think I should also, or we should also at that time, Mr. President, explain this Op Plan 34-A, these covert operations. There's no question but what that had bearing on. And on Friday night, as you probably know, we had four TP [McNamara means PT] boats from Vietnam manned by Vietnamese or other nationals, attack two islands. And we expended, oh, a thousand rounds of ammunition of one kind or another against them. We probably shot up a radar station and a few other miscellaneous buildings. And following twenty-four hours after that, with this destroyer in that same area, undoubtedly led them to connect the two events.

President Johnson: Well say that to Dirksen.

Secretary McNamara: That's what I know he'll like.

President Johnson: You notice Dirksen says this morning, that "we got to reassess the situation, do something about it." I'd tell him that we're doing what he's talking about.

Secretary McNamara: Well, I, I was, I was thinking doing this myself in personal visits. But I think your thought is better. We'll get the group together. You want us to do it at the White House or would you rather do it at State or Defense?

President Johnson: I believe it'd be better to do it uh up on the Hill.

Secretary McNamara: All right.

President Johnson: I believe it'd be better if you say to Mansfield, "You call"

Secretary McNamara: Yup

President Johnson: Foreign Relations

Secretary McNamara: Yup, OK.

President Johnson: Armed Services

Secretary McNamara: OK. OK.

President Johnson: and and get Speaker to do it over on his side [i.e., within the House of Representatives, as opposed to the Senate].

Secretary McNamara: We'll do it

President Johnson: And just say it's very, I'd tell him awfully quiet, though, so they won't go in and be making a bunch of speeches. And tell Rusk that a, that's my idea.

Secretary McNamara: Great. . . .

President Johnson: And he's in New York, so I don't know whether's he's got back.

Secretary McNamara: Well I just talked to George Ball a few minutes ago, and I'll have George arrange it. Or at least I'll tell him that, and then I'll call the Speaker and Mansfield himself.

President Johnson: Now I wish that uh you'd give me some guidance on what we ought to say. I want to leave an impression on the background in the people we talk to over here that we're gonna be firm as hell without saying something that's dangerous. Now what do you think? Uh, uh, the people that are calling me up, I just talked to a New York banker, I just talked to a fellow in Texas, they all feel that the Navy responded wonderfully and that's good. But they want to be damned sure I don't pull 'em out and run, and they want to be damned sure that we're firm. That's what all the country wants because Goldwater's raising so much hell about how he's gonna blow 'em off the moon, and they say that we oughten to do anything that the national interest doesn't require. But we sure oughta always leave the impression that if you shoot at us, you're going to get hit.

Secretary McNamara: Well I think you would want to instruct George Reedy this morning at his news conference to say that you you personally have ordered the, the Navy to carry on the routine patrols uh off the coast of North Vietnam, uh to add an additional destroyer to the one that has been carrying on the patrols, to provide an air cap, and to issue instructions to the commanders to destroy any uh force that attacks our force in international waters.

President Johnson: [speaks over McNamara] Bob, if you don't mind,

Secretary McNamara: . . . I think that's the way . . .

President Johnson: If you don't mind, call Walter Jenkins and tell him

Secretary McNamara: Sure

President Johnson: that you want to dictate this to me

Secretary McNamara: I'll do it right now

President Johnson: to give to my people or George Reedy because I'm over at the Mansion with some folks here

Secretary McNamara: I'll do it right now.

President Johnson: OK. Right.

Lyndon B. Johnson
Monday, August 3, 1964, 1:21 P.M.
Telephone Conversation with Robert McNamara, Secretary of Defense,
Regarding the Gulf of Tonkin Incident

President Lyndon B. Johnson: Yes?

Secretary Robert McNamara: Mr. President, I set up those meetings for this afternoon with the Senate and House leaders and I thought if it was agreeable with you, I would say to them that some months ago you asked us to be prepared for any eventuality in the Southeast Asia area and as a result of that we have prepared and just completed in great detail target analyses of the targets of North Vietnam. As a matter of fact in ten minutes I'm going over with the Chiefs [the Joint Chiefs of Staff] the final work on this. We have pictures, analyses, numbers of sorties, bomb loadings, everything prepared for all the target systems of of North Vietnam, and I would describe this to the the leaders, simply indicating your desire that we be fully prepared for whatever may develop. And furthermore we've prepared detailed movement studies of any contingency forces required, air squadrons, et cetera.

President Johnson: So obviously now, if you go put this in the paper . . .

Secretary McNamara: Yeah, and I, I'm going to tell 'em that

President Johnson: and your enemy reads about it then he thinks we're already taking off and obviously you've got us in a war. But I've got to be candid with you and I want to tell you the truth.

Secretary McNamara: Exactly. I was going to start my remarks by that, but be damn sure it doesn't, or try to be sure it doesn't get in the paper.

President Johnson: And uh, uh I think it's right, and I, I will tell 'em that yesterday morning that uh, uh they reported the *Maddox* incident and uh during the day yesterday we sent we sent out this order and read them the statement I made this morning.

Secretary McNamara: Right, I'll do that.

President Johnson: And, so that Dirksen doesn't think that we have to wait on him, and that we . . .

Secretary McNamara: Yeah.

President Johnson: did go out when . . .

Secretary McNamara: Yes, I'll tell them the order went out yesterday and you were simply repeating it to the press this morning.

President Johnson: OK.

AUGUST 4, 1964: THE GULF OF TONKIN INCIDENT CONTINUES— PRESIDENT JOHNSON DISCUSSES BOMBING NORTH VIETNAM WITH ROBERT S. McNAMARA (IN FOUR CONVERSATIONS)

Following the original incident of August 2, the Johnson administration wanted to underline its belief that U.S. Navy warships had the freedom to pass anywhere in international waters, naturally including most of the Gulf of Tonkin. Consequently President Johnson approved a move under which the destroyer *Maddox* was reinforced by the *C. Turner Joy*, and both ships entered the Gulf together. With the American warships in a state of hyperalert, on the night of August 3/4 the warships recorded a series of sound (sonar) and electronic (radar) readings interpreted to be attacking torpedo boats. Amid the confusion of that night, radio signals pertaining to the August 2 incident were read as Hanoi ordering a fresh attack, and expectant sailors on watch saw things they decided were enemy boats. Washington was initially told the warships were under attack. Although the commander on the scene, Captain John D. Herrick, quickly amplified the initial, excited reports with one stating he doubted the reality of the attacks, Pacific Fleet Commander Admiral Ulysses S. Grant Sharp nevertheless proceeded as if the attacks were genuine.

Because of the time difference between Washington and the Tonkin Gulf, and the time needed to transmit and receive messages from the remote naval forces involved, this sequence of President Johnson's telephone calls on August 4 begins at a moment when Washington was as yet unaware of the claimed second attack. McNamara's statement in the 9:43 A.M. conversation that "this ship is allegedly to be attacked tonight" is highly significant—it means that Washington was already operating on the basis of the radio intercepts mistakenly attributed to August 4th. Equally important, LBJ and McNamara discuss retaliatory action against North Vietnam in spite of the fact that no attack has yet occurred. Also of interest is President Johnson's statement that the United States "should pull one of these things that you've . . . been doing . . . on one of their bridges or something." This is a clear reference to the OPLAN-34A raids, confusion about which had been a factor in the initial Tonkin Gulf engagement on August 2. Here LBJ suggests a measure that would actually increase Hanoi's incentives to fight.

A little over an hour later, at 10:53 A.M., McNamara has a second conversation with the president in which Johnson's concern centers on the details of the supposed combat in the Gulf. McNamara tells LBJ that the U.S. aircraft carrier *Ticonderoga* sent out aircraft to help defend the two destroyers, and he mistakenly reports that the planes have seen two unidentified vessels and three planes near the American warships (Admiral John Stockdale, pilot of one of the *Ticonderoga* aircraft that night, affirms that the U.S. planes saw nothing at all). McNamara goes on to tell the president that he has developed a list of targets in North Vietnam that can be struck in retaliation. He promises to bring the list over to the White House.

Less than ten minutes later, McNamara comes back on the phone to tell President Johnson that Pacific theater commander Admiral Sharp has told him the destroyers are under torpedo attack. Here the secretary of defense reports information now known to be false, although McNamara did not know this at the time. LBJ responds by ordering the secretary of defense and other top officials to meet and coordinate a retaliatory bombing. There is no tape of that meeting, but a memorandum recording the meeting of the National Security Council that day notes McNamara entering the meeting and discussing the alleged attack. Secretary Dean Rusk comments that recommendations are being prepared but are not yet ready. Treasury Secretary C. Douglas Dillon warns, "There is a limit on the number of times we can be attacked by the North Vietnamese without hitting their naval bases."[5] For almost two hours following the NSC meeting, LBJ lunched with McNamara, Rusk, McGeorge Bundy, the CIA's John McCone, and Deputy Secretary of Defense Cyrus R. Vance. It was at lunch, according to a Pentagon chronology of these events, that LBJ agreed to a swift retaliatory air strike and a specific set of targets.[6] During this lunch (at 1:27 P.M.), Washington received the message from Captain Herrick on the *Maddox* that cast doubt on the veracity of the attack. This report had no effect on the actions of Washington officials.

By late afternoon the comings and goings at the White House and the Pentagon had put the press on notice that something was going on, and leaks became inevitable. Shortly after 5:00 P.M., President Johnson talked to McNamara again. This time they shared the news that the Associated Press and United Press wire services had both put out the story that another attack had taken place in the Tonkin Gulf. LBJ now approved an official Pentagon statement on the supposed attack (although as recently as twenty minutes earlier McNamara had been meeting with the Joint Chiefs of Staff to "overcome [the] lack of a clear and convincing showing that an attack on the destroyers had in fact occurred"[7]). The Joint Chiefs of Staff approved a message ordering execution of the retaliatory bombing and it was sent out at 5:19. A follow-up NSC meeting took place an hour later. That meeting gave pro forma consideration to the alleged North Vietnamese attack and the retaliation, again not taking into account the doubts of the on-scene destroyer commander, Captain Herrick. The White House meeting also tabled a prospective resolution approving the use of force by Congress. LBJ raised the matter of a resolution at a briefing of senior legislators which began at 6:45. The administration supplied a text as discussed by the NSC and then between LBJ and the legislators, and that draft became the Gulf of Tonkin Resolution which was subsequently used to justify the entire U.S. war in Vietnam.

There was a final conversation between LBJ and McNamara at 9:15 P.M., at which time the president was caught up in the drama of Mississippi. Then the questions were largely ones of coordinating the actual launch of the attack with LBJ's public statement. President Johnson finally made the statement at 11:36 P.M., approximately half an hour prior to the expected time of arrival of the U.S. strike aircraft over their targets in North Vietnam.

Thus the U.S. bombing of North Vietnam went forward based on the mistaken belief in a second attack in the Gulf of Tonkin. In a certain sense, because the resolution that passed Congress was used to justify the U.S. military commitment, the entire Vietnam War can be said to have been based on a misunderstanding. Just over a month afterward, when another pair of American warships in the Gulf of Tonkin also thought they had come under attack, LBJ began to express doubts about the reality of the August incident. In 1997, in Hanoi, Robert McNamara, in a conversation with Vietnamese Commander General Vo Nguyen Giap, also concluded that the August 4, 1964, incident had never occurred. That is now the general consensus among historians of the Vietnam War.

Lyndon B. Johnson
Tuesday, August 4, 1964, 9:43 A.M.
Telephone Conversation with Robert McMamara, Secretary of Defense,
Regarding the Incident in the Gulf of Tonkin with the Destroyers U.S.S.
Maddox and U.S.S. *C. Turner Joy*

Male Voice: Yes, sir. Off limits.

President Lyndon B. Johnson: Hello?

Female Voice: Secretary Robert McNamara's calling you again, sir. "O"

Secretary Robert McNamara: Mr. President, uh, General Wheeler and I are sitting here together. We just received a cable from Admiral Sharp [Ulysses S. Grant Sharp Jr. was the American commander for the Pacific] making three recommendations with respect to our destroyer tracks and enemy action responses. And I wanted to mention them to you with a recommendation. I've discussed this with with Dean Rusk [secretary of state] and he and I are in agreement on the recommendations.

Sharp recommends first that the uh, the track of the destroyer be shifted from eleven miles offshore to eight miles offshore. This makes no sense to us; we would recommend against it. His purpose, by shifting the track, is simply to make clear that we we believe the twelve-mile limit is not an effective limit on us. We don't, we think we do that adequately by sailing at eleven miles as opposed to eight.

Secondly, Sharp recommends that we authorize the task

President Johnson: What reason does he give for his eight?

Secretary McNamara: Simply that it more clearly indicates our, our refusal to accept a twelve-mile restriction. We think we've clearly indicated our refusal to accept a twelve-mile restriction with the, the eleven-mile limit; we see no need to change the track at this time.

President Johnson: Why, what, what other objections do you have?

Secretary McNamara: It, it, uh, changes a program that that uh shouldn't be changed frequently. These orders are very precise; the tracks are laid down very clearly; they go through the three command channels to get out there; this ship is allegedly uh to be attacked tonight—we don't like to see a change in operation plan of this kind at this time. And we don't think it achieves any any uh international purpose, so no, certainly no military purpose is served by it.

President Johnson: All right.

Secretary McNamara: Secondly, he recommends that the task force commander be authorized to pursue the attacking vessels in the event he is attacked and destroy their bases. In this case, it would be

President Johnson: Wait just a minute. [Speaking away from the telephone: I've got a call. I can't hear him. I've got a real important thing . . .]. Go ahead, Mac.

Secretary McNamara: Secondly, he recommends that the task force commander be authorized to pursue any attacker and destroy the base of the attacker. In this instance, if he were attacked by patrol boats, it would mean that he would pursue the patrol craft into the shore line, uh identify the base of the patrol craft and destroy that base. Now this is an action that we might well wish to consider after the second attack. But I think it would be inappropriate, and General Wheeler agrees, and Dean Rusk agrees, inappropriate to provide the task force commander that authority. There will be ample time for us, after a second attack, to bring this problem to your attention, and you can then decide how far you wish to pursue the attacker into his base area.

President Johnson: What objections do you have to pursuing it?

Secretary McNamara: With only the objection that if we give such authority, you have, in a sense, lost control of, of the degree of our uh response to the North Vietnamese. If you don't op, exactly what bases will be attacked, where they are in relation to population centers, how much force will be applied to attack them, when it will occur. I, I personally would recommend to you, after a second attack on our ships, that we do retaliate against the coast of North Vietnam some way or other. And we'll be prepared

President Johnson: What I was thinking about when I was eating breakfast, but I couldn't talk it—I was thinking that it looks to me like the weakness of our position is that, uh, we respond only to an action and we don't have any of our own. But when they, when they move on us, and they shoot at us, I think we not only ought to shoot at them, but almost simultaneously, uh, uh, pull one of these things that you've, you've been doing

Secretary McNamara: Right.

President Johnson: on one of their bridges or something.

Secretary McNamara: Exactly. I, I quite agree with you, Mr. President. And I'm not, not sure that the response ought to be as Admiral Sharp suggests

President Johnson: Well me not, I'm not either, I'm not either. I don't know, unless I knew what base it was

Secretary McNamara: Yes.

President Johnson: and what is compelled, but I wish we could have something that we already picked out, and uh

Secretary McNamara: We'll see

President Johnson: and just hit about three of them damned quick. Right after

Secretary McNamara: We will have that, and, and I, I've talked to Mac Bundy [national security adviser] a moment ago and told him that I thought that was the most important subject we should consider today, and, and be prepared to recommend to you a response, a retaliation move against North Vietnam in the event this attack takes place within the next six to nine hours. And we

President Johnson: All right. Now we better do that at lunch. There's some things I don't want to go in with these other, I want to keep this as close as I can. So let's just try to keep it to the two . . .

Secretary McNamara: I, I

President Johnson: three . . .

Secretary McNamara: I will be prepared to do so at lunch.

President Johnson: All right.

Secretary McNamara: Now, thirdly, Sharp recommends that, that, uh, the, uh, task force commander be authorized to engage in hot pursuit beyond the eleven-mile limit in as far as the three-mile limit, which we [i.e., the United States] accept as the definition of territorial waters. At present the instructions to the commander are: do not pursue an attacker, uh, closer to shore than eleven miles. Uh, Sharp recommends that that eleven mile limit be shifted to three miles. I've talked to Dean about this; he agrees, uh, as far as air pursuit is concerned. Pursue by air as close as three miles to shore. Do not pursue by sea closer than eleven miles. Uh, his reason for differentiating sea from air is that we can always argue that the, uh, the uh, air, uh, uh, was further out than three miles and he is concerned about taking the ships in as close as three miles to shore. I'm willing to accept his, his point for a different reason, however. I don't think ship pursuit uh, between eleven miles and three miles, would be effective anyhow because our ships travel at about twenty-seven knots, and these patrol boats travel at fifty knots, and the possibility of a ship being effective in that eleven to three mile area is not very great. The air power is likely the most effective power anyhow. And I would, therefore, recommend that we accept Sharp's recommendation but limit it to air.

President Johnson: All right. OK.

Secretary McNamara: Fine.

Lyndon B. Johnson
Tuesday, August 4, 1964, 10:53 A.M.
Telephone Conversation with Robert McNamara, Secretary of Defense,
Regarding the Gulf of Tonkin Incident

Woman's Voice: Secretary McNamara calling. Line "O."

President Lyndon B. Johnson: Yes.

Second Woman's Voice: Hello?

President Johnson: I'm trying to take this call.

Second Woman's Voice: Thank you. Yes. I'm sorry. Secretary McNamara.

Secretary Robert McNamara: Hello?

President Johnson: Yeah.

Secretary McNamara: Mr. President, we had, just had a report from the commander of that task force out there that they have sighted two unidentified vessels, uh, and three unidentified prop aircraft; and therefore the, uh, carrier launched, uh, two F-8s, two A-4Ds and four A-1s, which are prop

President Johnson: Go back over those again. What, what did we launch?

Secretary McNamara: We launched two F-8 fighter aircraft, two A-4D, which are jet attack aircraft, and four A-1Hs, which are prop-driven aircraft. So we have launched eight aircraft from the carrier to, uh, uh, examine what's in the vicinity of the destroyers and to protect the destroyers. The report is that they have observed, and we don't know by what means, whether this is radar or otherwise — I suspect it's radar — two unidentified vessels and three unidentified prop aircraft in the vicinity of the destroyers.

President Johnson: What else do we have out there?

Secretary McNamara: We have the, only the *Ticonderoga*, with its aircraft, uh, and a protective destroyer screen. I think there are three destroyers with the *Ticonderoga*. We have the *Constellation* [an aircraft carrier], which is moving out of Hong Kong, and which I uh sent orders to about an hour or two ago to move down towards South Vietnam. We don't know exactly how long it'll take; we guess about 30 hours. We have ample forces to respond not only to these attacks on the destroyers but also to retaliate should you wish to do so against targets on the land. And when I come over at noontime, I'll bring you a list of alternative target systems. We can mine the Swatow [a type of North Vietnamese patrol vessel] bases, we can — and I just issued ordered to Subic Bay and the Philippines to fly the mines out to the carrier, so we'll be prepared to do it if you want to do it. We can destroy the Swatow craft by bombing. There is a petroleum system that is concentrated, uh, uh,

Very faint whisper: seventy-two

Secretary McNamara: Seventy percent of the petroleum supply of North Vietnam we believe is concentrated in three, uh, dumps, and we can bomb those, bomb or strafe those dumps and destroy the petroleum system, which would be the petroleum for the patrol craft. In addition, there are certain prestige targets that we've been working on the last several months, and we have target folders prepared on those. For example, there is one bridge that is the key bridge on the rail line south out of, uh, out of Hanoi, and we could destroy that. And there are other prestige targets of that kind.

President Johnson: All right. Uh, good. Can I, I told, I told Rivers [Representative L. Mendel Rivers] the other day and I told him what's going to be in Charleston. He can announce that, can't he?

Secretary McNamara: Oh, surely, surely.

President Johnson: OK.

Secretary McNamara: Surely.

President Johnson: Bye. Thank you.

Lyndon B. Johnson
Tuesday, August 4, 1964, 11:00 A.M.
Telephone Conversation with Robert McNamara, Secretary of Defense,
Regarding the Gulf of Tonkin Incident

President Lyndon B. Johnson: Hello?

Woman's Voice: Secretary McNamara. Line "O."

President Johnson: Thanks a lot.

Secretary Robert McNamara: Mr. President, we just had word by telephone from Admiral Sharp that the destroyer is under torpedo attack.

Secretary McNamara: I think I might get, uh, Dean Rusk and Mac Bundy and have 'em come over here and we'll go over these retaliatory actions. And then we ought to

President Johnson: I sure think you ought to agree with that, yeah.

Secretary McNamara: And I've got a category here. I'll call the two of them.

President Johnson: Now where are these torpedoes coming from?

Secretary McNamara: Well, we don't know. Presumably from these unidentified craft that I mentioned to you a moment ago. We thought that the unidentified craft might include one, uh, one PT boat, which has torpedo capability and two Swatow boats which we don't credit with torpedo capability, although they may have it.

President Johnson: What are these planes of ours doing around while they're being attacked?

Secretary McNamara: Well, presumably, the planes are attacking the, the ships. We don't have any, uh, word from, from Sharp on that. The planes would be in the area at the present time. All, all eight of them.

President Johnson: OK.

Secretary McNamara: Thank you.

President Johnson: You get them over there and then you come over here as soon as you can.

Secretary McNamara: I'll do that, yes.

Lyndon B. Johnson
Tuesday, August 4, 1964, 5:09 P.M.
Telephone Conversation with Robert McNamara, Secretary of Defense,
Regarding the Gulf of Tonkin Incident

Secretary Robert McNamara: Bob, Mr. President. The story has broken on the AP and the UP [Associated Press and United Press, news wire services].

President Lyndon B. Johnson: Yeah, I see it.

Secretary McNamara: And, uh, uh, we tried to track it down. Jim Greenfield talked to the AP, I understand, and was told that it came from a source close to the Pentagon; it was alleged to be a chairman of a Congressional committee. I don't know what the source is. But, anyhow, it's broken. And uh, it seems to me, State and we and, and, George Reedy ought to agree now on a statement that could be made by one of the departments, I presume the Pentagon. But before doing that I wanted to ask your permission to do so. The statement that we would make, I would propose it simply say that during the night hours, the, the two destroyers were attacked by, uh, patrol boats; the attack was driven off; no casualties or damage to the destroyers; we believe, uh, uh, several of the patrol boats were sunk; details won't be available until daylight.

President Johnson: That's OK.

Secretary McNamara: All right. I'll take

President Johnson: I'd just go on and put that out.

Secretary McNamara: All right. I'll take care of it

President Johnson: Uh, anything else?

Secretary McNamara: No, I talked to Dillon [C. Douglas Dillon, secretary of the treasury] and he fully agrees with the action. I couldn't get hold of Bobby [Robert F. Kennedy, attorney general]; he's nowhere that he can be found. But I'll keep a call in for him.

AUGUST 4, 1964: FBI FINDS THE BODIES OF SLAIN CIVIL RIGHTS WORKERS—PRESIDENT JOHNSON DISCUSSES EVENTS WITH FBI DEPUTY DIRECTOR "DEKE" DeLOACH, POLITICAL ADVISER LEE WHITE, AND MISSISSIPPI GOVERNOR PAUL JOHNSON (IN FOUR CONVERSATIONS, INTERRUPTED BY ANOTHER CALL FROM ROBERT S. McNAMARA)

Ever since late June, when the FBI had reported finding the car belonging to missing civil rights workers James Chaney, Mickey Schwerner, and Andrew Goodman (a previous recording), bureau special agents had never ceased searching for the men or their bodies. President Johnson may have entertained briefly a hope that reflected the kinds of explanations put out by the segregationists and that had been related to LBJ himself by a member of the Mississippi congressional delegation—that is, the three men had simply gone off somewhere. But as the days passed after June 23, it became glaringly obvious that something had happened to the civil rights activists. Now, at the height of the Gulf of Tonkin Incident, with Johnson working hard to arrange the bombing strike he had been talking about all day, the president received bad news from the Federal Bureau of Investigation.

The big break for the FBI in its search had come in July, when they discovered that another African American man had been taken by the racists but released, and that he had been interrogated at a location that was a standard meeting place for the conspirators. The victim's name was Wilmer Jones, and he agreed to help the FBI, returning to Philadelphia, Mississippi, on July 21 to assist in identifying the place where he had been held. Within a few days of his arrival, Jones had found a place southwest of town that seemed familiar, and the FBI began to focus its search in that area. Then, on July 31, the bureau offered a substantial cash reward for information regarding the location of the bodies of the slain activists, and someone, never identified, told investigators about the Old Jolly Farm, owned by one Olen Burrage. The next day the FBI zeroed in on the farm, specifically on an earthen dam—20 feet high, 547 feet long, and 83 feet thick at its widest—that seemed unusual because it contained no water. A search warrant was served on the owner that morning, and the excavating equipment was moved onto the Old Jolly Farm. The actual digging, supervised by Agent Jay Cochran Jr., required just over six hours for the discovery first of the body of Schwerner, then Goodman (soon after 5:00 P.M., which was 6:00 P.M. in Washington), then Chaney's body moments later. Thus, when FBI Deputy Director Cartha DeLoach called President Johnson at 8:01 P.M., the news was just coming up the FBI chain of command. This is reflected in DeLoach's conversation with the president. In this and the following conversations with Mississippi Governor Paul Johnson and his own political staffer Lee White, LBJ primarily is concerned with the timing of the announcement of the discovery of the bodies; in an almost identical fashion, he is also preoccupied with the timing of the announcement of the Vietnam bombing. Here, however, LBJ's reasons were very different: the timing was important so that the families of the slain civil rights workers could be informed before the news was made public.

Lyndon B. Johnson
Tuesday, August 4, 1964, 8:01 P.M.
Telephone Conversation with Cartha DeLoach, FBI, Regarding the
Discovery of the Bodies of Michael Schwerner, Andrew Goodman, and
James Chaney, Three Civil Rights Workers Missing Since June 21, 1964

Cartha DeLoach: [Mr. Hoover wanted me to call you] sir, immediately and tell you that the FBI has, uh, found three bodies, six miles southwest of Philadelphia, Mississippi, the six miles west of where the civil rights workers were last seen on the night of June 21st. Our search party of agents turned up the bodies just about fifteen minutes ago, while they were digging in the woods and underbrush several hundred yards off Route 21, in that area. We're going to get a coroner there right away, sir, and we're going to move these bodies into Jackson, Mississippi, where we hope they can be identified. We have not identified them as yet as the three missing men, but we have every reason to believe that they are the three missing men. They were under a, they were inside of a dam that had been constructed near Philadelphia, Mississippi. Wanted to let you know right away, sir.

President Lyndon B. Johnson: When you gonna make the announcement?

Cartha DeLoach: Within ten minutes, sir, if it's all right with you.

President Johnson: Well, that's how you gonna make it. Where—from there, from

Cartha DeLoach: I plan to make it from Washington, here, sir.

President Johnson: All right. All right.

Cartha DeLoach: Just indicate that the FBI has, uh, found three bodies and does not identify them.

President Johnson: [Sigh] OK. If you can hold it about fifteen minutes, I think we ought to notify these families.

Cartha DeLoach: Well, Mr. President, uh, the only, uh, thing I'd, suggestion I have there is if you wish to do that prior to the time that they are identified. We think they're the ones, but, uh

President Johnson: Well I think we could tell 'em that we, we don't know but we found them, and that kind of eases it a little bit.

Cartha DeLoach: Yes, sir. All right, sir. Shall I wait till I

President Johnson: Yeah, I, I'll get right back to you.

Cartha DeLoach: Very good, sir.

Lyndon B. Johnson
Tuesday, August 4, 1964, 8:04 P.M.
Telephone Conversation with Lee C. White, Civil Rights Counselor to the President, Regarding the Discovery of the Bodies of Michael Schwerner, Andrew Goodman, and James Chaney, Three Civil Rights Workers Missing Since June 21, 1964

Woman's Voice: Lee White. And, do you want Walter Jenkins on?

President Lyndon B. Johnson: No, Lee White. Lee White.

Woman's Voice: All right.

President Johnson: [Not speaking into the telephone.] They found the three bodies in Mississippi. [Covers the phone and speaks to someone in the room.]

Woman's Voice: Lee White.

President Johnson: Lee.

Lee White: Yes, Mr. President.

President Johnson: They found those three bodies, six miles south of, uh, southwest of Philadelphia, Mississippi.

Lee White: Hmm

President Johnson: Six miles west from where they last seen. They don't know that these are the bodies. They moved them into Jackson to identify them.

They're off Route 21. Uh, eh, it's right near the site of a new dam that's been built. They have every belief they are the bodies, so, uh, call the families and tell them that there'll be an announcement in the next ten or fifteen minutes. We'll, as soon as you get proper identification, let 'em know further.

Lee White: All right. I'll call the three of them right now.

President Johnson: Yeah.

Lee White: All right.

President Johnson: Tell them I asked you to.

Lee White: I will, Mr. President.

AUGUST 4, 1964: THE GULF OF TONKIN INCIDENT CONTINUES— PRESIDENT JOHNSON DISCUSSES U.S. RETALIATION WITH DEFENSE SECRETARY ROBERT S. McNAMARA

With decisions made regarding bombing of North Vietnam, the evening conversation between LBJ and Robert McNamara focuses on the timing of the president's announcement of the attacks and the wording of his announcement. Johnson also discusses whether he should call opposition presidential candidate Barry Goldwater to inform him of the action. LBJ indeed made that call (not included in the present collection), and Goldwater expressed complete support for the president's decision. As already recounted, LBJ made his announcement late that evening.

Many of President Johnson's later Vietnam decisions, including the initiation of a regular bombing campaign against North Vietnam in February 1965 and his commitment of ground troops to a major war in South Vietnam that summer, showed this same careful attention to the public relations aspects of the issues. The methods of making and articulating a decision Johnson displayed regarding the Gulf of Tonkin express his standard operating procedure. The short time LBJ had to make his decision in August 1964 led to extensive use of the telephone, and thus assists our effort to illustrate his methods.

Lyndon B. Johnson
Tuesday, August 4, 1964, 9:15 P.M.
Telephone Conversation with Robert McNamara, Secretary of Defense,
Regarding the Gulf of Tonkin Incident(s)

Secretary Robert McNamara: Bob McNamara, Mr. President.

President Lyndon B. Johnson: Yeah.

Secretary McNamara: I just talked to, uh, Admiral Sharp again. He's been in contact with the carriers; they have not been able to launch yet. They won't launch for another, about forty-five minutes. They should launch at 10:00 P.M. I have this suggestion to make to you. That you make your statement at approximately 10:00 P.M. and that you leave out one sentence. It is the sentence that states "Air action is now in execution against gun boats and supporting facilities in and near four ports of North Vietnam." Without that sentence, you don't disclose the targets but you do disclose that action is presently underway.

President Johnson: Now, let me see where it's; what, what

Secretary McNamara: It's in the, it's in the fourth paragraph on the first page.

President Johnson: Yeah, I see. " . . . but repeat acts of violence against the armed forces. . . . Air action is now . . . "

Secretary McNamara: No, you would s—, you would read it, "But repeated acts of war against the armed forces must be met not only with alert defense but with a positive reply. That reply is now being given as I speak to you." Period. Then take out the next sentence.

President Johnson: Well, does that, uh, make it too indefinite?

Secretary McNamara: No, sir, I don't believe so. I think it's perfectly appropriate that while the action's underway, you not describe, uh, the specific targets or, or the type of action.

President Johnson: What do you think about, I don't see why we bring Goldwater in on this. Why don't we just say I felt it appropriate just to communicate my decision to the Republican candidate for president.

Secretary McNamara: Uh

President Johnson: And I'll say he's assured me of his

Secretary McNamara: Yeah

President Johnson: full support. I think it makes us sound like we're very much together and buddies and agreein' on bombing everybody.

Secretary McNamara: Well, in that case, I'd leave out the paragraph.

President Johnson: You wouldn't even say you'd communicated.

Secretary McNamara: I wouldn't say I communicated it.

President Johnson: Well, what do you think?

Secretary McNamara: I, I would, well, have you been able to talk to him?

President Johnson: No. Not yet

Secretary McNamara: I'd, I'd leave the paragraph out. You've talked up above about the leaders of both parties, and it seems to me that's the strong point.

President Johnson: Yeah. The trouble is, he's going to be calling in about 9:30

Secretary McNamara: Well, I'd keep talking to him, trying to talk to him all right, but, but I don't think I'd refer to it and say

President Johnson: What would you do, just wait until after, talk, talk to him until he's out on a [boat? slurred word] and they've gone to get him. Or would you talk to him as soon as he gets in and tell him I'm going to make a statement and I want him to know about it and then not refer to it.

Secretary McNamara: That's exactly what I'd do, Mr. President. I'd try to talk to him before I made it, but I wouldn't refer to having talked to him. And, and the purpose of talking to him would be to stop any opposition from him. And if you did that, I think you've accomplished your purpose. You don't have to tie him into your statement.

President Johnson: I think it's better not to, don't you?

Secretary McNamara: Yes.

President Johnson: And what's delayed them so?

Secretary McNamara: Just the, the limitations of time, Mr. President. We ask an awful lot of them. They said initially they could do it. But, uh, it's proven now they couldn't; they had to brief the crews and load the aircraft with specific types of weapons for these particular targets and it took more time than they anticipated.

President Johnson: And when they leave the carrier at 10:00, how long does it take them to get over the target?

Secretary McNamara: The last time, over the target, will be two hours from then, we believe.

President Johnson: Twelve.

Secretary McNamara: Which would be about 12 o'clock, our time. The first planes over the

President Johnson: Well, do we want to give them two hours notice?

Secretary McNamara: I don't believe there's any reason not to, Mr. President. I don't think there's any serious problem in that.

President Johnson: Better check that, Bob.

Secretary McNamara: I did. I just talked to Admiral Sharp about it. He, he did not want this particular sentence read, the one I'm suggesting be taken out, uh, prior to the time they get over the targets.

President Johnson: Well, won't they get there simultaneously, almost?

Secretary McNamara: They'll get the, the, uh, statement simultaneously, but they won't know what targets are being attacked.

President Johnson: Well, it looks like they'd think that they're liable to hit where those boats are coming from. Looks like they might get out there with some anti-aircraft guns. I'd sure as hell hate to have some mother say, "you announced it and my boy got killed."

Secretary McNamara: I don't think there's much damage, uh, uh, much danger of that, Mr. President. How late would you be willing to hold the statement?

President Johnson: I just, uh, I guess we could hold it till [the] 11 o'clock news. I don't know. We don't have to make it, do we?

Secretary McNamara: Oh, I think, uh, I think you need to make some kind of a statement at this time. Because tomorrow morning will be too late. Something will have to be on the news tomorrow morning. It ought to come from you.

President Johnson: Well let's see how it goes along, uh

Secretary McNamara: All right

President Johnson: He's told you that he's going to launch them at 10:00?

Secretary McNamara: That's right.

President Johnson: And [it] takes them two hours to get over the target?

Secretary McNamara: Well, the launch will take place over a period of time, and the last aircraft launched is estimated to be over the target at two hours after

President Johnson: Launch

Secretary McNamara: Launch.

President Johnson: Well, what do you think the first one will be?

Secretary McNamara: The first one ought to be over the target within an hour after launch, but the radar of the North Vietnamese should pick up the first aircraft, uh, a few minutes after launch. Say 10:30 our time, the North Vietnamese would be aware of, uh, attacking aircraft coming in.

President Johnson: So that would be all right then.

Secretary McNamara: I would think so then, and [if] you did it at 10:30, you could make the 11 o'clock news.

President Johnson: OK. And thank you.

Secretary McNamara: Right-oh.

AUGUST 4, 1964: CONVERSATIONS ABOUT THE SLAIN CIVIL
RIGHTS WORKERS CONTINUED

Lyndon B. Johnson
Tuesday, August 4, 1964, 9:35 P.M.
Telephone Conversation with Paul B. Johnson, Governor of Mississippi,
Regarding the Civil Rights Workers

Woman's Voice: Governor Johnson?

Governor Paul Johnson: Yes.

Woman's Voice: Thank you. One moment for the president.

President Lyndon B. Johnson: Yes?

Second Woman's Voice: Governor Johnson on 9–1.

President Johnson: Governor?

Governor Johnson: Yes, Mr. President.

President Lyndon B. Johnson: Uh, they, Hoover got a hold of me a while ago and tells me that, uh, they have found some bodies down there.

Governor Johnson: That's correct.

President Johnson: And, uh, they're going to take them into Jackson and see if they can, uh, identify 'em and, uh, I thought I'd, uh, I'd talk to you and, uh, see, see what's, see what they, I asked them to be sure that, uh, you were informed of it. And I assume you were.

[For a few moments Governor Johnson exchanges information with the president, who replies "Uh huh" several times, but the governor's comments are not audible.]

President Johnson: What, were they buried?

Governor Johnson: Uh, yes, sir.

President Johnson: How'd they locate 'em?

Governor Johnson: Well, I don't know. [inaudible] did the job [inaudible] I don't know all the details.

President Johnson: I've been in this Vietnam Security Council and we're, uh, we're having to retaliate out there tonight, uh, that this shooting that took place at our destroyer today, I'm goin' on television after a while, as soon as I get our planes off the ground, and

Governor Johnson: [inaudible]

President Johnson: tell the people about it, and I, I haven't eaten any dinner. I, I, just, um, it's, it's a, it's twenty minutes to elev-, twenty minutes to ten here, but I thought I'd better talk to you. I know you're gonna do everything you can to apprehend 'em. And any way in the world we can help, we want to do it.

Governor Johnson: Well, we've been doin' that all along, and we're gonna continue to do it. Now we just don't know where it's been [Johnson sighs, intones "Wha?" the governor's next words are not audible], we didn't know what in the world to do. And even though we had trouble in June [words inaudible] . . .

President Johnson: Well, we all got it, and you've, uh, you certainly, uh, acted fine under all the circumstances. And I certainly do appreciate your attitude and your cooperation. And I know what you've gone through, and it's been terrible for all of us, and we, uh, we just, we just got to do the best we can under these circumstances as the family gets pretty

[Again the governor's reply is not audible]

President Johnson: Fine! Couldn't be better. I, I just feel wonderful, and I, I got a good nap every day after lunch, and then I can work two shifts. I work one in the mornin' and take my nap and then work another'n that night and, uh, can't do anything very gay you know. They keep me locked up behind this black fence.

Governor Johnson: Well, that's all right. [Inaudible — "You can leave a man"?] for a while.

President Johnson: Well, we got, we got plenty of problems, and we gonna solve 'em, we're gonna solve 'em together, Governor, and I, I want to keep this line [of] communications open all the time. And anything that we can do here, you let us know.

Governor Johnson: [inaudible]

President Johnson: I know that. I, I know that. And it's been, it's been mighty good workin' with ya, and I know you're doin' the best you can. And we, we want to help you and not create any more problems. I'm gonna make a little speech tomorrow on this violence up at, uh, up New York, and it's gonna be pretty straightforward.

Governor Johnson: Well, I'll tell you uh something else. That some of those [inaudible]

President Lyndon B. Johnson: Yeah, that's right. Ah. Well. We'll, we'll continue to keep in touch with you.

Governor Johnson: [inaudible]

President Johnson: Thank you, Governor.

Lyndon B. Johnson
Tuesday, August 4, 1964, 9:40 P.M.
Telephone Conversation with Cartha DeLoach, FBI, Regarding the
Discovery of the Bodies of Michael Schwerner, Andrew Goodman, and
James Chaney, Three Civil Rights Workers Missing Since June 21, 1964

Woman's Voice: Sir. One moment.

President Lyndon B. Johnson: Yes.

Woman's Voice: Deke DeLoach on 9–0.

President Johnson: Deke?

Cartha DeLoach: Yes, sir, Mr. President.

President Johnson: I talked to the Governor in New Jersey and he thinks that, uh, that Italian came over from Brooklyn yesterday and, uh, started this riot up there in Jersey City, and they arrested him and he made bond right quick, $5,000, and they think that very suspicious people involved in this thing. I told him I'd ask Mr. Hoover to get some of his men up there to talk to him tomorrow.

Cartha DeLoach: Very good, sir.

President Johnson: And I wish you'd, uh, really show 'em.

Cartha DeLoach: I'll certainly do it, sir.

President Johnson: I talked to the governor of Mississippi tonight and told him I knew he was going to do everything he could to help apprehend those people. And he was very complimentary of you all. And said that, uh, he sympathized with us today with all of our Vietnam problems, and everything.

Cartha DeLoach: Yes, sir.

President Johnson: And, uh, he would do everything in the world he could. Do you pretty well have in mind, uh, who did this job?

Cartha DeLoach: Uh, Mr. President, we have, uh, some very excellent suspects in it. It's a matter of immediate digging of evidence now. We have some excellent circumstantial evidence but, uh, we don't have enough to cause any arrests right now.

President Johnson: Uh, how'd ya find the spot? Did somebody give you a lead?

Cartha DeLoach: Uh, yes, sir, uh, uh, someone that we have to protect, use a great deal of caution, of course. We got some information which led us to it, yes, sir.

President Johnson: You don't have much doubt but what these are the bodies, eh?

Cartha DeLoach: Mr. President, we feel very definitely these are the bodies, and the only reason we were very cautious in our press release is because of some fluke that might come up. But we have the coroner on the way there now, and we're going to move 'em to Jackson, Mississippi, which is seventy miles away, to the hospital, where we can possibly identify 'em, we think, through a, a previous broken leg of one of 'em and dental work on the other, and the third one has a defect, too, a physical characteristic.

President Johnson: Uh, were they all buried in the same grave?

Cartha DeLoach: It was not common grave, Mr. President. They were buried, uh, some few feet apart, at, uh, in this, uh, particular dam, which is a new dam on this farm. Uh, but it was not, uh, they were all not in the same grave, no. They were located about, uh, five to ten minutes apart. Indeed.

President Johnson: Were they under water?

Cartha DeLoach: Uh, no, sir. It was dirt. The damn, the dam site itself. And it took a, uh, it took a hell of a lot of shoveling and digging to, uh, get at them. As a matter of fact, for your information, sir, we had to get a contractor in there to help us out with heavy equipment.

[silence]

President Johnson: Uh, what's happened to Georgia thing? [Note: On July 11, 1964, Lemuel Penn, an African American U.S. Army Reserve officer, was killed by a gunshot from a passing car while driving through Madison County, Georgia, on his way home to Washington, D.C., from annual summer active duty at Fort Benning, Georgia. The car's driver signed a statement admitting his involvement and identifying Howard Sims and Cecil Myers as the ones who fired the shots. Members of the Ku Klux Klan, Sims and Myers were tried in state superior court and found innocent of murder charges by an all-white jury. Federal prosecutors subsequently charged Sims and Myers with violating Penn's civil rights. They were found guilty by a federal district court jury. Sims and Myers served about six years in federal prison.]

Cartha DeLoach: Um, Mr. President, that's been narrowed down to, uh, two suspects who actually pulled that job. And, uh, we have, uh, one of the man's name is Myers, the other man's name is Sims. They're both members of the Ku Klux Klan out of Athens, Georgia. They don't live in the city of Athens, but just on the outskirts of it. There were six suspects all together, but they've all been questioned and shaken down considerably, and, uh, one of 'em, two of 'em, have been able to, uh, provide the alibis for the two key subjects. Now the two men in question, just a matter there, too, of, uh, getting it just a little bit further evidence, and we'll be able to move on that case. But we have excellent, uh, chances of breaking that within the very next several days.

President Johnson: O-K.

Cartha DeLoach: I'll keep you constantly advised, sir, and, uh, I'll also notify Lee White and Walter Jenkins just the minute these bodies are identified so they can get in touch with you.

President Johnson: Thank you.

Cartha DeLoach: Yes, sir.

Richard M. Nixon

MARCH 26, 1971: PRESIDENT NIXON MEETS WITH HIS NATIONAL SECURITY COUNCIL ON VIETNAM, THE INVASION OF LAOS, AND OTHER ISSUES IN THE WAR

The conflict in Southeast Asia steadily expanded from the decisions LBJ made in the summer of 1964. With the beginning of large-scale ground combat a year later, the war assumed increasing importance for the United States, and for several years President Johnson reinforced the American military in his effort to win the war. By 1968, there were more than half a million American troops in the combat zone, while at home a rising tide of opposition to the war had begun to tie LBJ's hands and those of other leaders. In early 1968, a massive countrywide Tet Offensive mounted by the North Vietnamese and the guerrillas of the National Liberation Front in South Vietnam, though a military failure, proved a great political success in showing that a military solution to the Vietnam conflict was not practical. Lyndon Johnson stopped reinforcing the war, turned U.S. policy toward a negotiated settlement, and began a policy of turning over the war to our South Vietnamese allies. He also withdrew from politics, simplifying calculations for Richard Milhous Nixon, the Republican presidential candidate. Nixon won the election in November 1968 and confronted a political situation that made it impossible for him to further increase

U.S. forces, while the American people felt they had voted for an end to the war.

Nixon was understood to have promised a secret plan to terminate the war, but it was not clear to the public that the new president's intent was to end the conflict by winning it. The Nixon formula became a combination of initiatives, including holding out for a negotiating position that amounted to a surrender by North Vietnam, threatening force to secure agreement to that position, accelerating the turnover of the ground combat to the South Vietnamese (in the initiative known as "Vietnamization"), and gradually withdrawing U.S. ground forces from the conflict. The troop withdrawals cut down U.S. casualties, which bought time on the political front. Nixon's plans featured reliance on naval and airpower as the least vulnerable forces. Nixon expanded the war into nations adjacent to Vietnam by invading Cambodia in 1970, and by an energetic program of bombing in Laos from his first moments in office.

With U.S. troops reduced by more than half, and the airpower formula firmly in place, the invasion of Laos, carried out in early 1971, necessarily relied upon the South Vietnamese army (called ARVN for "Army of the Republic of Vietnam"), backed by U.S. airpower. They were supposed to cut North Vietnam's main supply route to the South, familiarly known as the "Ho Chi Minh Trail." This involved a thrust of perhaps thirty miles into Laos from the part of South Vietnam just below the Demilitarized Zone (DMZ). Instead, what happened in early February 1971, when the invasion occurred, is that the ARVN crossed into Laos, halted less than halfway toward their objectives, and sat still while North Vietnamese armies concentrated and hit them back. Some believe ARVN commanders were secretly under orders from Saigon leaders not to go the full distance, others that the ARVN simply did not have the stomach for a full-scale confrontation with the North Vietnamese army. Through the rest of that month and into March, the South Vietnamese remained immobile. Then, using U.S. helicopters, ARVN made a raid that reached its objective from the beginning of the operation, but the South Vietnamese quickly began to pull back under a hail of enemy counterattacks. On March 9, South Vietnamese commanders counseled President Nguyen Van Thieu that a withdrawal of all ARVN troops from Laos was the best course to take. Nixon sent his deputy national security adviser, Army Brigadier General Alexander M. Haig Jr., to South Vietnam to examine the situation, and Haig quickly agreed with the need for a withdrawal from Laos.

Soon after Haig returned from his trip, President Nixon held a National Security Council meeting to discuss the Laotian crisis. This meeting on March 26 is featured in our tape selection and includes a discussion of many issues, including the Laotian operation, progress in the Vietnamization initiative, press reporting of the Vietnam War, the dwindling congressional support for the war effort, and the demands of many to set a date for final U.S. withdrawal from Vietnam. These are the key issues in war policy throughout the Nixon administration, so that the discussion at the National Security Council that day represents a microcosm of the White House's political problems regarding Vietnam.

The meeting began at 4:09 P.M. and lasted about forty-five minutes. However, either something was wrong with the Oval Office taping system, Alexander Butterfield had orders to begin taping only upon some specific order, or the first part of this tape was destroyed or supressed for other reasons, for the taped record only begins in the middle of the meeting. Thus Henry Kissinger, who left at 4:25, features in just one brief comment on the portion of the meeting tape that survives. A memorandum for the files by Alexander Haig details the discussion in the Cabinet Room. (The written record shows that Kissinger's comments in the meeting, still sparse, are more extensive than apparent from the tape.) The meeting was attended by Secretary of Defense Melvin R. Laird, his deputy, David Packard, Joint Chiefs of Staff chairman Admiral Thomas H. Moorer Jr., Treasury Secretary John Connally, Kissinger, and Haig.

President Nixon opened the meeting with a bid for the group to consider the impact of Vietnamization. Plans already on the table envisioned radical reductions in U.S. military strength in Southeast Asia, and top secret memoranda from the JCS, MACV, and others had postulated different ways to bring strength down to about 60,000 by mid-1972. Nixon wished to be absolutely sure that when those troop levels were reached, the Saigon government had all it needed in the way of helicopters, planes, artillery and supplies. Nixon also wanted to talk about the scale of the U.S. air effort, insisting that the rate of air missions ("sorties" is the term of art) be kept at a high level through the U.S. presidential elections in November 1972. National Security Adviser Henry Kissinger then reported that the White House had received proposals on Vietnamization from Secretary Melvin R. Laird, but had yet to study them in any detail.

Laird replied for the Pentagon that existing plans already called for the high sortie rate through 1972. He mentioned the number of 700 sorties a month for B-52s, which he had as the general planning rate, but conceded the Joint Chiefs had held out for 800 (that number of B-52 sorties had been the monthly scale of U.S. effort at the height of the Vietnam War in 1968). As for providing helicopters and aircraft to the South Vietnamese, Laird pointed out that the principal constraints were the sufficiency of Vietnamese technicians and training for the pilots and air crews. The chairman of the Joint Chiefs of Staff, Admiral Thomas Moorer, linked the Vietnamese equipment issue with U.S. withdrawals by pointing out that due to the difficulty Laird had mentioned, the Pentagon planned to retain helicopter and tactical air units in Southeast Asia right through the end of the Vietnamization program. John Connally asked about spare parts for the equipment and was told these would be stocked at standard rates. Secretary Connally then observed that once a U.S. withdrawal had been completed, "it will be most difficult to get Congressional support for the provision of additional equipment for South Vietnam."[1] Connally advocated leaving large numbers of spares as the United States departed. Laird then objected that Pentagon ability to handle that aspect of the situation was limited by its responsibility for the worldwide military assistance program. President Nixon then asked Dr. Kissinger whether the military assistance program had been transferred to State Department control in a recent decision on the issue, only to be told that his decision had in fact been to retain the old system, which gave the responsibility to the Department of Defense.

Secretary Connally declared that if the South Vietnamese wanted 500 helicopters, the United States ought to leave them with 1,000. Richard Nixon agreed. Defense Secretary Laird, who actually had the responsibility, interjected that the South Vietnamese themselves disagreed on what they wanted, but he believed Saigon's president, Nguyen Van Thieu, would be content with 625 helicopters and a fifty-squadron air force.

The taped coverage of Nixon's Oval Office meeting on Vietnam issues begins at around this point, shortly after which Kissinger departs the room unheralded. There is discussion of the impending election in South Vietnam required by the Vietnamese constitution of 1967 (Nixon comments that "it is a shame" that "the U.S." is forcing Thieu to have an election in the middle of a war and John Connally agrees). There is an extensive discussion of support for the war, which is rapidly waning in the U.S. Congress, in which participants strategize on how to head off congressional moves to set an end date for U.S. participation in the war. Nixon, as he frequently did in meetings, postured and made claims that were not true—for example, that the war had not started until after he left Washington in 1961. There are also palpable contrasts. Asserting that he has cut back on the war ("we whopped it down" is Nixon's idiom), at two later points Nixon tells military leaders to consider new air attacks on North Vietnam and the passes crossing the mountains along the Ho Chi Minh Trail ("you might want to give 'em another whack"). Further, Nixon tells them to ignore political considerations. In fact, the Seventh Air Force in Southeast Asia carried out a special effort during this period specifically aimed at closing the mountain passes. Nixon insists that "if I were a politician," a certain tough rhetoric on ending the war would be appropriate, but he mandates a blatant political strategy—to blame Congress for any end to the war other than on the administration's terms. Nixon views the combat action as "taking risks for peace."

Admiral Moorer then takes the floor for a briefing that summarizes the results of the invasion of Laos, which has just ended with the last South Vietnamese troops pulling back across the border. Defense Secretary Melvin Laird jokes when Moorer confuses colors on the maps he is using for the briefing. Moorer's reference to thirty tanks at one point is confusing because he has been talking about South Vietnamese forces, but the figure actually represents an estimate of the number of tanks remaining on the North Vietnamese side. Moorer's mention of "Eagles" is a reference to the American 101st Airborne Division, nicknamed the "Screaming Eagles," which provided the vast majority of helicopter support for the South Vietnamese invasion. (It is during this portion of the meeting that President Nixon twice suggests new air attacks on North Vietnam and the mountain passes. Several large-scale raids on North Vietnam, involving about 1,000 air missions, actually took place during the invasion of Laos and were characterized as responses to North Vietnamese firing on U.S. reconnaissance aircraft. Moorer's discussion reveals that bombs targeted North Vietnamese artillery positions, missile sites and activity in the Demilitarized Zone between North and South Vietnam, not anti-aircraft positions.)

A full quarter of the entire National Security meeting is concerned with the media, denouncing press coverage of the Laotian invasion, particularly by Associated Press reporter Tammy Arbuckle, and how to counter reports of extensive losses. On March 22, President Nixon had given an extensive television interview on the invasion to ABC News commentator Howard K. Smith—which he refers to here ("the other night I was very careful about saying")—in which he had countered reports of poor performance by the South Vietnamese army by claiming that only four battalions of that force had done poorly. Nixon, who had spent that entire day preparing for the TV interview, here asks Moorer, "That's relatively accurate, is it not?" In fact, perhaps ten South Vietnamese battalions had to be completely rebuilt after Laos, the South Vietnamese armored brigade had suffered 60 percent equipment losses (a 30 percent loss would cause a unit to be rated "combat ineffective" in the U.S. Army), and the South Vietnamese Airborne and 1st Infantry Divisions had suffered about one-third losses while the ranger group engaged in Laos had casualties approaching one-half. At the meeting, Admiral Moorer states that the Pentagon has asked the U.S. command in Vietnam to explain the basis for its evaluation.

A statement issued in Saigon on March 24, as South Vietnamese troops recoiled to the border area, listed almost 14,000 North Vietnamese dead as an achievement of the operation. Admiral Moorer, however, tells this group in the White House, "We have no reliable information on their dead."

The U.S. Air Force official history for this period concludes, "President Nixon obviously erred on the side of optimism."[2] The meeting tape shows that the extravagant claims were to be made as a matter of policy. "People get more war weary," Richard Nixon says here, and he believed that had happened in the Civil War and World War II even before it happened in Vietnam. Nixon instructs the group, "So now is the time for all of us—we've got to be just strong and firm and confident."

In a speech on April 7, two weeks after this taped meeting, President Nixon would announce a further 100,000 reduction in U.S. troop strength in Vietnam, all personnel to be brought home before the end of the year, on the rationale that Vietnamization had succeeded. About a week later, Defense Secretary Melvin Laird attended a dinner with nine prominent congressional Republicans at the home of New York Senator Jacob Javits. One of the attendees, from Alaska, which he considered the most pro-war state in the country, told Laird that while he had run for election supporting the war in 1970, he would be unable to do so in 1972. Senate Republican leader Hugh Scott (R-PA) said he could no longer promise to defeat antiwar amendments to legislation offered in Congress, and that President Nixon had to begin thinking in terms of finality and advance some formula that indicated clearly an end to American participation in the war. "The hawks are all ex-hawks," Scott told Laird, "We just can't hold the line any longer on numbers."[3]

The Laotian invasion prefigured the end of the Vietnam war. Politics required President Nixon to continue Vietnamization and reduce U.S. force levels even below the 60,000 troops envisioned in the Pentagon's March 1971 planning. A negotiated ceasefire agreement with North Vietnam in 1973 brought the final U.S. withdrawal and the return of prisoners. South Vietnam fell to the North in April 1975.

Richard M. Nixon
March 26, 1971, 4:09 P.M.–4:53 P.M.
Meeting in the Oval Office
Present: Melvin R. Laird (Secretary of Defense), Admiral Thomas H. Moorer (Chairman of the Joint Chiefs of Staff), David Packard (Deputy Secretary of Defense), Henry A. Kissinger (National Security Adviser), General Alexander M. Haig Jr. (Deputy National Security Adviser), and John Connally (Secretary of the Treasury) Discussion about the Future of Vietnam and the Media

[Tape begins as conversation is already taking place.]

President Richard M. Nixon: When we get down to the point where American casualties aren't [unintelligible] he gets by with quite a bit. I tell you, he's going to be hit pretty hard.

Secretary of Defense Melvin Laird: Well, we'll see that, uh, when I spoke to Thieu about this, first objection is that is a little bit of disagreement with Thieu on this. Thieu believes that a helicopter force from, uh, about 625 is about as maximum that he can support. He will have the largest helicopter force of any nation in the free world.

President Nixon: Except us.

Secretary Laird: Except the United States. Uh, he'll have fifty air squadrons. He's got thirty-three right now. Uh, and, uh, he's gonna be in a position where we're willing to [unintelligible] fifty of them next year. Uh, so

President Nixon: All kinds?

Secretary Laird: Yeah.

President Nixon: I wouldn't want to tackle him.

Secretary Laird: The North Vietnamese have a real lot of nasty things down there. But if we can put more in there, we'll try to do it. But with the training

President Nixon: [unintelligible]

Secretary Laird: Everything, more emphasis on the training and the rest

President Nixon: I just feel that we give him whatever you can and leave now, Mel. Just leave it now. Figure we're gonna have one hell of a time getting them in.

Secretary Laird: What I would want Thieu to do, though, is to start cutting back on his force structure. Because he feels, you know, that he should make some reductions prior to this election and, uh, that he'd like to takes, he'd like to take some reductions. And I urged him [unintelligible]

President Nixon: Uh, [unintelligible] all of us want to hear. Is this, is this, uh, still a subject we all worked together on?

[unintelligible]

Henry Kissinger: Well, if we are going to work together we are a long [unintelligible — "North Vietnam has refused"?] pictures

President Nixon: Right

Henry Kissinger: of the Soviet radar thing.

President Nixon: Yeah.

Henry Kissinger: If he keeps the next thousand and eight hundred [unintelligible]

President Nixon: Right.

Henry Kissinger: Right.

Secretary Laird: We talked about that for '73. We didn't talk about that for '72. But I'm talking about '73.

Henry Kissinger: I must be going.

President Nixon: Fine. And, well, the, uh,

Secretary Laird: I don't think we'll need it in '73. We should plan on it. We'd like, we'd like to plan more. I, I can't, I can't select [unintelligible: "entrench"?] you 700 B-52s [noise interference] great exception.

Secretary of the Treasury John Connally: But before that, it's a little different [unintelligible] and appreciate the others, too. First difference seems to me, after this Laos-Chup confrontation [Connally refers to a battle in Cambodia being fought at the same time as Laos], you notice, marked articulation on the Hill on the Democrats. Now I don't have to withdraw that [noise interference] situation that you want.

President Nixon: Yeah.

Secretary Connally: I read it was December '72.

President Nixon: Yeah.

Secretary Connally: But they're anticipatin' the success of these moves all over [unintelligible: a reference to antiwar legislation] and I've begun to see this bill more and more and more; we've got to keep this off, my particular attitude, so that they don't just take the play away from us.

Secretary Laird: Well, I know that's the

Secretary Connally: It's the cutting season.

Secretary Laird: It's hard for responsible people like Carl Albert [D-OK-3, Speaker of the House] for one.

Secretary Connally: He has no

Secretary Laird: They're going to try to delay that decision in the Caucus next Tuesday on the motion that Tiger Teague's [Olin E. Teague, D-TX-6, chairman of the House Democratic Caucus] gonna make, that they think they should take no action. I talked to him about this. They'll ask for the President's counsel. They may be influenced [noise interference], that means they're going away for two weeks.

President Nixon: Yeah. Yeah. Yeah.

Secretary Laird: But, uh, Carl isn't allowing [unintelligible]

President Nixon: When is it, what day of the week is the 31st?

Secretary Laird: The 31st?

President Nixon: That's the date of the Caucus.

Secretary Laird: Tuesday, I believe. I'm not sure . . .

President Nixon: Wednesday

Secretary Laird: Tuesday or Wednesday

President Nixon: Well, it's very important that I know that, that, that, I would like to say the [unintelligible] from California, and

Secretary Laird: Day of the week

President Nixon: Six

Secretary Laird: Six

President Nixon: That's five days more. OK. Well,

Secretary Laird: I've talked them. I've worked with them closely. I've talked to them all. Almost every other day, Mr. President

President Nixon: I know

Secretary Laird: And I was up there talking to

President Nixon: I talked to Albert and Boggs [Hale Boggs, D-LA-2, majority leader] this morning. And they're going to do their very best, and let me tell you their line [recorder noise] I said, strongly, now, look, this is great; I appreciate it. Very, very key, to press for time. At first as far as Laos is concerned. In the final analysis we're gonna catch it. And as far as I am concerned, I survive. He said categorically that Laos would be judged by whether we continue our withdrawal, what happens also to the Vietnamization program. If it helps, full scores, then we'll raise [is it] worth doing; otherwise, not. So forth and so on. Then, we got to the key part. I said, now this withdrawal; let's just understand one thing. I said, I have a plan. I know the date that we're gonna be out of that. It's a reasonable date. It's one that *I* am convinced is the earliest possible date we can get out without risking a South Vietnamese debacle. Also it's the one that I think is essential for us to, uh, have, in terms of our, any possible regard to our position to what you're suggesting. Uh, then going on from there. You consider the situation, uh, uh [unintelligible] for the date you selected, you're doing two things. I said, One, you are inevitably giving [unintelligible: "Hanoi"?] the option to, uh, [unintelligible] terms that they'll say, well, we'll get out on the 31st if you give us back our prisoners. I said, That's not gonna be a good deal—well, they're not going to say, ah; they're going to say, Yes, get out on the 31st, throw out Thieu and Ky, and then it will be better business. That's the way it will be. That'll just be the starting place.

So, then this is where politics came in. I said, Now, let me tell you, I know you guys are not gonna play politics, but some of your colleagues will. But let's understand how it's gonna be played. I want you to be very clear on this [unintelligible]. I said, I've stuck this thing through; we took this war, started after I left Washington in 1961, and we whopped it down; and we have a proposed ending, an ending the way South Vietnam has a chance to survive. If you, on the other hand, decide you're going to take over and set an arbitrary date, over the objections, our objections, then [noise interference] but then *you* will have to take the responsibility for an American defeat in Vietnam, and for all these deaths, for the communization of South Vietnam. I said, This is what is on the line here. That anybody who wants to step in and view the play one way or another, you can let me—and I said it's a hell of a risk, I said it's a chancy thing to know whether South Vietnam can survive.

Another Voice: What else?

President Nixon: It's a chancy thing to know whether or not this withdrawal could go on. North Vietnamese will not bend. But I said, I'm willing to take it; and we're withdrawing on this kind of schedule. If it fails, then you, you'll have no, no sweat. You can just kick the hell out of me. You can say, He was wrong. He continued this war for four more years and because he could have got out four years ago, and we still lost to them. And that's one game to play. If I were a politician, I'd play that game. But we'll support the Commander-in-Chief in his best judgment because we know that he isn't gonna keep an American there any longer than he needs to. But if you play it the other way, I just want you to clearly understand that if there is any arbitrary day set, then *I* will have no choice but to put the responsibility on the Democrats in the

House and the Senate, on them, for losing everything that we fought for in Vietnam. And for bringing on a communist victory. If you want to fight it out on that gig, we'll beat the hell on it. Well they understood it. Understand. They're with us. That is the way to put it. Don't you agree [unintelligible name]?

[Voice responds, obscured by other voices, including Nixon's]

President Nixon: They are gonna [voices speaking over each other] there is no answer to this.

Voice: Well, Mr. President [voices again]

President Nixon: If they do it now, let me say this. This is [unintelligible]. Let us suppose the House and the Senate did pass a, the resolution or a call to defund or anything, bring all Americans home by January or by December of 1971, there would be a better than even chance then we lose the whole damn shebang. But believe me, if that happens, we ain't gonna get blamed for it; they are. That's the point now. And I talked a little cold politics to these guys. If you guys want to play that fine; on the other hand, play our game, it's risky is the difference, it may not work, but we believe it's the, that's the, we're, we're moving as fast as we can. But if it doesn't work, then you can kick us. But if it does work, then you cooperate. Now by God that's fair talk, isn't it?

Secretary Connally: It sure is. Nothin' wrong with that.

Deputy Secretary of Defense David Packard: It's gonna work, Mr. President.

President Nixon: I would hope so.

Secretary Laird: Mr. President

President Nixon: Also, we've all slept and worked hard, and, er, it's the right thing to do. That's the main thing.

Secretary Laird: There's no misunderstanding it, Mr. President. We can, even if when we get down to, say, the 50,000 force level in Vietnam, the way we have it planned out, we can maintain approximately the same level of air sorties because of the buildup of the South Vietnamese. As we did in '73 [Laird actually means 1970], we can still fly tactical air sorties at the rate of 17,000.

President Nixon: Yep.

Secretary Laird: And we can still, I'm told we have 700 B-52s, in there but we can go to the 800 that the Chiefs wanted in '73. We can do that.

President Nixon: Well, let's plan that.

Secretary Laird: There's no problem.

President Nixon: Yeah.

Another Voice: We gonna have some more guns exported this year?

President Nixon: By God, yes. Let's have those gun checks. The other thing I was gonna say is this now. Uh, that's, uh, uh, with regard to this Caucus thing, uh, the Democratic Caucus, that's important.

Secretary Laird: Well, I'm having them all over for breakfast. All the new Democrats. Tuesday morning, before the caucus.

President Nixon: And I, I think that you should talk with Bridges and say, now, look [unintelligible]. You should say that you and I have chatted. There's nobody that wants to get, there's nobody that has a greater interest in seeing to it that not one American is there longer one, there one day longer than is necessary. But I have looked it over and I am moving as fast as we possibly can, and a little faster than some think is wise. But we're doing it.

Secretary Laird: You're taking risks.

President Nixon: That's right. We're taking, we are taking risks for peace, and I think that should be emphasized. And say, now folks, here it is. You, you think we ought to move faster. All right. The President is moving in a way that he is convinced can get America out and still save South Vietnam. But if you have it move in your way, you'll get Americans out and you'll lose South Vietnam and the Communists will take it. And you've got to take the blame. By

God, if they don't sit that language, then it's gonna be, uh, if I were a politician, I'd, I'd listen, wouldn't you, John?

Secretary Connally: Yes, sir. They will.

President Nixon: Well, I'll let them understand it. There's no problem with, with our newspaper.

Voice: That's right.

[Numerous voices speaking over each other.]

Secretary Laird: He's worried about those damn votes.

President Nixon: He should be worried. But he should be reassured that, and also you can reassure him and say, look, now, eh [unintelligible] look, we're going to make another announcement. It'll be a good announcement. And, and, fellas, why don't you wait. You can take a look and then knock us.

Secretary Laird: Well, that's going to be their motion at the caucus. And they may carry that one. They'd, they'd rather not have a vote right now.

Secretary Connally: Well obviously I get word back to some of the liberals who are still [unintelligible, one voice says "a guy named"] what was yours? Uh, and just, uh, along the lines you're talking. You're idiots for taking on this responsibility [unintelligible] either one of you now.

President Nixon: And if you have to take on the responsibility, and I, incidentally, uh, I could very be [*sic*] nonpartisan in [another voice interferes] the war to date, but I could be just as partisan as hell if they want. But if they think partisan, believe me, they're gonna take the responsibility for it, for everywhere we lost [unintelligible] out there [unintelligible] forces. Us? We didn't lose it. Pretty good plan.

Secretary Laird: I don't like to be partisan about it.

[Laughter]

President Nixon: Ah, let me ask, uh, the, uh, Admiral, uh, before we go here, uh, the, uh, is there anything further to report on the general operations?

Admiral Thomas Moorer: I think we have [unintelligible]

President Nixon: Oh, sure, we got [noise interference] of the forces right now. . . . Would you like to

Admiral Moorer: [unintelligible] nothing I can do about it

Secretary Laird: [unintelligible] put it right next to that, sure enough. The trouble with the Chairman's request is that he has a little trouble with colors. You see, he didn't realize that if you mix green and orange, you get brown.

[Laughter]

Admiral Moorer: Mr. President, uh, the, the red is the North Vietnamese and the blue is U.S. Green are South Vietnamese [Moorer displays maps of military positions in Laos]. First, uh, let me, uh, uh, report once again that, uh, General Abrams says that of the 33 battalions that the North Vietnamese have, that only 17 are now effective. And, uh, they have suffered casualties. Uh, the estimate is that of the 17, uh, 9 of them are, are north of, uh, Nine, this Road 9 here, and, uh, 8 of 'em are south, in this area. Of course they have infiltrated across the border and halfway to Quang Tri. And, uh, along a, a, this Highway 9 [Nine, Road 9 and Highway 9 refer to the same road] here, as we really expect them to do. The South Vietnamese are positioning their forces, and then we are readjusting what they call the Area of Operations so that the South Vietnamese are taking positions along the border between the North Vietnamese and the U.S. forces. Uh, and so, uh, this will continue as the South Vietnamese are taking over beyond the DMZ [demilitarized zone], they're moving in here. Uh, this is the Airborne Division here in reserve and one of the regiments from the, uh, First Division which was not involved in the operation in Laos proper is now moved into the, the hot spot right here. In addition to that, the, we think there are about, uh, 30 [North Vietnamese] tanks, uh, left, upper left, about from their original forces of about a hundred and fifty.

President Nixon: We don't know where they are?

Admiral Moorer: Yes, sir. They, uh, they've been, uh, we attack them all the time. Uh, some would

President Nixon: Do we ever hit any?

Admiral Moorer: Yes, sir. They get killed plenty of times. Uh, a matter of fact, uh, I think there was 7, uh, out that way in here just a short time ago.

President Nixon: Good.

Admiral Moorer: But there are about 30 in, uh, in this zero area, and this indicated to the, uh, the, uh, flights being taken by the helicopters, uh, sent up to observe, uh, the, uh, motion of the North Vietnamese, and, uh, and to attack 'em when they see them. So far as Khe Sanh proper is concerned as you know, it's been getting attacked by fire again, it's getting attacked by fire about 12 hours ago. But no damage. We would expect that to continue.

President Nixon: Is this something we mentioned or know?

Admiral Moorer: Uh, Khe Sanh sir is, uh, uh, what, uh, is happening now is that, uh, we're, uh, withdrawing some of the forces in order to bring the, uh, the, uh, supplies to there and forces to there in balance with the activity that, uh, that, uh, is taking place throughout this area. In other words, we didn't want to leave the Eagles [Moorer refers to the 101st Airborne Division (Airmobile), nicknamed the "Screaming Eagles"] there and just have them, uh

President Nixon: Sure

Admiral Moorer: Uh, in jeopardy when they're not being used. So. What we're doing is moving our supplies, oh, to balance it out with the, uh, activity that is taking place in this area. Now, uh, there's an indication that the, uh, and particularly the tall [?], indication at all of any reinforcements coming in here so far as the North Vietnamese are concerned. Any additional forces. Secondly, uh, there, there are several inner steps indicating that they apparently, uh, uh, high-powered here, while trying to reconstitute this [unclear code name] and get it working again. And, as a result, they have erected, uh, uh, some of the forces that attached to the new battalions here to return and report back to these, uh, the General indicated this, pushing their supplies through. So that is taking place and we expected that. Now, during the next, uh, few days, uh, couple of weeks or so, there'll be, uh, I think, some patrol activity against this road, based on the ambushes, based on the shot of, uh, Khe Sanh, and, uh, the thing will finally gel itself out. Now, so far as the activity in the DMZ is concerned, uh, we see no, uh, change in what's doing around the, uh, uh, Laotian, uh, operation. Namely, there has been relatively

President Nixon: What, what about these stories about the, lot of guns being brought up and so forth, and the purpose of [unintelligible]. I saw something

Admiral Moorer: Yes, sir, you did. Uh, We're watching, uh, this, uh, movement that they did, uh, bring in, uh, a [unclear reference to a unit] of artillery over in this, uh, area here in the DMZ. They're moving back and forth, uh, and kind of, might as well be these blue tan colors [pointing to map with colored dispositions plotted on it]. Sir?

President Nixon: Do we intend to bomb?

Admiral Moorer: We will, yes, sir.

Secretary Laird: We have authority.

Voice: [concurs] We have authority.

Admiral Moorer: And we'll watch this, uh, they [now referring to the South Vietnamese withdrawal from Laos] are moving, uh, artillery or [word] the other day.

President Nixon: Are they doing reasonably well?

Admiral Moorer: I thought the, uh, first, uh, day went exceptionally well, sir. In terms of, uh

President Nixon: Second day didn't

Admiral Moorer: Uh, second day they had some weather problems. Now they have, uh, they put the artillery right inside; at this point they [the North Vietnamese] had a, a missile site that they, they established that was knocked out. And, uh, uh, the, uh, attack on the missile site, I think, was quite effective. In addition to that

President Nixon: Would we do this, uh, these, uh, I think, I think that would, I think that's very helpful now to have, have on one of these contingency plans for another one of those strikes up there. It certainly could fit in well with whatever we're thinking of diplomatically. I don't know when, but we ought to.

Secretary Laird: I don't know what the weather is, what is the weather going.

Voice: Let me give you an idea as to when we might be able to do it again.

President Nixon: Well the weather could be lousy in Laos.

Admiral Moorer: No, sir, I think it's better and better. We only had 2 days [of good bombing weather] in February. We expect 5 or 6 in March. But I, I

President Nixon: Yes. Could I ask, then, you direct reconnaissance flights to take those three passes [on the Ho Chi Minh Trail, entering Laos from North Vietnam], you keep them under constant surveillance, and so forth. When it gets real ripe, real ripe, if you let us know, you know, pass it on, and then we, we, we attack, consider we want to do it, [unintelligible] we want, you might want to give 'em another whack.

Secretary Laird: The weather is worse down in Laos and a little better up in, uh, it shifts over

Admiral Moorer: This is something we monitor. We keep, keep watching it.

President Nixon: 'Cause if you get a real good choke in there, then we'll knock the hell out of it.

Secretary Laird: That [unintelligible] artillery pieces, but, uh, they didn't *just* move in there

President Nixon: Oh.

Secretary Laird: They, they have been in there for a while, I think we had pictures, uh

Admiral Moorer: Yes, sir [unintelligible]. Over here they were referring to some, uh, black artillery that was, uh, moved over here. We have to

Secretary Laird: But we had heavy artillery right over

Admiral Moorer: Right. Yes, the Pentagon did it right. 100 and, uh, it was, 175 mm, I think. But, uh, we're watching this, uh, very carefully, Mr. President. All the, uh, strikes you could do, uh, ah, at any time and, uh, pointed out less which [unintelligible] strikes.

Secretary Laird: We have a good practical plan, so why is it necessarily to make another plan?

President Nixon: What I'm talking about is this, which is, the idea I assume you have, but, but, I want you to look for it.

Admiral Moorer: You want

President Nixon: Look [at] it, and if you think it's *real good*, be sure you, you bring it up. And don't think of the political considerations or any, let me decide that. When you think it's *real good*, real good, good weather and, and ready to move, you may want to give 'em another pop, this might be a good time to do it.

Secretary Laird: Looking at our [unintelligible] protective reaction [a type of air strike intended to retaliate for North Vietnamese antiaircraft fire]

President Nixon: I guess [unintelligible] a hell of a lot and they should get another pop.

Secretary Laird: We've had about three more

President Nixon: Back wherever [unintelligible]

Admiral Moorer: I look at that aerial data every morning.

President Nixon: All right. Good. What is the situation, I'd like to ask one other question. There is, that isn't smart [word]. What about this AP dispatch that came out yesterday to the effect that, uh, half of the ARVN [Army of the

Republic of South Vietnam] were casualties, that, er, uh, 20,000 out of the whole force. I understood that it only ran for the first, uh, first two leads.

Secretary Laird: Well, we called the AP on this charge. That was a guy named Arbuckle [Tammy Arbuckle]; he's been writing on

President Nixon: Arbuckle. There's a guy out there, an AP writer, he's from Laos. He's a son of a bitch.

[Voices overlapping]

Secretary Laird: He's writing from the beginning this way.

President Nixon: Well, what's the matter with the man?

Secretary Laird: Well, he's had a call, we've called the AP, God knows, and tried to talk to him, and tried to

President Nixon: What's the matter with him?

Secretary Laird: Well, he's just no damned good.

President Nixon: Well, is he, has he always been those problems?

Secretary Laird: Yes.

President Nixon: How long he's been out there?

Secretary Laird: Well, he's been out there

[Voices overlapping]

Admiral Moorer: all the hell down in Cambodia when we

President Nixon: Is that right?

Admiral Moorer: the problem we had with the, uh

President Nixon: Is he the same guy?

[Voices overlapping]

Admiral Moorer: isn't an American, either, I don't think.

Secretary Laird: What nationality is he? I'll find out.

President Nixon: All right. I knew there was something wrong. Remember, Al

General Alexander Haig: Yes, sir.

President Nixon: I told you to watch that son of a bitch when he was in Cambodia. Here he is up here. The AP has been responsible for most of the bad wire service and, of course, that gets on the TV, too. See, AP is the wire that usually used on TV. And he's the guy that wrote this story. It's not true, is it?

Admiral Moorer: No, sir.

[Voices overlapping]

President Nixon: The other night I was very careful about saying that 4 of the 22 battalions had taken flack.

Admiral Moorer: That's right.

Voice: Right.

President Nixon: The other 18 had come out in good, good form.

Voice: Right [Other voices overlap]

President Nixon: That's relatively accurate, is it not?

Admiral Moorer: As a result of that I sent, uh, General Abrams another message today asking about to, uh, send us a complete [unintelligible] let us know.

President Nixon: Yes. [unintelligible] What is he basing it on? Is it just gossip?

Admiral Moorer: God, what he had actually [unintelligible] and I, I, I don't know what he did. What he is basing it on. Because he doesn't have

President Nixon: He's just questioning them. It's an inaccurate

Secretary Laird: It's an inaccurate story. We called and told them this. We told them it was inaccurate. If they want to continue to run it, we told them here are the figures. This is not true.

President Nixon: What is this, yeah.

Admiral Moorer: And some of the, uh, South Vietnamese, obviously, that were, uh, wounded will, uh, die [word]

President Nixon: Well, of course!

Admiral Moorer: But, uh,

President Nixon: It's a tough battle.

Admiral Moorer: Tough battle

President Nixon: And, uh, and nobody reports from the side of the North Vietnamese. I understand it, and I might have glossed it over, but I just don't want the, uh, the real untruth to be, to be out there. John, you've [unintelligible]; don't you think it's shocking this damned reporting

Secretary Connally: Unbelievable. Whole war.

President Nixon: Yeah, well, it's worse right now. Now, what about the, the, uh

Secretary Laird: We just think it's worse, though, Mr. President. From time, if you go back and look over all the reporting, it is the same

President Nixon: Is that right?

Secretary Laird: You go back to Tet of 1968. Re-read those stories.

Secretary Connally: It's unbelievable. What's wrong with people

Secretary Laird: Read it. It, it's always been that way.

President Nixon: Well, [Voices overlapping] and we've got to realize is that each year that we're in this, people get more war weary. It was true in the Civil War, it's true of World War II; it's true of this war. As they get more war weary, then of course the, the reporters get a hell of a lot bigger audience for this kind of story. There is less and less support.

[Voices overlapping]

President Nixon: So now is the time for all of us—we've got to be just strong and firm and confident. Not, [unintelligible] hell, I will, I'm the last one you know to lie on this thing, we're not going to misrepresent anything. But my God, we must not *them* misrepresent anything. And I'm glad you called the AP. Would you agree, John?

Secretary Connally: Oh, sure, I think it's all we can do.

President Nixon: Let's try. You can't get your reporters from North Vietnam.

Secretary Connally: We have no reliable information on their dead.

[Voices overlapping]

Voice: Well, we told them we really find that . . .

Voice: Well, we know . . .

Admiral Moorer: Well I set up a press conference the other day. I said, Well I granted equal time to the North Vietnamese.

President Nixon: Good one. Good. Good. Well, now I think that you, I'm glad that you and, uh, the General [unintelligible] ask you to do this. You're going to meet with the Democrats

Secretary Laird: Tuesday morning

President Nixon: This Tuesday morning. Could you, all week long, the next week or two, keep quiet on this thing? Or is that going to be overreaction?

Secretary Laird: Oh, I don't know whether we could do it very [unintelligible] top editor list of all the people I've seen in this last week, uh [unintelligible] it's, uh, it's quite a

President Nixon: How about Senators, now, what do they, what are they up to this next week?

Secretary Laird: Well, these Senators aren't, no, they're not going to be doing anything in that area next week. But, you'd want to talk to the Senators; we'd, uh, take the briefing we gave the Armed Services Committee. They're supposed to be our friends. Hell, they thought it was a hell of a good briefing, brought up young Colonel that has been flying

[Voices overlap, including Nixon's]

Deputy Secretary Packard: Some of them run out to the TV cameras to talk about it. They just want to

[Voices overlap]

President Nixon: But you know what? They're afraid to get out there and prove to be wrong. Now, we're not being [unintelligible]. You see, the psychology is terribly important. Why did they handle it immediately, eh, when, when they started withdrawing and they shoved that one battalion so badly? Why did they scream victory? Because psychology has had this battle. And we can't do that. We can't, we can't lie and scream victory to the rest because we have to be held accountable.

Secretary Connally: They lose the damned war. And, and, but, but, uh

President Nixon: I think you're doing fine. Fine. Now is, uh, what about Bill [Secretary of State William Rogers]. Is he up, does he come up to bat next week at all, Mel? I want to be sure everybody in this administration is, you know, is, is,

[Voices overlap]

Secretary Laird: Well, I think he's cool. Bill's singing the same tune.

President Nixon: [unintelligible] If he's got it, if he's got it, so that, so that you don't go on a fact-finding [unintelligible]

Secretary Laird: Well I think Bill is, uh, gonna be out of town, at least before the, uh, the, uh

President Nixon: House

[unintelligible]

Secretary Laird: Decide he could be in the Middle East then. And it's just as well to have him talking about the Middle East.

President Nixon: We, we're doing rather well, we think.

[Deletion of 3 minutes and 40 seconds]

President Nixon: Well, thank you a lot. And, I, uh, I, I, uh, I've got to go to California. I don't have any much desire, they say the weather is lousy out there. [Voices overlapping] Well, I promised to go and I'm going to see movie people; see Sam Goldwyn's "The Battle of Freedom" before he dies. [Voices overlapping]

Secretary Laird: Going to play a little golf?

President Nixon: No, I, uh, just, I've given it up.

Secretary Connally: Have a nice trip, sir.

President Nixon: We appreciate all your hard work. Thanks, John. Good party.

FEBRUARY 1, 1972: PRESIDENT NIXON MEETS WITH EVANGELIST BILLY GRAHAM

Born into a Quaker family, Richard Milhous Nixon professed Christian beliefs and had a particularly strong connection with the evangelist Billy Graham. A North Carolina boy who had made his self-professed "decision for Christ" at age sixteen in 1934, Graham had built a ministry beginning in Charlotte, near where Billy had grown up the son of a prosperous dairy farmer. As early as 1949, Graham had made a national impact with a Christian crusade in Los Angeles, press coverage of which garnered major media attention. He soon became a national religious figure and was among the first evangelists to use large public rallies, radio, and then television to reach more of the public and build a mass fellowship. With Graham's following came political connections, and he met with every president from Harry S. Truman on. In the conversation included here Graham tells a story from the Eisenhower years, when Richard Nixon was vice president, featuring then-secretary of state John Foster Dulles.

Richard Nixon continued to have numerous contacts with Graham. In December 1967, in fact, when Nixon made his final decision to run for the presidency in Key Biscayne, Florida, Graham was one of the two men Nixon invited (the other was businessman and confidant Charles "Bebe" Rebozo) for the three-day-long brainstorming session at which the politician firmed up his choice. Although Graham did not make an open political endorsement in the 1968 campaign, he was present at the outset, was with Nixon at campaign headquarters in New York City the day of the election, and said a prayer with Nixon and family members in their private suite the next morning. Graham also attended Nixon's inauguration on January 20, 1969. Thereafter President Nixon hosted a series of prayer meetings at the White House where Billy Graham often officiated. The conversation between the two men that is included here followed one such prayer breakfast.

The Nixon-Graham relationship was political, practical, and personal, as well as spiritual. Graham became a supporter long before the 1968 campaign. The two also played golf together. At the time of Nixon's invasion of Cambodia at the end of April 1970, Billy Graham was among those persons whom the president consulted by telephone, stiffening Nixon's resolve for an action accurately expected to be inflammatory. Shortly thereafter Graham invited Nixon to be the major speaker at a religious rally in Knoxville, Tennessee, which was attended by 88,000 people. Later that year, based on its alleged harassment of Graham's ministry, Nixon is recorded as having complained to aides that the Internal Revenue Service (IRS) was dominated by bureaucrats left over from the Democratic administrations of Lyndon Johnson and John Kennedy. In the fall of 1971, at Nixon's request, Billy Graham taped television messages in favor of voluntary desegregation of schools, an action that Nixon credited with helping to ensure compliance with court orders in the American South. That October, President Nixon appeared at a "Billy Graham Day" celebration in Charlotte.

By February 1972 Nixon's attention was focused on the coming presidential election campaign, and that is the underlying theme of their conversation recorded here. Strident professions of the necessity of a Nixon electoral victory feature in Graham's comments. Graham's analysis of Nixon's political situation is that the only issue that could hurt him, at least on the international level, is the U.S. government's inaction in the India-Pakistan War at the end of 1971. The Vietnam War oddly goes unmentioned. Graham's troubles with the IRS also come up in passing in this conversation and lead to a comment comparing postage costs for religious literature versus those for pornographic publications.

A major theme in this conversation, and a recurrent one for Nixon, who frequently railed about the press and its assumed distaste for him, is the media. Nixon and Graham both discuss the supposed concentration of ownership of media sources in Jewish hands, so serious in their view that, as Graham says, "This stranglehold has got to be broken or this country's going down the drain." When the tape of this conversation was opened to the public in early 2002, Billy Graham's comments proved so controversial that, on March 1, 2002, Reverend Graham felt obliged to issue a statement to the press disavowing them.

Richard M. Nixon

February 1, 1972, 10:00–11:37 A.M.

Meeting in the Oval Office with the Rev. Billy Graham, Chief of Staff H.R. Haldeman, and Press Secretary Ronald L. Ziegler

President Richard M. Nixon: What do you have your people say to prepare [unintelligible].

Rev. Billy Graham: No, and that in my scheduling I just don't take it. I just don't take it. I mean, I we're, we can be rougher than you can, in a way

President Nixon: Oh, I know all about that.

Rev. Graham: Not any more as president. It's [unintelligible].

Press Secretary Ronald Ziegler: As a person, he can. As the candidate . . .

Rev. Graham: That's right.

President Nixon: He'd have a real problem. There you always just gotta be available to every . . .

Rev. Graham: But I, they know that while, your politics is all for the President of the United States' responsibility

President Nixon: Sure

Rev. Graham: And I would like to see you this Fall, as of now, I mean this may change, but I'd like to see you this Fall when you campaign, uh, take control of situations, such as being televised and, uh, not this frantic racing back and forth across the country that you had to do last time. I don't think you need that. I think that your record this time, uh, being President is going to do it. Now, I may be wrong. Things may change. Polls may look uh different, but, uh, I think that if you pace yourself and under control situations, uh, where it's televised and where, if you didn't have big crowds, having maybe two or three a week or something like that, rather than

President Nixon: Yeah

Rev. Graham: going to every town, which you've gotta do

President Nixon: The rest of the time is

Rev. Graham: Doing your work as President, making you, you can make some events. Right here. But you don't have to race around the country. I think that people will not take any more the President of the United States frantically running from place to place. I think, you know, I wrote you a letter which I never mailed; I've still got it, after you came back from England last time. And I was right, I wrote you, suggesting that you not get involved in the, in the campaign last time

President Nixon: Yeah.

Rev. Graham: because I felt that it was, that you were at the height of your popularity and I thought it was gonna hurt you.

President Nixon: Well that was after my trip to Europe.

Rev. Graham: After your trip to Europe. Right. And, uh, I feel that this, uh, this, uh, that it's a little bit, uh, beneath the dignity of the, uh, of, of the

President to find him traipse around the country like a candidate does. Let them do the fighting.

President Nixon: You don't agree that, uh, people want to see their man, whoever he is, fighting for what he believes in?

Rev. Graham: Oh, well, I, I think you can fight [raising voice], but it it's a different tactic. You have different tactics.

President Nixon: You have to find a theory you know. What's your theory? You think your man ought to get out there and fight?

Rev. Graham: Yeah, but you were the candidate. You were not the President of the United States.

President Nixon: You think it's different now?

Rev. Graham: I think it's different now. I think that you have a, a dignity to maintain. You have to, and you're doing the job. That's the thing they want to see. And I think there's got to be, and I think you have been able to get over integrity, I think the only thing that has hurt your integrity has been this Pakistan-India situation, and the so-called Anderson papers. But, uh, that has passed over in my judgment. That's not going to hurt. But your overall impression is one now of integrity. You've brought dignity to the office, and I think people are, uh, uh, impressed by that.

[The tape is excised for nine minutes, forty seconds, followed by thirty-four seconds of conversation with a woman, presumably Rosemary Woods, and an informal exchange with Graham, followed by a second tape excision of four minutes, twenty seconds.]

Rev. Graham: By the way, Hedley Donovan [Editor-in-chief, *Time*, Incorporated, 1964–79] has just invited me to have lunch with all their editors here on March the 7th, and I was quite amazed because this is the first time I've heard from *Time* and *News* . . . I mean, *Time* Magazine since Henry Luce died [cofounder, managing editor, and later editor-in-chief, *Time* magazine; date of death: February 27, 1967].

President Nixon: Yeah. If you need to call their editors you better put your Jewish [unintelligible].

Rev. Graham: [Laughs] Is that right? I don't know any of them now.

President Nixon: It's become, it's become almost due. . . . It's a very interesting thing, they're all Jews, you can't talk about it in public with them. You don't fault [unintelligible]

Rev. Graham: Yeah.

President Nixon: Needless to say [unintelligible] generational [unintelligible], a level of politics all [unintelligible] by Jews.

Rev. Graham: That's right.

President Nixon: In the media now, money, it's totally dominated by the Jews. *Newsweek* is totally, is all by Jewish and dominated by their editorial pages. *The New York Times, The Washington Post*, totally Jewish. [unintelligible] the owners of *The Los Angeles Times* [unintelligible] in our system about [unintelligible]. The other thing, you know, is that all three [television] networks except for, say, they have top men, in our case, men per [name] or [Walter] Cronkite may not be of that persuasion. But the writers going, 95% are Jewish. Now, what does this mean? Does this mean that, uh, that, uh, that all of Jews are bad and all, but it does mean that all Jews are left wing, way particularly the younger ones like that. They're way out, they're radical, they're peace at any price except for where [unintelligible] is concerned. Uh, the only thing that you could tell me would be that [unintelligible] uh, the Middle East. The best Jews actually are the Israeli Jews.

Rev. Graham: That's right.

President Nixon: Because Israel, the reason is Meir [Golda Meir, prime minister of Israel, 1969–74] supports me, which she does. And, I handled a series for her fundamental reasons, as I do, they, they, they know the Democratic candidate is weak-kneed and interested in the domestic Jewish vote. But she supports me. Because she knows the greater danger to Israel is Russia, and she knows that if the crisis following Lebanon,[4] uh, the Charter [of the Palestine Liberation Organization], that I face the Russians down for her. So I'm the only one who'll do it. She knows that a democrat will give you the communists, the Russians. She doesn't want it. She's tough. We talked about this. But [name] the same way for me, of course.

Rev. Graham: Oh, yeah.

President Nixon: Russian Jew, boy the, does she know that? Now, however, the détente reading [?] we must be under no illusion [unintelligible] our efforts. You're, uh, you're aware of the fact the, that in the media, we, we confront almost a solid block of people that they don't, it isn't the aim in the Middle East, [unintelligible] the point of the thing. They're arrogant because he took the whole thing off, and, and it has nothing to do with the other sentiments. It happens, though, that insofar as media is concerned, the powerful media . . .

Rev. Graham: They've got it.

President Nixon: They've got it right by

Rev. Graham: And they're the ones putting out pornographic stuff. And putting out everything.

President Nixon: I don't know why they do it . . .

[Tape is excised for one minute, thirty-two seconds.]

Rev. Graham: Answer me this. They had the whole thing, you see, and if he went about it wrong. But, but this stranglehold has got to be broken or this country's gonna go down the drain.

President Nixon: Do you believe that?

Rev. Graham: Yes, sir.

President Nixon: Boy. I can't ever tell you, but I believe

Rev. Graham: Nobody's

[Voices overlapping]

Rev. Graham: the second time. We might be able to do something.

President Nixon: Let me tell you something, Billy. All, every Democratic candidate will go, who was the last one of these. I won't. Never. 'Cause they know we're gonna, they didn't buy us off. You know I thought that you matched, that you

Chief of Staff H.R. Haldeman: That the old Jewish support he had was different kind of people and maybe

Rev. Graham: They are. Like Barney Laska, he's a terrific guy.

President Nixon: Oh, Barney Laska. Oh, and Max Fisher, and uh, uh, Pat Macarthur and [unintelligible]. I can go up 55%, that's all I'll ever get. But [unintelligible] insists that the difficulty is it, that not only are they Jews, but, but, but boy they take care of each other. Now every group has a tendency to do that, Catholic tends to hire a Catholic, and a, a, and Quaker perhaps tries to, wants to hire a Quaker. But the Jews. We would see [unintelligible] too bad. Boy, they [unintelligible] hire Jews.

Rev. Graham: And they affect the [unintelligible] hire Jews.

President Nixon: All things else being equal. Now, what we've got to remember about [unintelligible] written on this is this: the media in this country is extremely dangerous. I mean you, you've talked about the media network and so forth, but everybody's working on that. If we get into the act, believe me, we're going to take care of it.

Rev. Graham: Nah

President Nixon: Wait a moment, there's a way to do it. But we can't do it now, we can't do it before the election [of 1972], but with blood in it. But believe me, if you don't, you're going to hell. You look at television, how filthy it is?

Rev. Graham: Terrible. If I [Nixon speaks over Graham, overlapping] in the last year.

President Nixon: I won't look at it. I won't look at it. And movies. They're filthy.

Rev. Graham: Oh, I don't even go to movies.

President Nixon: Now, now, [unintelligible] I don't even like the movies on TV now. Now we [unintelligible], when we see movies, we see, usually the old ones, but we, we reason with it in advance, and we show. We, we agreed to that in advance, but I never go to the movies. But whatever the gap is that, that the media today, the filth, the anti-Americanism, the Red thing, is, is for me [unintelligible]. And Time-Life [a large media corporation] isn't good to you. Believe me.

Rev. Graham: No, I know it [laughing]. When Henry Luce died, they dropped me just like a [snaps fingers], you know, he sort of promoted me for years.

President Nixon: Well.

Rev. Graham: In my opinion, in my work. But since you've been President, I had to be quiet on just about everything that would make any news due to the fact that I didn't want to look like I was critical of some policy

President Nixon: Sure

Rev. Graham: of yours. Or being interpreted as political and so forth.

President Nixon: Yeah.

Rev. Graham: So I have had to, you know, uh, watch a little bit on the things that I would say that normally made news. For example, even when Mr. Eisenhower was President, I spoke out against the way we were giving to India; Mr. Dulles called me up to his home to explain it to me, and I would talk out against this or that or the other thing . . .

President Nixon: Yeah.

Rev. Graham: Well, it would make news.

President Nixon: [unintelligible]

Rev. Graham: But with you as President, I feel like, you know, I can't do that.

[Tape is excised for one minute, thirty-three seconds.]

President Nixon: The, uh, the remark I think this morning [at the presidential prayer breakfast that both Graham and Nixon had attended just before their private conversation] that, er, asking for calm, uh, uh, uh, but there was much more to it than that if any sophisticated person was listening to our greatest meditation. The point being that, that we are in a situation at the present time where, as it's the last time when the United States through its power can create conditions which, uh, lead the peace for, eeeeh, perhaps twenty-five years. Nobody can look beyond that. That would be a great deal. Now, what is important is that the United States use that power and use it effectively; that, that, I, that I said something which, which many people, of course, don't . . . like to hear. All people like to think that if we just get to know each other better we'd have no differences. But the people that have the biggest spite for people that are married [?], they don't usually do well. The problem that we have, of course, is [unintelligible] the Chinese by [unintelligible]. It's not that we not know each other, but the fact that we do know each other. They believe in one thing, we believe in another. They believe in one kind of work, we believe in another. But, if you start talks with that in mind then there is a chance to find those areas where you live much better, which is about the way the world is gonna hand these, uh, uh, the millennium will come some day, people, ah, when everybody may want peace for the right reasons. But at the present time, we may want peace for reasons that are secondary. They're not necessarily wrong. Men want a lot, but people do. The only, the only, thing I didn't give to the other side is what I say about the fact that, that any man, no matter how well [not clear] should park wherever he is. Probably that doesn't sit with young people, the kids. I mean, the Russians must think of the Russian kids and the Chinese must think of the Chinese kids. I would hope that they not be incinerated. And they know, as we know, that if you got war, it would be mass incineration. So we think that, now.

The point that I make, however, is there's never been a time when the United States needed, in this office, somebody who knew the communists, who knows our strength. Take Vietnam. But, who, who is more keenly aware than I am that on a political standpoint, we could have flushed it down the drain three years ago. Blame Johnson and Kennedy. Kennedy got us in. Johnson carried us in. I could have much been [word] a national hero as Eisenhower was for ending Korea. Anyone could have imagined that. Sure. The North Vietnamese would have probably slaughtered, castrated, two million South Vietnamese Catholics. And, I know I shouldn't care, these little brown people, so far away, as you know very well as you say. But on the other hand, we couldn't do that. Not because of Vietnam. But because of Japan, because of Germany, because of the Middle East. Once the United States ceases to be a great power, ah, acting responsibly, to restrain, uh, uh, aggression, which is exactly what we did essentially in India and Pakistan,[5] our problem was [unintelligible]. You know, I can count. There are a lot more Indians than Pakistanis and I prefer the Indian government to the Pakistani government. We could not allow anyone, with the support of Russia, to gobble up its neighbor. So we said, Stop. And we tried . . .

[Tape is excised for thirty seconds; the first twenty-one seconds of the following exchange are also omitted.]

President Nixon: But Luns [Joseph Luns, secretary general of the North Atlantic Treaty Organization, appointed in October 1971] said, Thank God he was mentioned in my speech, you know, you just thank God. I'm amazed. There is a difference between surrender and suffering. Somebody had to say that. He said all over Europe today, they look to *you* to see how strong that is. He said, believe our office, you know [unclear] around with the Russians, and the British, of course, are trying to get into the Common Market, so they will understate, and he's a good man, he can't be very strong [unintelligible]. But they have other strengths. But my answer to [name] is the Italians don't have a government. Probably never will have. And nobody else matters. They're too small. And so here we sit, for better or for worse, the United States is the only nation in the free world that can act. And act powerful to restrain Russians or the Chinese, who *do* know what they want

Rev. Graham: I, indeed

President Nixon: And who will wait for it. And are out to get it. So, what do you need? That's why we got to be stronger to convince, that's why, as a matter of fact, that's why I think he needs trips. Because uh, uh, regardless of what happens [in the] election, the Russians and the Chinese need to see one America. And perhaps they need to see as the first American, somebody who knows them. And that they know him, is not a sucker. That's really what it gets down to. So, you see, the stakes are very high. That's the stakes in the international [word] — peace in the world, it's freedom for the world press. Yet the message is probably something else, too. It's a, and it need not be accomplished [unintelligible] rest of those things.

Rev. Graham: No, of course.

President Nixon: But I wouldn't mind, one way or another. Terror that you call [unintelligible]. But here [unintelligible]. The real question is whether this country's gonna believe me in there. Now we all have different degrees from which, we have different ways of expressing them, not necessarily the same. But the [unintelligible] incident that Bob [Haldeman] will have to verify. The thing that concerns me about interest in [unintelligible] that maybe it's Stanford, other places, these changes occurred. I hope it is. But a lot of the professors and the associate professors in the colleges and the universities, in the junior colleges and the high schools, I think 90% of them are atheists or worse. They have no confidence in themselves. They have no faith in this country. And

Rev. Graham: So they're undermining the country

President Nixon: And they're [word]. Now, therefore, you see, we simply cannot allow the, that sort of thing to prevail. Now, thank God, that the homeland there's still a majority of American citizens [unintelligible].

Maybe 55% of the American people still will support those decent, strong virtues. Let's say. That 55%, however, would have to be very strongly modified in some areas. And in order to use this top 50%, in New York, very problematic whether it is. Pennsylvania, often on the edge. And in the mid-West, probable, but going down. Pennsylv, uh, Ohio, and so forth. The South, that's the strongest. The South, uh, is, is, [word] is religious, it's the most patriotic, decent part of this country today. Really is. Without the South, the country would be in terrible shape. California, big bad [word] because of Hollywood and because the lousy colleges and universities. California's over educated. Every one of them. Uh, that's what we say today in this country. And what we have to do about it, of course, is to fight it skillfully. You gotta get in it first. But, believe me, once in it, then we got to *really* then start to, start to, to, to, re, reward the decent people, and, and, and frankly throw, throw out the, the, uh, "Me, too."[6] Take that [Jack] Anderson column, that thing in the press.

Rev. Graham: He was right, he understated it. It was worse.

President Nixon: But you had the [unintelligible]?

H.R. Haldeman: No.

President Nixon: [unintelligible] newsletters. Now that was bullshit, except

[Voices overlap]

Rev. Graham: I probably have it down in my home

President Nixon: Send it to him and have him read it.

Voice [Possibly Ron Ziegler]: I, I, I've read a review of it.

President Nixon: All right.

Rev. Graham: I've read excerpts.

[Voices overlap]

President Nixon: Well, we'll send that and send the, the Grace review of it

Rev. Graham: One thing that, uh, I

President Nixon: Anyway, don't, don't

H.R. Haldeman: You know what's even better?

President Nixon: Where is Clara White?

H.R. Haldeman: She's, she's testifying today, I guess, that, uh, or tomorrow, at Ervin's Committee, and her testimony is, is, is better than her book, 'cause it gets it all in a compact phrase and, uh

Rev. Graham: That's great

H.R. Haldeman: So she's

President Nixon: [unintelligible] I wonder if she's Jewish.

Rev. Graham: I didn't know that.

H.R. Haldeman: Married to [name] Hill?

Rev. Graham: Is that a po—I didn't know that.

[Voices overlap, laughter]

President Nixon: That's a first.

Rev. Graham: That's a big point.

H.R. Haldeman: Go ahead. A professor from what, Columbia, or some place.

Rev. Graham: Uh, I was going to say with the, uh, with the, the

President Nixon: You understand, I'm not overstating this, don't you?

Rev. Graham [chuckling]: Oh, I know, I know that, you know. I

President Nixon: You're [unintelligible] is that the really scary thing is that the media's control used to be certain places. The writers on television have always been Jewish, Jeff Haddies, writers and all those people. They are, they've always been.

Rev. Graham: Yeah.

President Nixon: But the, now, what's become of the old time press corps, old time White House press corps, was Jewish.

Rev. Graham: Yeah.

President Nixon: It was, uh, that, you know, you had your, a lot of liberal, lot of friends that had been very close.

Rev. Graham: For instance, the Gridiron Club was not Jewish.

President Nixon: That's right, the Gridiron was very much, very much, frankly very much uh Wasps.

H.R. Haldeman: Who's that?

President Nixon: The Barons, the Smiths, the Dick Wilsons, the Kirkpatricks. All that kind of people. But you look at, at what covers the President today and, indeed, find it scary. *Time* Magazine is Jerry Schecter.

Rev. Graham: Mm-hmm.

President Nixon: For the Los Angeles

Voice: It's incredible.

President Nixon: For the *LA Times* or the *New York Times*, it's a Max Frankel. That's telling you. For the *Washington Post* it's Karnow, Stanley Karnow, Karnow. And uh, these are the people who are going with me on these trips. At NBC it's Herb Kaplow.

Rev. Graham: Yeah.

President Nixon: From CBS, uh, it's Ra, Dan Rather.

[Tape is excised for one minute, ten seconds.]

Rev. Graham: You know, I mean, I don't care how conservative, I'm sure I'm more conservative than you are. At least you told me that one time, and I think that's true. But, I have to *lean* a little bit, you know, I go and I keep friends with Mr. Rosenthal at *The New York Times* and people of that sort, you know

President Nixon: [speaks over Rev. Graham, unclear what he says]

Rev. Graham: And, uh, all the, I mean not all the Jews, but a lot of the Jews are great friends of mine. They, they swarm around me

President Nixon: Rosenthal

Rev. Graham: They're friendly to me, uh, because they know that I'm friendly to Israel, too. But they don't know how I really feel about what they're doing to this country. And I have no power and no way to handle 'em.

President Nixon: You must let them know.

Rev. Graham: But I would stand up, if it, it, it, you know, under proper circumstances.

President Nixon: But you do have a way to handle them, 'cause the only way to handle them is to have an effective counterforce. You've got to reward the people that start promoting, you know what we have to do, Billy, we've got to go push separate issues aside. New God and so forth. I was thinking, for example, of our sea tragedy last [unintelligible]. Good enough. We just got to get this better with this. And I don't know where, I don't know where they are, duh, but, let me [unintelligible] maybe they are, maybe just can't find feature conservative writers. Ah.

Rev. Graham: They are hard to find because

Press Secretary Ronald Ziegler: We have to try to find a conservative columnist to take on the China trip.

President Nixon: That's right. Bill White is [unintelligible]. Bill White [unintelligible].

Rev. Graham: By the way, there's quite a big, um, there's quite a big, uh, protest among religious people, you might check this out. Uh, religious magazines, that no religious, uh, person has been invited in the press thing. And the one that they chose, that the Religious News Service and all of them sort of agreed on, was a fellow by the name of Gene Kerchevsky who is *really* conservative, and I was amazed that they chose him. They thought maybe he might have a chance. And I don't know whether you've got another place or not

President Nixon: I doubt if China but he could go to Russia. But if he can't do the China, Russia

Rev. Graham: You see, uh, out of, uh,

[President Nixon talks over Rev. Graham]

Rev. Graham: it's a religious, the religious papers

President Nixon: These papers were submitted [voices overlap] months ago.[7]

Rev. Graham: The religious, uh, papers in this country, by the way, there's another thing, you know I brought up to you about the fact that, uh, a lot of these papers are going out of business and so forth.

H.R. Haldeman: We could investigate that [unintelligible].

Rev. Graham: Yeah.

President Nixon: We're totally irrational. We were supporting legislation for a professional subsidy where

Rev. Graham: My own magazine, if that went through, was going to rise 700%, my postal rates. Pornography rise 25%. Somehow they had a discrepancy and then I got our lawyer. They're drawing it up right now to submit to the proper people. But, uh,

President Nixon: I'll arrange to talk to my person.

Rev. Graham: But, uh, I told you that we could absorb it. My organization can absorb that.

President Nixon: Yeah.

Rev. Graham: It'd be hard on us, but we can

President Nixon: [unintelligible].

Rev. Graham: 'Cause our income is very large.

President Nixon: What is the situation there, that legislation package can

Rev. Graham: But the religious

President Nixon: [Voice obscured by Graham]

Rev. Graham: people are really howling over it.

President Nixon: Hmm.

Rev. Graham: And lot of 'em ought to close. You know.

President Nixon: I really don't

Rev. Graham: It is, in fact, *The Christian Century*'s just about out of business.

President Nixon: Horrible.

Rev. Graham: It's gone out of business.

President Nixon: That's damned interesting.

Rev. Graham: And our *Christianity Today*

President Nixon: I used to read it as a kid, it was out of Union College, but no more.

Rev. Graham: No more. It's, well, it's well, well, the most left-wing of all the religious press in the country

President Nixon: Is it? Who publishes that?

Rev. Graham: Uh, it's published in Chicago by a foundation and the man that's been the angel back of it is a fella who supported you, is J. Irwin Miller. [The ecumenical weekly *Christian Century* was initiated by the Christian Church, known as Disciples of Christ. Industrialist J. Irwin Miller was the first lay president of the National Council, 1960–63.]

President Nixon: Who?

[About seven minutes of the conversation are excised at this point. When the conversation resumes Nixon and Graham are still discussing individual political, business, and religious figures and their connections with them. Reverend Graham then takes his leave, after which H.R. Haldeman stays behind to go over White House business with Nixon. Beginning with the excision the meeting recording continues for a total of about twenty minutes.]

JUNE 23, 1972: PRESIDENT NIXON HOLDS MEETINGS WITH WHITE HOUSE CHIEF OF STAFF H.R. HALDEMAN ON HANDLING THE WATERGATE BREAK-IN CONTROVERSY—THE "SMOKING GUN" TAPE (IN THREE CONVERSATIONS)

On Saturday, June 17, 1972, five men were arrested in the Democratic National Committee headquarters, situated at the Watergate, a two-building complex of offices, apartments, commercial space, and a hotel along the Potomac River in the northwest quadrant of Washington. The five, in business suits complemented by surgical gloves, had broken into the committee offices. Many theories have been advanced for their action. The most plausible among these is that the group was attempting to repair a monitoring device placed on one of the telephones there. What White House Spokesmen quickly dismissed as a "third-rate burglary" equally rapidly assumed the dimensions of a political scandal and major headache for the Nixon administration when it emerged that one of the men, James W. McCord Jr., was an employee of the Committee to Re-Elect the President, Richard Nixon's campaign organization.

Investigation soon established that a sixth man, H. Howard Hunt, had helped in the break-in, and he too was a Committee to Re-Elect the President staffer. Both Hunt and McCord were former CIA officers; the other four burglars were Cuban Americans from Miami. Hunt had worked on the Bay of Pigs invasion for the CIA and, it transpired, had hired the Miami Cubans for the Watergate operation. At least one of the Cubans, Bernard Barker, still received retainer payments from the CIA as an inactive agent while he worked on Hunt's political operation. In addition, Hunt and G. Gordon Liddy, the director of the bugging project, had until recently been White House employees as part of a special investigations unit called the "Plumbers," formed to counter information leaks and carry out efforts to discredit or actively hurt leakers. It would later develop that the Watergate bugging had been part of Project Gemstone, a political intelligence operation by the Committee to Re-Elect the President. The Gemstone material went directly to the chairman of the committee, John N. Mitchell, who had been Nixon's attorney general until moving over to the campaign job. Furthermore, the bugging had been financed by illegal cash contributions to the Nixon campaign, some of them laundered through Barker's Miami bank account. There could be no doubt that investigation of the Watergate break-in had the potential to inflict huge damage on Richard Nixon's political prospects.

President Nixon read about the arrests on vacation in Key Biscayne. In his memoirs Nixon recalls he dismissed the report as "some sort of prank" and "preposterous."[8] He spent one more day in Miami, much of it on the telephone, including at least one call to Billy Graham. Then he returned to Washington, arriving late on June 19. In an entry Nixon quotes in his memoirs, his diary shows that far from dismissing the Watergate burglaries out of hand, he thought about them in enough detail to compare the problem with another recent political scandal and to tell his chief of staff who to keep away from the matter. Shortly before noon the next morning, by which time the newspapers had already connected Howard Hunt with the White House, he held his first known meeting on the Watergate affair with the staff chief, H.R. Haldeman. The content of that meeting has been hidden by the notorious "18 1/2 minute gap" audiotape erasure.[9] That afternoon they met again, with Haldeman giving Nixon a rundown of who had been arrested and how the press had been able to connect Howard Hunt with the White House. Haldeman was already indicating that Hunt, who had not yet been arrested, could disappear, and that the Watergate break-in could be made out to be connected to the Bay of Pigs — that is, that it might be a CIA operation. Uncontradicted by President Nixon, this already hovered at the edge of an obstruction of justice.

By the next morning, when Nixon met again with Haldeman along with presidential aide Charles W. Colson, broad outlines of a strategy to limit the damage were becoming apparent. Haldeman reports John Mitchell's concern that the FBI inquiry into the Watergate matter be turned off, and Nixon expresses his desire to "get a little better protection for the White House."[10] The president nevertheless clung to the hope that Watergate was going to be a narrow Washington story, not one that engaged Americans all over the country. That afternoon, in a further discussion of the implications of the Watergate arrests with Chuck Colson, the aide suggests emphasizing the CIA angle. In these and other discussions, there was also some expectation that Gordon Liddy might step forward and assume all responsibility for the bungled political intelligence effort, and there were repeated pleas to keep the White House out of the line of fire. Within five days of the Watergate break-in, the main elements of an attempt to head off an investigation had been suggested. Then, on June 22, acting FBI Director L. Patrick Gray told White House Counsel John Dean of a suspicion of his own that the CIA might be behind the break-in. As Haldeman put it in his diary entry that day, "The Democratic headquarters break-in case took some good bounces today. . . . They're going to continue cranking up the Cuban operation, leave Liddy out of the line of fire and get the FBI situation straightened out."[11]

John Dean called Haldeman at 8:15 A.M. of the 23rd to report Gray's suspicion of the CIA, as well as the FBI's interview with Chuck Colson, which had been satisfactory from the White House point of view. Haldeman very quickly told Nixon of this on the telephone, setting the stage for a series of conversations on June 23 that have come to be called the "Smoking Gun tapes." In these conversations recorded on the Secret Service's tape recorders, President Nixon agrees to and works on a deliberate attempt to obstruct justice by having the CIA stop the Watergate investigation on the grounds of national security, essentially that the FBI investigation might uncover agency sources and methods. The tapes consist of several conversations between the president and Haldeman throughout the day. These talks centered around another meeting at the White House, to which Central Intelligence Agency Director Richard M. Helms had been summoned.

For an hour and a half beginning a little after 10:00 in the morning, Nixon and Haldeman discuss the "problem area" of the investigation—which is the potential for Watergate links to implicate White House officials, in particular (at that stage) Charles Colson, the president's hatchet man. The FBI was out of control, in Haldeman's view, in the sense that Director Gray could not prevent his special agents from pursuing their investigation into the problem area. He suggests the only way to head off that possibility is through White House instructions, and they have to be addressed to Helms and his deputy, General Vernon Walters. President Nixon says, "All right, fine." Then he rationalizes why the CIA ought to go along with this: "Well, we protected Helms from one hell of a lot of things." Nixon then articulates why the strategy of having the CIA claim its operational security was at risk in the Watergate investigation was a plausible one, and that is because (supposedly) Howard Hunt and the Cuban contract agents had been mixed up in projects the agency would not want to have revealed, starting with the Bay of Pigs and its successor anti-Cuban project, which had been code-named Mongoose.

"You call them in," Nixon ended, referring to Helms and Walters. "Good. Good deal. Play it tough. That's the way they play it and that's the way we're going to play it."

Director Helms and General Walters were scheduled to meet the officials in the office of John D. Ehrlichman, Nixon's domestic policy chief, around 1:00 P.M. Haldeman popped into the Oval Office at 1:04 P.M. for a last-minute check on his instructions. Nixon emphasized that the CIA people should be told they had to shut down the FBI investigation of Watergate due to the involvement of Howard Hunt.

Ehrlichman had crossed swords with Helms the previous fall on one of the Plumbers' schemes, which had involved getting the CIA to declassify documents that could be used to implicate previous Democratic administrations in follies in Vietnam. He had no wish to get into any new fights. Although Ehrlichman's office on the second floor of the West Wing was being used, the domestic council chief said little. As he writes, "One reason I was quiet was that I simply didn't know why we were having the meeting and I didn't know why I was attending it, beyond the fact that Haldeman had told me the President wanted me to sit in on it."[12]

Haldeman sat to wait with Ehrlichman for the CIA officials and exchanged banter. "Guess what?" he threw out. "It's Bay of Pigs time again."

The chief of staff quotes John Ehrlichman's reply: "The man will never quit." This referred to Nixon's almost constant railing about the CIA since he had taken office, which had previously included similar invocations of alleged prevarications about the failed Cuban operations. John continued, "Well, the President has a point. It will put pressure on Helms. But this time you're going to push the red button, not me. I've had it on that route."[13]

By Director Helms's account to the Senate Watergate investigating committee, it was he and Walters who awaited Haldeman and Ehrlichman in the West Wing second floor office, not the other way around. Helms testified that the White House officials never mentioned the Watergate case itself, and Vernon Walters affirmed that assertion. Both CIA men testified that Haldeman instead made the point that Democratic politicians were attempting to exploit the situation, that the FBI was investigating, and that the investigation of money laundering in Mexico might uncover agency officers. Director Helms avowed that he did not understand what the reference to Mexico was, but that he assured Haldeman the CIA had nothing to do with Watergate and no problem with investigations in Mexico (these figured in Nixon's "problem area" because of the illegal political fund-raising and the resulting cash that had been used to finance the Watergate break-in). According to a memorandum for the record that General Walters prepared five days later, Haldeman also said, "It was the President's wish that Walters call on Acting Director L. Patrick Gray and suggest to him that, since the five suspects had been arrested, this should be sufficient and that it was not advantageous to have the inquiry pushed, especially in Mexico."[14]

On the Bay of Pigs connection, Helms testified that Haldeman's mention of that, much like his insertion of the Mexican matter, seemed to the CIA director an "incoherent reference." Helms said, "I assured him that I had no interest in the Bay of Pigs that many years later, that everything in connection with that had been dealt with and liquidated as far as I was aware."[15]

Haldeman's account is rather more colorful. In his version—and in this Helms would have agreed—the CIA chief declared the agency had no connection with the Watergate incident (Helms had met with Patrick Gray himself the previous day to say that very thing). Then Haldeman brought out the Bay of Pigs, which he saw as Nixon's trump card. Haldeman recollected what followed: "Turmoil in the room, Helms gripping the arms of his chair leaning forward and shouting, 'The Bay of Pigs had nothing to do with this. I have no concern about the Bay of Pigs.' "[16] Silence followed. Haldeman professed to be puzzled at the "violent reaction" by the CIA director. He assured Helms he was just following instructions and that that is what Nixon had told him to say. "Again I wondered," Haldeman recollected later, "what was such dynamite in the Bay of Pigs story."

As they left the White House, Director Helms and Deputy Director Walters talked briefly as they got into their CIA limousine. Helms told Walters to see the FBI director, but to remind him of a long-standing agreement the two agencies had that neither was supposed to uncover the operations of the other. Their meeting took place at 2:30 P.M. According to the record Walters made of it on June 28, he told the FBI director, "I was aware of [Helms's] conversation with him the previous day and while the further investigation of the Watergate affair had not touched any current or ongoing covert projects of the agency, its continuation might lead to some projects."[17]

At 2:20 P.M., H.R. Haldeman appeared again in the Oval Office to report to Nixon on his conversations with the CIA officials. It was not long after the meeting in Ehrlichman's office had broken up, indicating the urgency with which the president expected Haldeman's account, and their meeting continued even as General Walters arrived at FBI headquarters and met with L. Patrick Gray there. President Nixon and Chief of Staff Haldeman in their conversation share satisfaction that the FBI investigation will now be contained through intervention by the CIA. Kenneth Dahlberg, whose name comes up in the course of Haldeman's talk with Nixon, was one of those who had solicited illegal cash contributions for the reelection campaign. Haldeman's diary entry commenting on this day's work reads: "The FBI is convinced it's the CIA which is doing this [i.e., Watergate], and Gray's looking for a way out of the investigation. So we talked to Walters and had that worked out."[18]

It would be characteristic of the Watergate affair that none of the increasingly desperate efforts by Nixon and others to keep investigations out of the "problem area" worked, and their conspiracy to obstruct justice was itself a criminal offense. Watergate brought about the destruction of the Nixon presidency. On August 4, 1974, just ahead of congressional action to impeach Richard Nixon, the president resigned his office.

Richard M. Nixon
June 23, 1972, 10:04–11:39 A.M.
Meeting in the Oval Office with H.R. Haldeman

President Richard M. Nixon: Uh. Good. That's a very good paper that he's turned us. At least he thought it through. One thing you haven't got in there is the thing we mentioned regarding the Armed Services.

H.R. Haldeman: As it comes out of Ervin [Senator Sam Ervin, D-NC; Chairman, Government Operations Committee, 1954–75] who says that can be done, and he's moving. Not only Armed Services, but the whole government.

President Nixon: GSA [General Services Administration]. All we can [word]

H.R. Haldeman: All government does general.

President Nixon: Yeah.

H.R. Haldeman: And, uh, apart from John [Ehrlichman, senior domestic affairs adviser to the president] but uh, so that was a good idea.

President Nixon: Uh huh.

H.R. Haldeman: Uh, Henry [Henry Kissinger, special assistant for National Security Affairs, December 1968–November 1975] gets back at 3:45.

President Nixon: Yeah, I told, uh, Haig [General Alexander M. Haig, military assistant to Kissinger at the National Security Council, deputy national security adviser, 1970–72] today, I'd see Rogers [William P. Rogers, secretary of state, January 1969–September 1973] at 4:30.

H.R. Haldeman: Oh, good, OK. [Pause]

President Nixon: Well, if he gets back at 3:45, he won't be here 'til 4:00, 4:30.

H.R. Haldeman: It'll be a lot [unintelligible], 5:00.

President Nixon: Well I, at that time, I think I'm supposed to go to Camp David at 5:00, but Rogers doesn't need a lot of time, does he?

H.R. Haldeman: No, sir, picture.

President Nixon: Posing, that's all.

H.R. Haldeman: And he—now this is pretty. He called me about it, the other, yesterday; and he said, "I don't want to sit in the meeting with Henry. I understand, I put, there may be a couple of points Henry . . . "

President Nixon: Yeah. Sure. [Haldeman and Nixon speak over one another]

H.R. Haldeman: "wants me to be aware of"

President Nixon: Send us, that bill that, [name] bill that we've [words] right before we should tell the [Republican congressional] caucas to send against the [word]. We'll, we'll call him as soon as Henry gets here, which will be between 4:30 and 5:00.

H.R. Haldeman: Fred's always on time. Because.

President Nixon: Good. [Pause]

H.R. Haldeman: OK. That's fine. Now, on the investigation, you know, the Democratic break-in thing, we're back to the—in the problem area, because the FBI is not under control, because Gray [L. Patrick Gray, acting director, FBI, May 1972–April 1973] doesn't exactly know how to control, and they have their investigation is now leading into some productive areas, because they've been able to trace the money, not through the money itself, but through the bank. You know, sources.

President Nixon: Mm-hmm.

H.R. Haldeman: The banker, saw them, and it goes in some directions we don't want it to go. Uh, also there have been some, things like an informant came in off the street to the FBI in Miami, who, uh, is a photographer, who has a friend who's a photographer who develops films for this guy Barker [Bernard Barker, subsequently convicted as one of the Watergate burglars]. And the films had, uh, pictures of Democratic National Committee letterhead. Documents and things. That, so you s . . . , you've got, there's things like that are gonna, that are filtering in. Mitchell [John Mitchell, attorney general of the United States, January 1969–February 1972; chairman, Committee to Re-Elect the President (CREEP), February 1972–July 1, 1972] came up with, yesterday—and John Dean [counsel to the president, July 1970–April 1973] analyzed very carefully last night and concludes, concurs now, with Mitchell's recommendation that the only way to solve this, and we're set up beautifully to do it, uh, in that, and that's the only network that paid any attention to it last night is NBC [National Broadcasting Corporation television network] who did

President Nixon: Cuban

H.R. Haldeman: a massive story on the Cuban

President Nixon: [word—"fail"?]

H.R. Haldeman: trial. That the way to end all this now is, for us to have Walters [Vernon Walters, deputy director, CIA, April 1972–July 1976] call Pat Gray and just say, "Stay the hell out of this. This is uh, this business here we don't want you, going any further on it." That's not an unusual development. And, uh, that would take care of that

President Nixon: What's the matter with Pat Gray? Uh, he doesn't want to?

H.R. Haldeman: Pat doesn't want to. He doesn't know how to. And he doesn't have, he doesn't have any basis for doing it. Given this, he will then have the basis. He'll call Mark Felt [deputy associate director, FBI] in, and the two of them, and Mark Felt wants to cooperate because he's

President Nixon: Yeah

H.R. Haldeman: ambitious.

President Nixon: Yeah.

H.R. Haldeman: Uh, he'll call him in and say, "We've, we've got the signal, across the river[19] to, to put the hold on this." And that'll fit rather well because the FBI agents who are working the case, at this point, feel that's what it is. This is CIA.

President Nixon: But they've traced the money to 'em.

H.R. Haldeman: Well, they have, they've traced to a name, but they haven't got to the guy yet.

President Nixon: Would it be somebody here?

H.R. Haldeman: Ken Dahlberg [Kenneth H. Dahlberg, treasurer, Finance Committee to Re-Elect the President].

President Nixon: Who the hell is Ken Dahlberg?

H.R. Haldeman: He's a, he gave $25,000 in Minnesota. And, um

President Nixon: Yeah.

H.R. Haldeman: the check went directly in to, to this guy Barker.

President Nixon: Maybe he's a . . . bum? He didn't mean this is from the committee dollars, from Stans [Maurice Stans, finance chairman of the Committee to Re-elect the President]?

H.R. Haldeman: Yup. It is. This, it's directly traceable, and there's some more through some Texas people in, that went to the Mexican bank which they can also trace through the Mexican bank, they'll get their names today. [Pause] And,

President Nixon: Well, I mean, uh, there's no way that, I'm just thinking, if they don't cooperate, what do they say? They, they were, torched by the Cubans? That's what Dahlberg has to say, and the Texans, too. That idea.[20]

H.R. Haldeman: Well, if they will. But then we'll rely on more and more people all the time. It's the problem. And, uh, they'll stop if we could, if we take this other step.

President Nixon: All right.

H.R. Haldeman: And,

President Nixon: Fine.

H.R. Haldeman: And, and

President Nixon: All right

H.R. Haldeman: They seem to feel the thing to do is to get 'em to stop.

President Nixon: Right, fine.

H.R. Haldeman: They say the only way to do that is the White House instruction. And it's got to be to Helms [Richard Helms, director of Central Intelligence], and, uh, what's his name? Uh, Walters.

President Nixon: Walters.

H.R. Haldeman: And the proposal would be that Ehrli [clears throat] Ehrlichman and I call in.

President Nixon: All right. Fine.

H.R. Haldeman: And say, uh

President Nixon: How do you call him in, I mean you just, well, we protected Helms from one hell of a lot of things.

H.R. Haldeman: That's what Ehrlichman says.[21]

President Nixon: Of course, this is, uh, this is uh, Hunt [E. Howard Hunt, until recently a White House operative under Charles Colson, former CIA officer, currently co-manager of the Watergate break-in, subsequently convicted], you will, that'll, uncover a lot of sc—, a lot of sl—, that scab there's a hell of a lot of things in it, we just feel that this is, would be very detrimental to have this thing go any further. This involves the Cubans, Hunt, a lot of hanky-panky that we have nothing to do with ourselves. But what the hell, did Mitchell know about this thing to any much of a degree?

H.R. Haldeman: I think so. [Pause] I don't think he knew the details, but I think he knew.

President Nixon: He didn't know how it was going to be handled, with Dahlberg and Texans, and so forth. Well, who is the asshole that did [unintelligible]? Is it Liddy [G. Gordon Liddy, plotted and managed the Watergate break-in; convicted Watergate conspirator]? Is that the fellow? He must be a little nuts.

H.R. Haldeman: Yeah.

President Nixon: He just isn't well screwed-on, is he? That the problem?

H.R. Haldeman: No, but he was under pressure, apparently, to get more information, and as he got more pressure, he pushed the people harder to move harder on

President Nixon: Pressure from Mitchell?

H.R. Haldeman: Apparently. [Pause]

President Nixon: Oh, Mitchell, Mitchell was at the point that you made on this, that exactly what I need from you is on the

H.R. Haldeman: Doin' something. Yeah.

President Nixon: All right. I understand it all. We won't second-guess Mitchell and the rest. Thank God it wasn't Colson.[22]

H.R. Haldeman: The FBI interviewed Colson yesterday. They determined that that would be a good thing to do. Uh, to have him take a

President Nixon: Uh-huh

H.R. Haldeman: interrogation, which he did, and *that*, the FBI guys working the case had concluded that there are one or two possibilities: one, that this was a White House [initiative], they don't think there's anything about the Election Committee; they think it was either a White House operation and that some obscure reasons for it, non-political. Or, was a, uh,

President Nixon: Cuban

H.R. Haldeman: The Cubans and the CIA. And after their interrogation of, of

President Nixon: Colson

H.R. Haldeman: Colson, yesterday, they concluded it was not White House but are now convinced it's a CIA thing. So the CIA turnoff would [Haldeman and Nixon speak over each other]

President Nixon: Well, I don't agree with their analysis. [Word] hypothetical.

H.R. Haldeman: OK.

President Nixon: I don't get involved.[23]

H.R. Haldeman: No, sir. We don't want you to.

President Nixon: You call them in. Good. Good deal. Play it tough. That's the way they play it and that's the way we're gonna play it.

H.R. Haldeman: OK. [Pause] We'll do it.

President Nixon: Yeah, when I saw that news summary item, I of course knew it was a bunch of crap, but I thought that, well, it's good to have them off on this wild hare thing 'cause, listen, when they start bugging us, which they have, we'll know our little boys will not know to handle it. I hope they will though.

H.R. Haldeman: You never know. Maybe, you think about it.

President Nixon: Good.

[Conversation on other matters proceeds for about thirteen minutes.]

H.R. Haldeman: I think that's the irony. Mitchell says, "Hell, yes." Anything we can hit on at anytime we get the chance, and we've got a reason for doing it—do it.

President Nixon: When you get in, when you get in, these people, say, "Look, uh, — the problem is that this will open the whole, the whole Bay of Pigs thing, and the President just feels that," uh, I mean, without going into details, don't, don't lie to them to the extent to say there is no involvement, but say this is sort of comedy of errors, it's bizarre, without getting into it. "The President's belief is it's going to open the whole Bay of Pigs thing up again." And, uh, because these people are playin' for, for keeps, and that they should call the FBI in and say that "We wish for [for the sake of the] the country, don't go any further into this case." Period!

H.R. Haldeman: OK. [Noise]

President Nixon: That's the way to put it, do it straight.

[Nixon and Haldeman proceed to talk about the election campaign for the remainder of this meeting, about half an hour. They cover points such as how to use First Lady Pat Nixon and daughters Tricia and Julie—what events they should be scheduled for and whether they should have motorcades—as well as the effect of the media. Nixon returns to that theme in comments on the presidential elections of 1968 and 1960 and tells Haldeman that everyone in his campaign should get copies of Nixon's book Six Crises, *which contains his recollections of the 1960 campaign. The president also voices his desire to host a reception for members of the Secret Service in the near future and shake hands with one or two hundred of them. They discuss a paper on the economy prepared by adviser George Shultz and the president's schedule for the rest of the day. Toward the end of this conversation, Press Secretary Ronald L. Ziegler enters and the group discusses certain journalists.]*

Richard M. Nixon
June 23, 1972, 1:04–1:13 P.M.
Meeting in the Oval Office with H.R. Haldeman

[Background noise, paper shuffling.]

President Richard M. Nixon: [evidently on the telephone] Are those people now OK?

[silence]

President Nixon: Where are they? OK, I'll be up in just a minute.

[Writing, silence, about 40 seconds.]

H.R. Haldeman: I see[24] a time way back [unintelligible] might find out about that report before we do anything.

President Nixon: [unintelligible] Sorry.

[Silence and background noise, almost 40 seconds.]

H.R. Haldeman: OK

President Nixon: And this, this, just postpone the [unintelligible] and all that sort of [unintelligible] garbage. Just say that I have to take a look at the primaries [unintelligible]. I just don't [unintelligible] very bad to have this fellow Hunt, uh, OK, [unintelligible] aah, er, Jeez, he knows too damn much. And he *was* involved, we have to know that, and it gets out that the whole, this is all involved with the Cuban thing, and it's a, it's a fiasco, and it's gonna make the FB— the CIA look bad, and it's gonna make Hunt look bad, and it's likely to blow a hole in the Bay of Pigs thing, which we think would be very unfortunate for CIA and for the country at this time, and for American foreign policy, and he's just gotta tell 'em to lay off.

H.R. Haldeman: Yeah, that's, that's the basis we're gonna do it on, just leave it at that.

President Nixon: I don't want them to get any idea we're doing it because our concern is political.

H.R. Haldeman: Right.

President Nixon: And at the same time, I wouldn't tell them it is not political.

H.R. Haldeman: Right.

President Nixon: I would say, "Look, it's because of the Hunt involvement," just say [unintelligible] the whole cover is, uh, basically this [unintelligible].

H.R. Haldeman: Well they've got some pretty good ideas on this need thing. I thought Shultz [Secretary of the Treasury George P. Shultz] did a good paper [unintelligible].

President Nixon: I read it. . . . Of course you know better, I don't know.

[Conversation trails off in noise.]

Richard M. Nixon
June 23, 1972, 2:20–2:45 P.M.
Meeting in the Oval Office with H.R. Haldeman

H.R. Haldeman: Well, it's no problem. Had the two of them in, and they'd be scared going to [word] anyhow.[25] Well, it's kind of interesting. Walters sat there, uh, I just made the point, and didn't mention Hunt in the opening, I just said that, that, uh, this thing will just lead in the directions that were gonna create some very major, potential problems. Because they were exploring leads that led back into, to uh, to uh, areas that would be harmful to the CIA, harmful to the government, if they were [telephone rings]. Didn't [telephone rings] have anything to do with, with the Cubans, with the Cuban [word].

President Richard M. Nixon: [Speaks into telephone]: Chuck, I wondered if you would, uh, give John Connally a call. He's on his trip. I don't want him to read in the papers before Monday about this quota thing and say, "Look, uh, we met, uh, we're gonna do this, but, that, I, uh, checked, I asked you about this situation, and you personally checked your calendar date, and made, have an understanding. It's only temporary, it's won't affect, I mean [unintelligible] people." OK? I didn't want him to read in the papers. Good. Uh. [Hangs up telephone.] He's tough.
     Walters could send, send a visa [?]. I think Helms did too.

H.R. Haldeman: Helms said, Well, uh, I've had no contact with this at first, and, uh, said Gray called and said, uh, yesterday, and said, uh, that he thought

President Nixon: Who had, Gray?

H.R. Haldeman: Gray called Helms, which we knew, and he said, uh, I think he, "I think we've run right into the middle of a CIA covert operation here."

President Nixon: Gray said that?

H.R. Haldeman: Yeah. And Helms says, "I think nothing, nothing we've got at this point," and uh, uh, Gray said, "Well, it sure looks to me like that's what we did," or something, and Dick said, "Well, we have, you want me to just review our," and all, and, uh, that was the end of that conversation. Dick should say, "We don't." There's not a [words] on this [words] so you've got to be polite.

President Nixon: Um-hmm.

H.R. Haldeman: Said, "Well the problem is it tracks back to the Bay of Pigs, it tracks back to some other, if the leads run out, to people who have no involvement in this except by contact or connection, but it gets to areas that are here emphasized, that we'll raise." It's a whole problem with this fellow Hunt. Yes. So at that point, Helms kind of gets the picture, he said. *He said it*. He said, "We'll be very happy to be helpful. We'll handle anything, anything you want. I would like to know the reason for being helpful." And we made it clear to him he wasn't gonna get it, explicitly, he was gonna get it generality, and, and so he said, "Fine." And, uh, Walters.

Voice [Nixon? Ron Ziegler?][26]: Walters can do it? Walters said that?

H.R. Haldeman: Ya. Walters is gonna make a call to Gray. I think. That's the way we put it, that's the way it was left. And, uh, just leave 'em alone. Walters [unintelligible].

President Nixon: How would that work, though? How would—for example, they're desperate, run back a powerful, got somebody from Miami bank to be here, available [unintelligible].

Voice: Probably.

H.R. Haldeman: The point John made was the Bureau doesn't, the Bureau is going on on this because they don't know what they're uncovering. [Unintelligible] continue to pursue it. Uh, they don't need to because they've already got their case as far their, their charges against these men, has nothing to do with whether they're guilty or not. And, um, as they pursue it they're uncovering, starting to look in [unintelligible]. But we didn't in any way say we had an operational interest or concern or [word]. One thing Helms did raise is, he says, well, that Gray wants, he asked for it, why he felt they'd run into a CIA ... thing, and Gray said, "Well, because of the characters involved and the amount of money involved." He said, "There's a lot of dough in this somewhere."[27] [noise interference] That probably makes Helms suspicious [noise].

President Nixon: Well, we'll cross that bridge

H.R. Haldeman: Well, I think they will 'cause our, see th-there isn't any question

President Nixon: If it runs back to the bank, what the hell, they, who knows? [Maybe] Dahlberg's contributed to the CIA you know what I mean, in all seriousness.

H.R. Haldeman: CIA gets money as we know, 'cause, I mean their money moves in a lot of different ways, too.

President Nixon: Yeah. [Pause] However we thought, it did a lot of good. All right. [Brief pause] Can you imagine what Kennedy would have done with that money? Well, you remember what the son of a bitch did on my vote. When I brought out the fact, you know, about, the uh

H.R. Haldeman: Dulles

President Nixon: that he knew all about Dulles. Shit, Dulles knew it. Dulles told me. I knew. I mean Fred Seaton [assistant secretary of Defense for Legislative and Public Affairs during the Eisenhower administration] had had the telephone call. Remember, I had a call put in. Dulles just blandly said something. Called me on the phone, and for why?[28]

H.R. Haldeman: Yeah.

President Nixon: Well now, what the hell. Who told him to do it? President, of course. I am going to try to get Harry to send a referral call.

H.R. Haldeman: At least Dulles was no more Kennedy's man than Helms is your man.

President Nixon: But he was told then [noise]. Better check on that [unintelligible]. Call down [unintelligible]. That is all. [Unintelligible] on Cuba rather than Helms. But, the [words — "crime is"?] CIA briefing Helms on Cuba — they did not brief him on the covert operation, do anything else — *that* involves culpability.[29] He's not in control [unintelligible].

H.R. Haldeman: The Democratic nominee, we're gonna have to brief him.

President Nixon: Yes, sir. But, I wouldn't brief him about a single thing we don't want him to have.

H.R. Haldeman: Oh, no. Just tell him what we want to tell him. But, but, uh, I don't think you ought to brief him.

President Nixon: Me? Oh, hell, no!

H.R. Haldeman: Now, after you were nominated, Johnson called you in, er.

President Nixon: Johnson was out of office.

H.R. Haldeman: I mean, that's the point, he was [President Nixon talks over Haldeman]

President Nixon: Eisenhower didn't brief, Eisenhower did not brief Kennedy.

H.R. Haldeman: And it wouldn't, wouldn't be proper anyway

President Nixon: No, I'm his opponent.

H.R. Haldeman: because you're, you're his opponent

President Nixon: We simply said I will follow the same thing that Eisenhower did. 'Course Eisenhower was not [telephone rings][30]

H.R. Haldeman: That guy wasn't running either, but

President Nixon: [Answers telephone] Yeah. Ah, I'll call him tomorrow [hangs up].

H.R. Haldeman: But we didn't, it isn't that I just, uh, I'm sure you didn't have any thoughts that you'd want to

President Nixon: No.

H.R. Haldeman: But, I think we should

President Nixon: No. I just simply say yes, I would provide for briefings from the appropriate authorities, and then say, Well, are you going to brief him? Of course not, and, uh, I don't think we ought to [have] Kissinger brief him.

H.R. Haldeman: Just Helms?

President Nixon: I'd just have Helms. [Pause] Just Helms.

Voice: Maybe somebody would say, What do you think of it?

[Tape excised for sixteen seconds.]

H.R. Haldeman: He can't, you see, he would have no reason, no possible reason to put Senator Hubert [Senator Hubert H. Humphrey, D-MN, 1949–65 and 1971–78; vice president, 1964–68; a contender for the Democratic presidential nomination in 1972] in.

President Nixon: Hmph, that's true.

Voice: Uh, but they'll just find out that [unintelligible]

President Nixon: Brief those things.

H.R. Haldeman: He asked specifically, "What did you say to that poll, Gallup [unintelligible].

President Nixon: [Unclear exclamation] [Pause]

H.R. Haldeman: It's out. It's been mailed for two weeks, poll released.

President Nixon: Wonder why he got it, why he got it off so quickly. Usually lead time is two weeks.

H.R. Haldeman: Well, actually, this where lead time u-usually was until the last few months when he's spent a lot for some percentage. At this time he's putting it out fast.

President Nixon: [Unintelligible] for protection?

H.R. Haldeman: Well, because he's got trial heats, and he wants to put this out probably before he puts it, set the stage for the trial heats. [Noise]

President Nixon: Back before the Convention, the obvious thing [unintelligible] 60. The polls are high. [Unintelligible] God damn [unintelligible] nobody even appreciated it. Remember, we sat here and talked about trying to conduct a search because we were, that was a year and a half ago. But we had no idea. We thought they were gonna do it through going on the "Today Show" and [name of a media outlet] and all that bullshit. Remember at that time, we didn't know that we were going to have the other thing.

H.R. Haldeman: Took events, didn't we?

President Nixon: Yeah.

H.R. Haldeman: They've always said you've known it's the case, but

President Nixon: The great event, it could be China, May 8th and Russia.[31] That's all.

H.R. Haldeman: If you don't have the event, you gotta, you gotta make everything you can. Well obviously you're better off to put three months' or three years' effort against one event than you are to put the same amount in, in a, a tenth of that effort, against, uh, a non-event type thing. Then, maybe

President Nixon: I was really impressed with Shultz [George P. Shultz, secretary of labor, January 1969–June 1970; director, Office of Management and Budget, June 1970–May 1972; secretary of the treasury, May 1972–April 1974] and all those guys at the meeting.

H.R. Haldeman: I told them, and, uh

President Nixon: [Speaking over Haldeman] Shultz [unintelligible]

H.R. Haldeman: I talked to Shultz about calling Connally, and, and, uh

President Nixon: Yeah.

H.R. Haldeman: I said that you had mentioned how impressed were with the paper that John [Connally] had done on the whole [unintelligible, then noise].

President Nixon: Eisenhower [unintelligible] shows you how elections [unintelligible] and then in November, just before the election, he dropped to 57–23. I remember the [unintelligible]. The reason for that was nothing *he* did, it was Congressional, where they were kicking shit out of the Republicans.

H.R. Haldeman: Yeah.

President Nixon: That's why we're saying to you that McGovern candidate, the race, taking on some [word—"balls"?]. The problem is we've got to take it on [words].

[Noise]

President Nixon: [Unintelligible] But in 1958, of course it was recession [unintelligible]. He started the year, he started the year, at, uh, 23, with 60–30. It was Eisenhower. Most people forget. 58 in December, March, 52–33, April 49–31.[32]

H.R. Haldeman: Eisenhower?

President Nixon: Eisenhower.

H.R. Haldeman: Was that the fourth time?

President Nixon: That was his third time. Yes, sir.

H.R. Haldeman: Have we got any [unintelligible].

President Nixon: Unemployment. May 54–31; June 53–32; July 52–32; August, [unintelligible] 80, September 60–28; October 70–26; November, election, 52–30; and '59, it's the time we have the coverage, coverage of from below, [word] 60, 57, 56. In January of '60, we got up to 71 [unintelligible] no election.

[unintelligible]. 57, of July 57. In August 61, uh, for example, here's the early July 61, late July is 57. Nothing, nothing happened.

This is, this is, this is phony. This has got to be phony. August 61.

H.R. Haldeman: That's just, just like [words].

President Nixon: Sep-September, September 58; October 58; November 58. That's when we were running.

H.R. Haldeman: [Unintelligible]

President Nixon: Now there was Eisenhower in '60. We were running lower than, well, lower than, as low as July. [Unintelligible]

H.R. Haldeman: As low as July?

President Nixon: A little lower, yeah. Except that was off at the end of '59. Kennedy, you really can't tell about that. Uh, at the eve, of, of, his, his low in '62, in the election of '62,

H.R. Haldeman: Yeah

President Nixon: '62, was 62 yeah. But in '63, at the end, he was 57, 59, 57 [unintelligible] Johnson, then, of course, he massively higher than Kennedy, in the 80's. We've never been very high, but never as low as recently with Johnson.

H.R. Haldeman: [word — "Signalizing"?] that's inevitable. I don't think you ever will get up. Are you sure you want 80.

President Nixon: Yeah. [Pause] But *not*, these days. Johnson, of course, was 66–46, 50–56. Then in September, 48; October, 46; October, 44; November, 44; December, 48; December, 46; that's all. That's, that's 56 — now, of course, we can pull in 49 by the nearest count.[33]

H.R. Haldeman: Yeah.

President Nixon: Except his negatives were higher: 46, 42, 44, 41, 44, 42. Our negatives have never been that high. We run around 49–36, and that, uh, ballpark record, 36 to

H.R. Haldeman: Yeah.

President Nixon: 37, 38, 39. Then it goes on: 46, 48, 45, 44, 39, 39, 38, 41, 46, all [words — "of some concern"?], 48, 48, 39, but we, 43, and 41, 48, [word] action, 46 there, then back up to 49, 46, 41, 42, 40. [Unintelligible, then pause, sound of hammering.] The point that I'm trying to make here is that the money does inevitably, ah, [hammering]

H.R. Haldeman: Yeah

President Nixon: Because you're under attack.

H.R. Haldeman: Sure.

President Nixon: The issues, you know, that's what you hear.

H.R. Haldeman: Well. So then, what's before the public eye —

President Nixon: There's

H.R. Haldeman: the focus of attention is on things that are negative to the Administration. Uh, uh, that's, it's an interesting point. Buchanan [Patrick J. Buchanan, special assistant to the president, 1969–73], in response to the, response to his, you know, attack memo

President Nixon: Yeah.

H.R. Haldeman: argues quite strongly that, the point that the attacks should always be turned to the positive side, that, he argues that that's wrong; and that the attacks should stay on the negative side. Do not try to weave in also the positive, maintain there are positive points. That we should, that there should be an attack program that is purely attack. That's one of the understandings he was out to fix.

President Nixon: Except on foreign policy. I, I just don't, uh,

H.R. Haldeman: [Speaks over Nixon] But, Uh, I just didn't see

President Nixon: He's talking about

H.R. Haldeman: Huh?

President Nixon: He's talking about primarily domestic problems

H.R. Haldeman: Foreign, you hammer *your* strong point [both speak over each other]

President Nixon: I just think you've got to get that over and over again, 'cause God damn it, we gotta win our election

H.R. Haldeman: He doesn't argue against our hammering our strong points on everything, but his argument is when you are attacking, like if we do, uh, you've got to, uh, view it, we should do some of our advertising should be an attack on McGovern [Senator George McGovern, D-SD, a Democratic contender in the campaign and the eventual Democratic candidate in 1972] advertising.

President Nixon: Yeah.

H.R. Haldeman: And that attack did not try to make any Nixon strong points. It should only

President Nixon: Right.

H.R. Haldeman: make McGovern negative point.

President Nixon: Yeah.

H.R. Haldeman: His argument being that it's impossible in this election for you to get less than 40% of the vote; and that's equally impossible for you to get more than 60.

President Nixon: Yeah.

H.R. Haldeman: They set up over there?

Ron Ziegler [White House press secretary, 1969–74]: It's ready to go.

H.R. Haldeman: If you could go over early, if we could get this for sure on the networks. If we wait till 3 o'clock, we got a problem because of proc-, what is it, proc-, film processing. Because they're shooting, you know, they shoot with one camera, then they got to service all three networks out of the pool so that we keep rolling out, therefore. We're better off than if we wait [word].

Voice: Get ready.

President Nixon: OK.

Voice: Clear over there at the other side of the [words]? You get the word to them.

Ron Ziegler: Yes, sir. But I don't want to take your time to do it.

President Nixon: [Unintelligible] my time. I'll go across, at this point [words].

Ron Ziegler: Yes, sir.

[Unintelligible]

President Nixon: And, uh, based on the thing this morning, do you feel it's, uh, worthwhile to, um [unintelligible] till Monday?

Ron Ziegler: Yes, sir. [Pause]

H.R. Haldeman: Well, let's do it earlier in the day, because we are completely jeopardizing [unintelligible].

Ron Ziegler: 2 o'clock.

President Nixon: I'll do it. I'll be five minutes. Have you set it up? You want me to come right this minute?

Ron Ziegler: Well, I don't, anytime you feel comfortable, we'll [words—"do it"?]

President Nixon: OK. Scuff mark.

Ron Ziegler: As soon as possible.

H.R. Haldeman: His argument is if you, if you start with him, you got 40% of the people who will vote for you no matter what happens.

President Nixon: I agree.

H.R. Haldeman: And you got 40% of the people who will vote against you no matter what happens. So you got 20% of the people left in the middle who may vote for you or may not, and that 20 is what you gotta work on. His argument is that you're so well known, your pluses are as clear as well as your minuses; that getting one of those 20, who is an undecided type, to vote for you on the basis of your positive points is much less likely than getting them to vote against McGovern by scaring them to death about McGovern; and that that's the area we ought to be playing.

President Nixon: Well. If I could

H.R. Haldeman: I have to admit that these people are in the business, you know

President Nixon: That's right, by God, I am not going to do it. I really want you to bring in Flanigan [Peter M. Flanigan, White House Political and Economic Adviser, 1969–74] and these others about that and lay it to 'em. I'm *not* going

H.R. Haldeman: Yup.

President Nixon: to do it.

H.R. Haldeman: Yup.

Voice: Don't you think he'll agree?

President Nixon: Yup. Oh, you don't?

H.R. Haldeman: No, I think he will. They'll agree with the lobby; they think, heh, I agree with them. The conclusion, they'll say, why not do it anyway?

President Nixon: No, no, no, no, no, nothing, never. I'd say that. Can't take them for granted.

H.R. Haldeman: Listen, he could think I'm setting a Muskie [Edmund S. Muskie, United States senator, D-ME, 1959–80; another contender for the Democratic Party nomination in 1972; secretary of state, 1980–81].

President Nixon: He couldn't unless you're a reasonable man. God damn it, for all concerned.

H.R. Haldeman: Our best [words]. Buchanan's just getting back [Nixon and Haldeman speak over each other]

President Nixon: Buchanan's where he is. Have him be against Muskie. Don't give a shit about Nixon.

H.R. Haldeman: Yeah.

President Nixon: Because Muskie, screw 'em otherwise! All right, fine, Bob! [Pause] I don't know whether our people have scared the people enough about Muskie or [name].

H.R. Haldeman: Not yet.

President Nixon: You're, where, yeah

H.R. Haldeman: We feel that they are.

President Nixon: Yeah.

H.R. Haldeman: They are, but I mean, you got to build that up. His point is that so little is known about McGovern, you'll have a better chance of changing people's minds about him than you do [unintelligible, voices fade].

Gerald R. Ford

JULY 17, 1975: PRESIDENT FORD TALKS TO AMERICAN AND
RUSSIAN ASTRONAUTS ABOARD THE DOCKED *APOLLO* AND
SOYUZ SPACECRAFT ON A JOINT ORBITAL MISSION

Richard Nixon's political difficulties grew steadily as revelations of Watergate misdeeds piled one atop another. Nixon sought to protect his tapes, especially the "smoking gun" conversations that showed the president of the United States actively participating in an obstruction of justice. Nixon ultimately resigned to avoid a bill of impeachment in August 1974. He was succeeded by Vice President Gerald R. Ford, whose tenure in the Oval Office would complete the second term to which Nixon had been elected. The business of the Ford administration would be the fulfillment of programs begun under Nixon, or responses to crises already acute during Nixon's time. Both of the two surviving Ford tape recordings represent these continuities from the past. As discussed in the introduction, these are the *only* Ford tapes known to exist.

The first selection presented is a conversation between President Ford and the American and Russian astronauts orbiting the earth in linked-up space capsules in what was known as the *Apollo-Soyuz* project. *Apollo* was the U.S.-manned program designed to explore the moon, which U.S. astronauts reached in July 1969. The program ended in December 1972 after seventeen missions, including several moon walks. However, at a summit conference in Moscow that June, the same meeting at which a treaty regulating ballistic missile defenses and an accord on nuclear offensive forces were reached, President Nixon and Russian leader Leonid Brezhnev agreed to carry out a joint manned space flight.

To make the joint mission work, National Aeronautics and Space Administration (NASA) in the United States had to take the *Apollo* space capsule, a three-person craft, and modify its docking and mating equipment to be compatible with a Russian craft. The Soviet Union had to do the same with its own two-person spacecraft called *Soyuz* (hence the name for the joint venture). These engineering tasks took time, and both nations had to train crews for the mission as well. Design and production work extended through early 1975. Americans manufactured the docking and clamping gear. The Russians prepared a complete backup *Soyuz* capsule in case anything went wrong with the primary mission craft. A dress rehearsal for the launch occurred at the U.S. space center at Cape Canaveral, Florida, as early as November 1974. In the end the mission would go well, with no worse mishaps on the U.S. side than some cracks in the fins of the Saturn N-1 booster rocket (discovered months in advance) and a last-minute leaky valve.

Each country's crews, aside from their own training, spent three-week instruction periods in the other nation several times during the period of flight preparation. The American crew first traveled to Russia in the summer of 1974. Members of the crew were Air Force Brigadier General Thomas P. Stafford, Donald K. ("Deke") Slayton, and Vance D. Brand. The Russian crew consisted of Colonel Alexei A. Leonov and Valery N. Kubasov, and they came to America for an initial stint of training at Houston's Johnson Space Center in September 1974.

President Ford first met the Russian spacemen (Russians termed their crewmen "cosmonauts") on that visit to the United States, as they reached the East Coast. He took them to the annual "crab pick" of the Alexandria Police Department on September 7. There Ford introduced the Russians to hard-shell crabs, demonstrating how to pry off the shell with a knife and use a mallet to dig out the meat. Ford handed samples to Leonov and Kubasov and told them, "Out in Michigan we don't have crabs, but we have a few crabby people."[1] President Ford also introduced his Russian guests to hot dogs. The president would refer to this event in his conversation with the astronauts in orbit.

After all the preparatory work, the *Apollo-Soyuz* mission began on July 15, 1975. The Russian rocket launched first, from Baikonur in Kazakhstan. Almost eight hours later, the American astronauts launched from Cape Canaveral. Times were carefully calculated to permit the two spacecraft to draw closer with minimum fuel expenditure. In fact this meant a lengthy process of gradual orbit changes and slight maneuvers, so that it was July 17 when the *Apollo* and *Soyuz* spacecraft actually docked in earth orbit. The craft were 140 miles above the earth, over the Atlantic Ocean (620 miles west of Portugal) when the docking took place at 12:09 P.M. eastern daylight time. General Stafford was the first to visit the *Soyuz* craft, and Colonel Leonov was first to return the visit. While Leonov remained aboard *Apollo*, President Ford telephoned.

Gerald Ford's conversation suggests the president was torn between regarding the phone call as a ceremonial occasion, a private visit, and an official exchange on the operational aspects of rendezvous in space. All these elements are present in his questions and comments. The astronauts momentarily lost their ground link during the talk but quickly regained it. President Ford subsequently issued a statement from the White House terming the *Apollo-Soyuz* docking "a momentous event."[2]

Gerald R. Ford
July 17, 1975
Telephone Conversation with Apollo-Soyuz Test Project Crews Following
Rendezvous and Docking of the Spacecraft

President Gerald R. Ford: Yes.

Male Voice: The astronauts are on the line, sir.

President Ford: Gentlemen, let me call to express my very great admiration for your hard work, your total dedication in preparing for this first joint flight. All of us here in Washington, in the United States, send to you our very warmest congratulations for your successful rendezvous and for your docking; and we wish you the very best for a successful completion of the remainder of your mission.

Your flight is a momentous event and a very great achievement, not only for the five of you but also for the thousands of American and Soviet scientists and technicians who have worked together for three years to insure the success of this very historic and very successful experiment in international cooperation. It's taken us many years to open this door to useful cooperation in space between our two countries, and I'm confident that the day is not far off when space missions made possible by this first joint effort will be more or less commonplace.

We all look forward to your safe return and we follow with great interest the success so far, and we look forward to talking with you on earth again when you do end your flights.

General Stafford, uh, Tom, now that you've had, uh, an opportunity to test the new docking system, do you think, uh, it will be suitable for future international manned space flight?

Brig. Gen. Thomas Stafford: Oh, yes, sir, Mr. President, I sure do. Out of the three docking systems I've used, this was the smoothest one so far. It worked beautifully.

President Ford: About three and a half hours ago, I sat here in the Oval Office and watched the docking procedure. It looked awfully simple from here, I'm sure it wasn't that simple, uh, for the five of you. Let me, if I might

Brig. Gen. Thomas Stafford: [unintelligible]

President Ford: Yes, Tom. Let me say a word or two, if I might, to Colonel [Aleksei] Leonov. Uh. The docking was a critical phase of the joint mission. Uh, Colonel, could you describe it, and would you describe the reaction of the crews on meeting in space, after such a long preparation?

Col. Aleksei Leonov: Mr. President, I am sure that our joint flight is the beginning for future cooperation in space between our countries. Thank you very much for very nice words, eh, to us. We'll do our best.

President Ford: Uh, Colonel, I think you and the other four have done very, very well so far, and may I congratulate you and your associates on this great achievement.

Now, Dr. Slayton, Deke, you've had a very, very long record of distinguished service preparing other astronaut crews for various space missions, and we're extremely pleased to see you on the crew of the first international manned space flight. As the world's oldest space rookie, do you have any advice for young people who hope to fly on future space missions?

[Unintelligible noise from the space ship.]

President Ford: Deke, did you have a chance to hear my question?

Donald K. "Deke" Slayton: Uh, No, sir, Mr. President, unfortunately . . .

President Ford: Can I repeat it and um

Donald K. "Deke" Slayton: . . . went too long.

[Unintelligible noise from the space ship.]

Donald K. "Deke" Slayton: Tom just repeated it for me, sir. Well, uh, yes, I have a lot of advice for, uh, young people, but I guess, uh, probably one of the most important bits is to, number one, decide what you really want to do, and then secondly, never give up until you've done it.

President Ford: Well, you're a darned good example, Deke, of never giving up and continuing; n, and I know it is a great feeling of, um, of uh success from your point of view to have made this flight and to be on board with your four associates.

Donald K. "Deke" Slayton: Yes, sir.

President Ford: Vance Brand, I know that you are still in the *Apollo*, holding the fort there. It's been my observation, uh, that the crews on both sides have w, uh, worked very hard to learn either Russian on the one hand or English on the other. Uh, has this training period, which is so important, stood the test in the complicated procedures that all of you must execute in this very delicate mission?

Vance Brown: Mr. President, I believe it really has. I think in a way, uh, our project, and in particular the training that we've undergone, has been a sort of a model for future, uh similar projects. I think, uh, it's been a real pleasant experience to, uh, work on learning Russian and, uh, to be able to, uh, work with the cosmonauts; and I think, uh, we'll have some ideas that would probably help people in the future on similar paths.

President Ford: Thank you very much, uh, Vance. I might like to say a word or two to, uh, Valery Kubasov, the other, uh, member of the cosmonaut crew. I might say to him, uh, as well as, uh, Colonel Leonov, I remember both of you on that enjoyable Saturday last September when both crews visited the White House and joined me in a picnic over in Virginia. We flew from the White House over to this picnic, uh, just across the river. We had some crab specialties that I enjoyed and I think you, uh, did. I'm sure you're having a little different menu, somewhat different food on this occasion. What are you having over there, uh, out in space?

Valery Kubasov: We have good, eh, space, eh, food. There are some Russian food, some Russian music, some juice, some coffee and a lot of water—no beer, no crab.

President Ford: Let me say in conclusion, we look forward to your safe return. It's been a tremendous demonstration of cooperation between our scientists, our technicians and of course our astronauts and their counterparts the cosmonauts from the Soviet Union. I . . . congratulate everybody connected with the flight and particularly the five of you who are setting this outstanding example of what we have to do in the future to make it a better world. And may I say in signing off, here's to a soft landing.

Valery Kubasov: Thank you very much.

Brig. Gen. Thomas Stafford: Thank you, Mr. President; it has certainly been an honor to serve the country and work here.

President Ford: We'll see you when you get back.

Brig. Gen. Thomas Stafford: Yes, sir.

SEPTEMBER 1, 1975: PRESIDENT FORD DISCUSSES MIDDLE EAST TRUCE AGREEMENTS WITH SECRETARY OF STATE HENRY A. KISSINGER, ISRAELI PRIME MINISTER YITZHAK RABIN, AND EGYPTIAN PRESIDENT ANWAR EL-SADAT

The October War of 1973 began with an Egyptian-Syrian attack upon Israel on the Yom Kippur religious holiday. After initial successes—most important was Egypt's successful assault across the Suez Canal and attempt to break through into the Sinai—Israeli forces struck back. The war ended after about three weeks. In the Sinai it produced a very confused situation in which Egyptian forces held most of the Sinai bank of the canal, but Israelis were across the canal themselves, on the African side, interposed behind the Egyptians in the south. The Israelis had a narrow and vulnerable corridor into Africa, but the Egyptians had been unable to crack it and their forces in the south were surrounded. Diplomacy following the war faced the challenge of disentangling the forces. In addition, there remained the larger question of peace between Israel and Egypt—especially involving the Sinai peninsula—which Israeli forces had taken from Egypt in the Six Day War of 1967. This tape selection concerns an intermediate stage of the post–October War diplomacy.

In January 1974, an initial move occurred when Israel and Egypt reached a disengagement agreement. Israeli forces pulled out of Africa and conceded Egypt a narrow strip of land on the Sinai side of the Suez. There were strict limits on the number and types of Egyptian troops permitted on the Sinai bank; the two sides were separated by a demilitarized zone, and a United Nations unit monitored the separation of forces. Israel's military held a line several miles back from the Canal, along with the mountainous region approximately twenty miles to the east, crossed by the Mitla and Giddi passes, which afforded a spectacular view of most of the Suez region. Egypt sought the return of half the Sinai, later all of it, with Israel reluctant to yield further territory, yet desirous of peace with Egypt.

The United States became involved in the Middle East negotiations from the beginning. The Nixon administration had not quite run its course when the separation of forces agreement took effect, but Nixon's August 1974 resignation left further efforts to President Gerald R. Ford. There were notions of a comprehensive Middle East peace negotiation that might be held at Geneva, but this avenue was rejected by both Israel and the United States. Instead Secretary of State Henry A. Kissinger engaged in intense diplomatic efforts, making a number of trips to the Middle East where he would fly among the Israeli, Egyptian, Syrian, and other capitals carrying the latest versions of the various nations' proposals and attempting to mediate among them. In fact, the term "shuttle diplomacy" was coined at this time to describe Kissinger's missions and has come to signify a diplomatic mediation of this sort. Kissinger's first exhausting shuttle mission took place in March 1975, but it failed.

Despite failure Egypt made certain conciliatory gestures. Under President Anwar el-Sadat, the Egyptians moved steadily to a more flexible position on its demands. Toward the end of March, the Egyptians returned the bodies of twenty-nine Israeli soldiers who had been killed in the October War and were considered missing-in-action by Israel. Between Syria and Israel, hostility remained high, leaving no chance for progress, so that diplomatic efforts increasingly focused on the Israeli-Egyptian sides. Under Prime Minister Yitzhak Rabin, a former general and army chief of staff, Israel was willing to negotiate with Egypt, though it continued to resist significant concessions. Leaks from the Israeli capital Tel Aviv sought to associate the United States with its own position, infuriating President Ford, who publicly ordered a reassessment of Middle East policy in Washington, hinting that the United States had soured on Israel's intransigence. As Ford set this context in his memoirs, his comment was, "When Rabin and his colleagues saw that I wasn't about to bow to any home-front political pressure they could exert, they were ready for serious bargaining."[3] The basis for another Kissinger shuttle was laid when both Israel and Egypt declared a preference for another interim agreement on the Sinai rather than a Geneva conference.

President Ford met with Egypt's Sadat at Salzburg, Austria, during May 1975. Kissinger pressed the Egyptian leader on several points and found Sadat amenable to guarantees for Israeli security. In June, Prime Minister Rabin visited Washington and found both President Ford and Secretary Kissinger united in insisting that Israel could move safely forward on negotiations. Rabin's explanations of Israel's concerns led Ford to instruct Kissinger to meet them as far as possible, but Ford also told the Israeli leader that unless progress were made toward an interim agreement, the United States would have to begin working toward a Geneva conference and comprehensive settlement. Negotiation then focused on identifying a new line in the Sinai to which Israel would withdraw, a process that consumed much of the summer.

To allay Israel's security concerns, President Ford took two major actions. The first was to approve increases in military and technical aid to Israel, which was requested by Rabin's defense officials. The second was to instruct Kissinger to build special security provisions into the interim agreement. Teams of American experts in a "Sinai Support Mission" would staff several observation posts in the Egyptian-controlled part of Sinai that covered the main routes troops would have to take if they were assembling for an attack. Israeli experts would be permitted major radar and listening posts high up in the mountains near the Mitla and Giddi passes that could furnish further warning of any Egyptian troop buildup (even under later agreements these posts were retained, staffed by Americans, with their information provided to both Israel and the United Arab Republic). The passes themselves would fall in the buffer zone between the Israeli and Egyptian lines, and that zone would have its own contingent of United Nations observers. As before, specific types of weapons and forces were restricted in the area of the sides' front lines. Israel would also withdraw from some oil fields in the Sinai that were located in an area away from the Suez Canal. Secretary Kissinger resumed his shuttle diplomacy in August and discussed the details of all these points. Negotiations also involved the American ambassadors and other diplomats in both Israel and Egypt. Talks went on right up until the interim agreement was finalized and initialed.

President Ford considered the interim agreement fair and balanced and hoped it would build confidence and generate movement toward a more fulsome peace. The agreement was initialed in both Tel Aviv and Cairo on September 1 (it would be officially signed in Geneva on September 4). Henry Kissinger telephoned the president from Tel Aviv, initiating our tape selection. President Ford refers to Ron Nessen, his press secretary, and informs Kissinger that the White House Communications Agency (WHCA, but pronounced "Waca") is recording the call. He also refers to a congressional briefing ("Thursday") on the interim accord he would give on September 4, the date of the Geneva signing. President Ford then successively calls Prime Minister Rabin and President Sadat.

A certain frustration in listening to this tape is quite justified. Not only is President Ford able to speak easily with astronauts in orbit but not to another world leader right on earth, but their telephone problems had practical consequences. Most of the persons on this tape are speaking more or less ceremonially, but Egyptian President Anwar Sadat attempted to do real diplomatic business. Sadat asks Ford for two things: to keep the Middle East negotiations going on parallel tracks and to begin a dialogue with the Palestinian people. Either President Ford did not, or professed he did not, understand Sadat's words owing to the bad telephone connection. Ford provided vague reassurances of America's good intentions. Sadat's request for a dialogue with the Palestinians here was made in 1975, many years before the Intifada and the rise of terrorism (frequently confused with Palestinian rebellion) made progress on the Palestine issue nearly impossible. Had President Gerald R. Ford heard Sadat and acted on the Egyptian leader's requests, the shape of the Middle East today might be quite different.

Despite the optimism, the 1975 interim agreement did not lead to a comprehensive settlement. The Sinai remained under occupation by both Israel and Egypt until after the Camp David Accord, a key breakthrough mediated by the Carter administration in 1978 that provided for a framework of peace and for normalization of relations between Israel and Egypt. Except for a small part of the Sinai near Eilat, called Taba, and the Gaza Strip, the peninsula had been returned to Egypt by 1981, and peace restored between the two countries. President Sadat was himself assassinated that year by Islamic fundamentalists. A peace process was revived during the 1990s but failed to bring about a final settlement. Yitzhak Rabin, who became a major Israeli proponent of peace, was assassinated in 1995. Ironically, the leaders on both sides who agreed to this early step toward peace would fall victims to extremists who opposed ending the strife. The Middle East continues in turmoil today, with no peace yet between Israel and Syria, and with intense conflict within Israel and in the Palestinian territories.

Gerald R. Ford
September 1, 1975
Telephone Conversations with Secretary of State Henry Kissinger, Prime
Minister Yitzhak Rabin of Israel, and President Anwar el-Sadat of Egypt on
the Egyptian-Israeli Agreements

Secretary of State Henry Kissinger: Hello, Mr. President.

President Gerald R. Ford: Henry, how are you?

Secretary Kissinger: I'm fine. How nice to hear from you.

President Ford: Well, the same to you. I've just been warned by, uh, uh, Ron,[4] that, uh, I have to tell you, and later, uh, when I tell, or talk to, to the prime minister and to the president, that WHCA[5] is recording this conversation. You don't have any objections, I trust.

Secretary Kissinger: No, I don't have any objections.

President Ford: Well, I think they wanted it for historical purposes.

Secretary Kissinger: Right.

President Ford: Well let me say, Henry, very, very deep, uh, very deeply, how very grateful I am for the tremendous effort that you made in this last, uh, round of negotiations, but I know how long and how hard and devotedly you have spent many, many hours not only with me but with, uh, uh, Prime Minister Rabin and President Sadat. I think this is a great achievement—one of the most historic, certainly, uh, of this, uh, decade and perhaps in this century. And I know that the American people, uh, will be most grateful for the successful efforts that you've made, n, I just want to express it very strongly and very deeply for myself.

Secretary Kissinger: And I appreciate this very much, Mr. President. And of course we spent more time on the Middle East, you and I, than on almost any other problem.

President Ford: I think if we added up the hours, it would be a good many days, and the fact that we finally made, uh, a successful conclusion, I know, gives you as well myself and many, many others a great deal of satisfaction. It's in the best interests of not only the two countries, ourselves, but in my judgment Henry, one of the great achievements for the world at this time.

Secretary Kissinger: I think it gives peace a chance in this area, and the consequences, as you have pointed out repeatedly, of stalemate were simply unacceptable.

President Ford: I'm sure there'll be some critics, but I think in all honesty, *they* have to understand what the alternatives would have been.

Secretary Kissinger: Exactly, Mr. President. That is the problem, that the continuation of the stalemate would have had both military and economic consequences for the world that we had to do something about.

President Ford: Are you, uh, you're leaving very shortly as I understand, for the actual initialing?

Secretary Kissinger: I'm going to see Prime Minister Rabin now and then we are going to initial the documents.

President Ford: Right.

Secretary Kissinger: Then shortly after that, I will go to Egypt to meet with President Sadat and participate in the initialing of the documents there.

President Ford: You'll uh, you'll actually carry the documents with you to Alexandria then?

Secretary Kissinger: Exactly, documents and maps.

President Ford: Well, I'm going to call, uh, the Prime Minister, uh, after talking with you, and, um, I'll express to him my appreciation; but if you will do it, uh, in person for me, I would also be very grateful.

Secretary Kissinger: I will do that, Mr. President, and I look forward very much to seeing you on Thursday.

President Ford: You're getting in Wednesday night, as I understand?

Secretary Kissinger: That's right. I'm getting in Wednesday night about 9 or 10 o'clock.

President Ford: Well I will be at the airport to meet you.

Secretary Kissinger: Aren't you nice.

President Ford: And it is arranged for us to have a bipartisan leadership meeting on Thursday morning at 8:00 A.M.

Secretary Kissinger: Good.

President Ford: And, uh, I'm sure that their reaction, uh, will be the same as mine, that this is a great achievement for not only the parties involved but, uh, for the world as a whole. And I, uh, I just can't express deeply enough my appreciation for your own magnificent efforts in this area.

Secretary Kissinger: Well, Mr. President, it's, we've worked together on this, and your strong support and your leadership and your talks with Sadat and Rabin made this possible.

President Ford: Well, you go over there and um, uh, participate with the prime minister, give him my best, and at the same time give Nancy my very best.

Secretary Kissinger: Thank you, and the best to Betty.

President Ford: Thank you very much, and we'll see you Wednesday night.

Secretary Kissinger: See you Wednesday night.

President Ford: OK. Thanks, Henry.

Secretary Kissinger: Bye.

President Ford: Bye.

❉   ❉   ❉

Prime Minister Yitzhak Rabin: Hello?

President Ford: Mr. Prime Minister, how are you, sir?

Prime Minister Rabin: I am fine, Mr. President. How are you?

President Ford: I am excellent, thank you, and I just finished talking with Henry and I understand he's coming over to meet with you very shortly, uh, for the actual initialing; and let me congratulate you for the superb efforts that you've made under most trying circumstances. I think your role has been one of great statesmanship, under terribly difficult circumstances, and I congratulate you and compliment you on the achievement of I think an outstanding uh negotiation that's culminated in a a document that will lead to uh great progress in the Middle East for the benefit of the world as a whole.

Prime Minister Rabin: Mr. President, thank you very much for your kind words. It was not an easy decision. It was a very complicated uh, complicated negotiations. But, uh, we have decided this time ah to take risk, and I stress *to take risk*, for an opening for peace. I hope that, uh, what we have decided will set a new pattern in the area, and I, we all hope here that, uh, the agreement will really lead to both tranquility in the area and to bring eh closer the positions of at least Egypt and Israel. I eh would like eh to thank you very much for the role that you personally, the United States, uh, and your envoy Dr. Kissinger, uh, have served in the achievement of eh eh this agreement.

President Ford: Well I thank you very much, Mr. Prime Minister and, let me assure you that you can count on us to continue to stand with you. Uh, We have a close relationship, and it will continue as we move forward under the basis of this outstanding agreement. You have laid a solid foundation with this agreement in my judgment on which we can build for real peace efforts in the future.

Prime Minister Rabin: Well, we all hope for it here, and we really hope that will be the beginning of something which we have not yet experienced in this area. And uh we hope that uh the other side, Egyptian side, uh, feels the same.

President Ford: Well, you can rest assured that we will work with you uh to make certain that the agreement is carried out not only in the spirit but in the letter; and that we uh expect uh to continue the relationship that we have had over a good many years, your country and ours. You have heroic people, and the American people are most sympathetic to those uh uh that you so ably represent, Mr. Prime Minister.

Prime Minister Rabin: Mr. President, as you are fully aware, we appreciate very much you; we appreciate very much eh the special relations that eh have the signif, so significant in the past and at the present between our two countries. And I am sure that what we have done there today will add a new dimension to the relations between your our two countries.

President Ford: Will you give my very best to Mrs. Rabin; uh, and uh I hope that in the near future you can come back and see us again, sir.

Prime Minister Rabin: Thank you very much, Mr. President. And please, convey our best wishes to Mrs. Ford.

President Ford: Thank you very much; and uh we'll see you, I hope, soon.

Prime Minister Rabin: I hope so, too.

President Ford: Thank you.

Prime Minister Rabin: Thank you very much, Mr. President.

President Ford: Goodbye.

Prime Minister Rabin: Bye

*   *   *

President Ford: Hel—President Sadat?

President Anwar el-Sadat: Hello?

President Ford: Oh, President Sadat?

President Sadat: This is President Sadat.

President Ford: How are you this morning? President Sadat, I wanted to call you and congratulate you on the great role that you played in the negotiations that have culminated in this agreement.

President Sadat: Hello? [unintelligible]

President Ford: Unfortunately, I don't hear you too well, Mr. President, uh. I hope that my uh conversation is coming through more clearly. Let me uh express most emphatically on behalf of my government the appreciation for your statesmanship despite uh adversity and some criticism, the spirit with which you have approached the need for an agreement. I am most grateful for the leadership that you've given, and I look forward to continuing to work with you in

President Sadat: Hello?

President Ford: Hello!

President Sadat: Sir?

President Ford: Can you hear me, Mr. President?

President Sadat: No, I can't hear you very well.

President Ford: Well, uh I know that you and I recognize that stagnation and stalemate in the Middle East would have been potentially disastrous, and your leadership in working with Secretary Kissinger and with the Israelis, all of us are most grateful for. And as we continue to work together, personally as well as government-to-government.

President Sadat: Hello?

President Ford: Hello!

President Sadat: Hello, hello, Hello!

President Ford: Yes, I can hear you, Mr. President.

President Sadat: Hold on please.

President Ford: I hope you can hear me, Mr. President.

President Sadat: President Ford? Hello?

President Ford: Yes?

President Sadat: [unintelligible]

President Ford: I don't hear too well, Mr. President.

President Sadat: President Ford speaking? . . . Hello?

President Ford: Hello.

President Sadat: President Ford Speaking?

President Ford: Yes! This is President Ford.

President Sadat: Hold on please.

President Ford: The connection unfortunately is not uh, uh, too good for me to hear your uh comments, Mr. President. Let me say, [clears throat] if I might, despite the difficulties, that Mrs. Ford and I hope that Mrs. Sadat and you and your children will visit the United States uh sometime this Fall. The Secretary Kissinger has told me of the very warm hospitality that you've extended to him and Mrs. Kissinger, and we look forward to reciprocating uh when you come to the United States uh in the Fall of 1975. This will be

President Sadat: [unintelligible]

President Ford: I regret that I can't hear; the connection is very bad. I hope that you can hear me and my comments from the United States . . . The . . .

Unidentified Voice: Is there any

President Ford: Yes. I can't hear him at all.

Unidentified Voice: [unintelligible]

President Ford: All right [to Unidentified Man] . . . Well, Mr. President, I understand that Secretary Kissinger is coming to Alexandria uh, to personally delivery the document for your initialing. And I've asked Henry to extend to you on that occasion uh the gratitude and appreciation of the American people uh for your patience, your leadership, and um your understanding of the need and necessity for uh a forward step, an important step, in the ultimate aim of total peace in the Middle East.

President Sadat: Hello.

President Ford: Hello, Mr. President.

President Sadat: Hello, Mr. President.

President Ford: I can hear you better now, sir.

President Sadat: Very well. Mr. President?

President Ford: Yes.

President Sadat: I hope you and your family are well.

President Ford: I am feeling very well, Mr. President, and I hope you are, too.

President Sadat: I greatly appreciate your call. I must thank you for your personal message. [Lengthy undecipherable statement.]

President Ford: Mr. President, I couldn't hear every word distinctly, but I got the uh thrust of your kind comments and your encouraging words. And I can assure you that we will work with Egypt, not only in seeing that the uh agreement is implemented uh with the spirit as well as the letter; that we will continue to develop the good relations between Egypt and the United States, uh working to make sure that we expand trade, tourism and our help to the maximum degree possible; and that this is the way that United States can continue to play a constructive role in the most uh important area, the Middle East.

And you have my personal assurance, and I'm sure the Congress will cooperate, because it *is* recognized in the United States that the Middle East is a vitally important area of the world, and that our participation in a constructive way is an important element in the tremendous success that has been achieved in the negotiations between your country and Israel. And I wish to thank you very, very much.

And I said a few moments ago, Mrs. Ford and I look forward to having Mrs. Sadat, your family and yourself here in the United States early this fall.

President Sadat: Mr. President, I am looking really forward to this visit with you and your family [unintelligible]. And I should like, Mr. President, to ask a point, if you, if you agree, I also assure you we accept this agreement as a further step toward a just and peaceful solution. I consider it a a turning point in the history of the country. And this, again, thanks to you; but it is essential, Mr. President, uh uh that we must keep the momentum of the peace process uh, uh, uh, and continue it.

President Ford: I can assure you, Mr. President, we're going to keep the momentum going in the peace process. We will not tolerate stagnation or stalemate. The momentum is on the way for a peaceful solution on a permanent and an equitable basis; and you have my pledge that we will make sure that that momentum keeps going.

President Sadat: Thank you very much, Mr. President.

President Ford: I look forward to seeing you after that wonderful visit we had in Salzburg; and give my very best to Mrs. Sadat if you will, please.

President Sadat: Thank you very much, Mr. President.

President Ford: Thank you, sir.

President Sadat: Uh, uh, I should like another two points, Mr. President.

President Ford: Yes.

President Sadat: [unintelligible] until I leave, uh, uh, I think I would like to emphasize the importance of uh uh retaining talks on a, on a uh uh parallel spokes [unintelligible] and I also urge you to begin a dialogue with the Palestinians uh [unintelligible].

President Ford: I unfortunately could not hear as well as I would like the last comments you made. The connection from here is not, apparently, as good as I hope you have there, but

President Sadat: I hear you quite uh, quite good. I also commend [unintelligible]

President Ford: Well, the efforts of Secretary Kissinger and myself, we feel, were completely worth what we've done, but our efforts could not have been successful without the leadership and the statesmanship by you and the equally uh fine actions by the Israeli government and Prime Minister Rabin, uh. But, as you said a moment ago, Mr., President Sadat, the momentum is moving in the right direction, and you have my personal assurance that we will continue that movement because it *is* vital, uh, not only in the Middle East but elsewhere for the benefit of all peoples.

President Sadat: Thank you, Mr. President, *very* much.

President Ford: And we will see you soon, I hope.

President Sadat: Sure, I shall be coming with pleasure, and convey my good wishes to your family.

President Ford: Thank you, and the best to yours, sir.

President Sadat: Thank you very much.

President Ford: And have a good day; and Henry'll be there shortly, I understand.

President Sadat: I am waiting for him.

President Ford: OK!

President Sadat: Thank you.

President Ford: Bye bye.

President Sadat: Bye.

Ronald Reagan

NOVEMBER 25, 1986: PRESIDENT REAGAN'S PUBLIC STATEMENT
ACCEPTING THE RESIGNATION OF NATIONAL SECURITY
ADVISER ADMIRAL JOHN POINDEXTER OVER THE
IRAN-CONTRA AFFAIR

On October 5, 1986, during a civil war in the Central American nation of
Nicaragua, an intruding aircraft was shot down by government forces deep
inside the country. Examination of the wreckage revealed the aircrew had been
Americans, and recovered documents showed that the pilot had previously
flown in Laos for the Central Intelligence Agency (CIA) proprietary Air America. Search of the surrounding area also resulted in the capture of one survivor,
the crew chief, who had parachuted to safety. He too was an American, one
Eugene Hasenfus, who had also flown for Air America in Laos. Every aspect
confirmed what government forces thought they knew in advance: that the
plane had been engaged in a resupply flight to help contra (a contraction for
the Spanish word *contrarevolucionario*, or counterrevolutionary) forces that for
some years had been supported by the United States.

Speculation immediately centered upon an undercover CIA operation, but
the Reagan administration vehemently denied any connection with the enterprise. Indeed, although there had been a CIA project backing the contras from

1981 through 1984, by this time anything other than humanitarian assistance was prohibited by U.S. law (in the fiscal year 1983 intelligence authorization act, P.L. 97-377 Section 793; and the 1985 defense authorization act, P.L. 98-473, Section 8066). Hasenfus quickly told Nicaraguan authorities of his connection with an individual—another of those Miami Cubans—who bragged of connections with Vice President George H.W. Bush. Press inquiries quickly established the truth of that claim, while the State Department's denials of any connection with the contra resupply enterprise disintegrated under a barrage of revelations of relationships between the operators and U.S. military attachés and diplomats in El Salvador and Honduras. Investigation of the tail number of the airplane led to Southern Air Transport, another former CIA proprietary, and it later turned out the plane had also been used in an earlier CIA sting aimed at proving the Nicaraguan government complicit with drug trafficking.

While controversy swirled around the events in Nicaragua, on November 5 a newspaper in Beirut, Lebanon, published a story claiming that the United States had sold weapons to Iran—an archenemy since the Iranian Hostage Crisis of 1978–80—and that President Reagan's own former national security adviser, Robert C. McFarlane, had traveled to Teheran for negotiations on some of the weapons deals. This story also turned out to be accurate. McFarlane had even taken a Bible inscribed by Reagan and a cake shaped like a key on the Teheran trip. So began the Iran-Contra Affair, a scandal that nearly brought down the Reagan presidency and, like Watergate, contained the threat of impeachment for the president. Our Reagan-era tape offerings all highlight moments in the opening months of this intense controversy.

Before it came to a close, the Iran-Contra Affair would include separate investigations by the House and Senate intelligence committees, by a presidential commission, by a joint special committee of Congress, and by a court-appointed special prosecutor. The national security adviser, an NSC staff member, a deputy director of the CIA, and an assistant secretary of state would be indicted on felony charges and put on trial. Other State Department, CIA, and Pentagon officials came close to indictment, while a former national security adviser, diplomats, and persons associated with the contra resupply enterprise pled guilty to criminal offenses. The head of the CIA would undoubtedly have been indicted also had he not died suddenly at the outset of the affair. Allegations of involvement reached as high as the vice president of the United States, and, as indicated, Ronald Reagan would be accused of violations of laws governing the export of weapons by the U.S. government, and of participation in a cover-up of the other crimes. Among the dubious policy innovations conjured to legitimize the actions that had been taken were the notion of a presidential finding, a notification to the intelligence community that furnishes legal authority to engage in a covert operation, that is "mental" (never written down), and others that applied retroactively to actions already taken.

In bare essence the Iran-Contra Affair began with twin headaches in the Middle East and Nicaragua. One horn of the dilemma started in Beirut, where between March 1984 and June 1985 seven Americans were kidnapped and held hostage, including a CIA station chief. Arms sales to Iran, understood to control the Islamic groups that had taken the Americans, were supposed to free all the hostages and also to foster a rapprochement in Iranian-American relations. The Nicaraguan horn of the White House dilemma, born of excessive zeal in pursuit of the contra rebellion, which resulted in the restrictions on the CIA already mentioned, meant that the contra rebels President Reagan had promised to support were starved for weapons, ammunition, and other military support after 1984. National Security Adviser McFarlane and his successor, Admiral John M. Poindexter, put one of their staffers, Marine Lieutenant Colonel Oliver L. North, in charge of helping the contras in addition to assigning him other duties as NSC director for counterterrorism. U.S. government officials solicited money from friendly governments (chiefly Saudi Arabia but also including Brunei and Taiwan) and private citizens to be donated to the contras, while North created a network of arms dealers to procure military items and created an organization to deliver them in the field in Nicaragua, Honduras, and Costa Rica. North's delivery enterprise also engaged in arms buying, and then in delivery of the weapons being sold to Iran. In all, more than $40 million was collected, but even that amount proved insufficient. As funds for contra military aid fell short of needs, money from the Iran sales was then diverted to contra support, hence the linkage of the two horns in the "Iran-Contra" Affair. All of this was done bypassing standard procedures and with quiet assistance from the CIA ordered by its director, William J. Casey. On the Iran side of the ledger, the arms sales never resulted in freeing all the hostages but rather in the selective releases of one or two (the CIA station chief and a military attaché were killed), and more hostages were taken as well. In Beirut the hostage business became just that, a business, and this business was conducted in the face of the official U.S. policy of making no deals with terrorists.

The crash of the Hasenfus plane began the unraveling of this operation. As leaks and press inquiries revealed more aspects to the cabal, administration denials sounded more and more hollow. On November 6 Reagan deflected a question with the comment that "speculation" on the story coming out of Beirut, where a hostage had been freed four days earlier, "that to us has no foundation," was making it more difficult to get the hostages released.[1] Forced to take some public position, President Reagan began with a nationwide television speech on November 13, 1986, in which he defended the Iran initiative and declared, "We did not—repeat—did not trade weapons or anything else for hostages, nor will we."[2]

At that very time a renewed negotiation between North and associates and Iranian representatives was underway in Germany. Reporters were also already aware that on the three occasions in which hostages had been released, weapons shipments had preceded the releases. The Iran arms sales again dominated when Reagan held a press conference on November 19, where the president refused to acknowledge any miscarriage: "I don't think a mistake was made. It was a high-risk gamble, and it was a gamble that, as I've said, I believe the circumstances warranted. And I don't see that it has been a fiasco or a great failure of any kind."[3] The press conference included a number of Reagan statements contradicting items that were already public knowledge, so much so that that night both the State Department and the White House were obliged to issue statements changing what the president had said. Even this White House statement contained the major inaccuracy that all the weapons sold to Iran by the United States or any third country (Israel had provided weapons that were shipped at U.S. behest in September 1985 and were replaced with more advanced versions from U.S. stocks) could have fit in a single airplane.

Secretary of State George Shultz had warned Reagan before his press conference against too-strenuous denials that arms had been traded for hostages, and afterward demanded a meeting with the president. The evening of November 20, Shultz and White House Chief of Staff Donald Regan met in the White House family quarters with Reagan. There Shultz told the president of discrepancies between his own recollections and what CIA Director Casey intended to tell Congress in sworn testimony the next morning. Casey went ahead with that testimony, relying upon a chronology that had been extensively doctored, with inaccuracies deliberately added and other items deleted, by Poindexter, North, CIA officers and lawyers, and other persons. Poindexter also gave false accounts to congressional investigators. On November 21, at another White House session with Regan, Poindexter, and Attorney General Edwin Meese, President Reagan ordered the Justice Department to conduct an inquiry into whether arms had really been traded for hostages. That order led to extensive destruction of documents and deletion of computer files by both Admiral Poindexter and Colonel North. The records destroyed included thousands of pages of documents and almost 6,000 electronic messages. Until this time the use of money from the Iranian weapons sales to benefit the contras had remained unknown, but Justice Department lawyers found documents that referred to the diversion. The destruction of evidence had been inadequate. Documentary evidence gathered over that weekend showed that Oliver North had in fact diverted money from the Iran arms sales to the contras.

At a Monday morning summary of the investigation, Meese had not the heart to tell the president of the diversion, though he had already informed Don Regan. That afternoon, at an NSC meeting, Meese presented a version of the affair that the Iran-Contra special prosecutor later concluded was fraudulent because it maintained that the 1985 arms shipments had not had presidential approval and was obstructive of justice because Meese had warned others that the president needed to be shielded from any mention that he had known of the Hawk missile shipment before it took place, which made him culpable. Don Regan saw Reagan again and laid more cards on the table. Regan insisted upon the immediate resignation of Admiral Poindexter. He also urged President Reagan to show he was in charge, which led to the notion of a blue ribbon committee to uncover the facts and make recommendations.

At the morning national security briefing on November 25, Poindexter told Ronald Reagan, "I'm sorry it's come to this, Mr. President."[4] They did not shake hands when he left. Minutes afterward Reagan convened his National Security Planning Group, a subcommittee of the NSC. The group strongly supported the idea of the blue ribbon inquiry. President Reagan accepted these recommendations.

The first recording of President Ronald Reagan presented here is that of his opening remarks on the morning of November 25 at a news conference where he announced the resignation of Admiral John Poindexter as national security adviser and the simultaneous firing of Colonel Oliver North. Here Reagan declares, "I was not fully informed" of "one of the activities undertaken"—the diversion of arms sale money—which raised "serious questions of propriety."[5] Reagan also announces that he will appoint a special review board, or presidential commission, to look at both aspects of the evolving Iran-Contra Affair. The situation had become serious indeed.

President Reagan's Opening Remarks
at a Press Conference
November 25, 1986

[Voices overlap]

Voice 1: Bob, the President is in the hall just behind us waiting for his queue to come on here in about thirty seconds. With him is the Secretary of State,

Mr. Shultz, and the Secretary of Defense. We don't see Mr. Admiral Poindexter. A high administration official told CBS News earlier today that Poindexter had been fired. We expect the President to tell us why and Attorney General Meese to provide the explanation that his '

Voice 2: Ladies and Gentleman the President of the United States.

Voice: Here he is, come on.

President Ronald Reagan: Last Friday, after becoming concerned whether my national security apparatus had, provided me with a security or a complete factual record with respect to the implementation of my policy toward Iran, I directed the Attorney General to undertak, undertake a review of this matter over the weekend and report to me on Monday, and yesterday Secretary Meese provided me and the White House Chief of Staff with a report on his preliminary findings, and this report led me to conclude that I was not fully informed on the nature of one of the activities undertaken in connection with this initiative. This action raises serious questions of propriety. I've just met with my National Security Advisors and Congressional Leaders to inform them of the actions that I'm taking today. Determination of the full details of this action will require further review and investigation by the Department of Justice. Looking to the future I will appoint a special review board, to conduct a comprehensive review of the role and procedures of the National Security Council staff in the conduct of foreign, and national security policy. I anticipate receiving the reports from the Attorney General and the special review board at the earliest possible date. Upon the completion of these reports I will share their findings and conclusions with the Congress, and the American people. Although not directly involved, Vice Admiral John Poindexter, has asked to be relieved of his assignment as Assistant to the President for National Security Affairs and to return to another assignment at the Navy. Lieutenant Callha [stumbles] Colonel Oliver North, has been relieved of his duties on the National Security Council Staff. I am deeply troubled that the implementation of a policy aimed at resolving a truly tragic situation in the Middle East has resulted in such controversy. As I have stated previously, I believe our policy goals toward Iran were well founded. However, the information brought to my attention yesterday convinced me that in one aspect implementation of that policy was seriously flawed. While I cannot reverse what has happened I am initiating steps including those I've announced today to assure that the implementation of all future foreign and national security policy initiatives will proceed only in accordance with my authorization. Over the past six years we've realized many foreign policy goals, I believe we can yet achieve and I intend to pursue, the objectives on which we all agree a safer more secure and stable world. And now, I'm going to ask Attorney General Meese to brief you.

Member of the Press 1: [Voices overlap] Do you still maintain that you didn't make a mistake Mr. President.

President Reagan: Hold it

Member of the Press 1: Did you make a mistake in sending arms to Tehran sir?

President Reagan: No, and I'm not taking any more questions and, just a second I am going to ask Attorney General Meese to brief you on what we presently know of what he has found out.

Member of the Press 2: Is anyone else going to be let go sir?

Member of the Press 3: Can you tell us?

Member of the Press 2: Is anyone else going to be let go?

Member of the Press 3: Is Secretary Shultz?

President Reagan: No one was let go, they chose to go.

[Voices overlap]

Member of the Press: Is Secretary Shultz going to stay sir, can you tell us if Secretary Shultz is going to stay?

Member of the Press: Can you give Secretary Shultz a vote of confidence if you feel that way?

President Reagan: May I give you, Attorney General Meese.

[Voices continue to overlap as reporters struggle to ask questions]

Attorney General Edwin Meese: That's what I'm going to say what it's all about. Why, why, why don't I tell you what, what is the situation and then I'll take your questions. On Friday afternoon, or Friday at noon, the President asked me to look into and bring together the facts ah, concerning the ah, particularly the implementation of the strategic initiative in Iran, and ah, more precisely, anything pertaining to the transfer of arms. Over the weekend this inquiry was conducted, this, uh, yesterday evening I reported to the President, we continued our inquiry and this morning the President directed that we make this information immediately available to the Congress ah, and to the ah, public through this medium at this noon, ah, let me say.

DECEMBER 1, 1986: PRESIDENT REAGAN MAKES OPENING REMARKS AT THE INITIAL MEETING OF THE SPECIAL REVIEW BOARD (TOWER COMMISSION) CREATED TO REVIEW WHITE HOUSE PARTICIPATION IN THE IRAN-CONTRA AFFAIR

Once the National Security Council officials had resigned, there was the matter of picking up the pieces. There was immediate public demand to get to the bottom of Iran-Contra. Late in the afternoon of November 25, Donald Regan gathered senior officials to consider who might participate in the presidential commission. While the White House canvassed the possibilities, President Reagan left for California, where he planned to spend Thanksgiving at his Rancho Cielo near Santa Barbara. On November 26, in Reagan's absence but with his approval, the White House issued a statement in Reagan's name on the Review Board and announced its membership. Reagan's statement declared, "I have asked the Board to review the NSC staff's proper role in operational activities, especially extremely sensitive diplomatic, military, and intelligence missions. Specifically they should look at the manner in which foreign and national security policies I established have been implemented by the NSC staff."[6]

Three men were appointed commissioners on the board. It was chaired by former Texas Republican Senator John Tower, a sixty-one-year-old politician originally elected to fill the seat vacated by Lyndon B. Johnson when LBJ moved into the White House with John Kennedy. Tower had served on the Senate Armed Services Committee from the beginning of his Washington tenure until his retirement in 1985. To give the group a bipartisan cast, there was another former senator, Edmund S. Muskie, a Democrat from Maine first elected in 1959 who had figured on the Foreign Relations Committee. Muskie had sought the Democratic presidential nomination in 1972 but lost out to George B. McGovern. He had also been President Jimmy Carter's last secretary of state from May 1980 to the end of Carter's term in office. A national security expert completed the group. He was retired Air Force Lieutenant General Brent Scowcroft who had previously (1983) led a presidential commission studying strategic nuclear forces. General Scowcroft had headed the White House military office under Nixon, had been deputy national security adviser during the Ford administration in 1974–75, and had succeeded Henry Kissinger as national security adviser from November 1975 to January 1977. The Tower Board would eventually assemble a staff of twenty-three persons.

On December 1 the members of the board gathered at the White House for their first working meeting. Back from California, President Reagan joined the commissioners. This selection contains the president's remarks on that occasion. The TWA hijacking and the *Achille Lauro* affair, respectively, which President Reagan refers to in these comments, were terrorist seizures of an American airliner and an Italian cruise ship, both of which occurred during 1985. Reagan's reference to Grenada is to the U.S. invasion of that Caribbean island in October 1983. The mention of Iran is a direct reference to the matters at issue in the Iran-Contra Affair.

President Reagan's express orders to the board members were, "I say, go to it!" The president also stated his commitment to "learn how this happened," with his full support and cooperation. If an independent counsel (i.e., a special prosecutor, as in Watergate) proved necessary, Reagan said he would welcome that appointment. But the executive order President Reagan issued simultaneously to govern the activities of the Review Board (No. 12575, December 1, 1986) proved much less expansive. The order provided that government officials would only give information to the Tower Board "upon request" and "to the extent permitted by law."[7] The investigators were given a sixty-day time limit. In practice he refused to permit the board access to his own diary notes except as approved by his lawyer Peter Wallison. Reagan also rejected the possibility of the board utilizing his authority as commander in chief to compel testimony from either John Poindexter or Oliver North, which meant the commission made its investigation without input from either of the officials accused of orchestrating the Iran-Contra Affair. Congress ultimately deemed this inquiry insufficient and created its own joint committee to look into Iran-Contra. A special prosecutor was also appointed.

President Reagan's Opening Remarks
at the First Meeting of the Special Review Board
December 1, 1986, 11:08 A.M.

President Ronald Reagan: Well, Senator Tower, Secretary Muskie, General Scowcroft, I am grateful to all you for agreeing to serve on this board, I know it will take a lot of your time, but your experience and expertise in this inquiry are extremely important in evaluating the National Security Council's staff operations and, providing recommendations on how it should operate.

The purpose of your undertaking is to review past implementation of Administration policies and to conduct a comprehensive study of the future role and procedures, of the National Security Council Staff in foreign and national security policy. I would like you to focus on that staff and one, develop policy; two, coordinate with other agencies; and three, implement the President's policies; and four, oversee the implementation of these policies by others. I hope that you would take particular care to look into the question of whether and under what circumstances the National Security Council staff, was and should be directly involved in the operational aspects of sensitive diplomatic military or intelligence missions such as the *Achille Lauro*, the TWA hijacking, and, Grenada, and Iran.

In addition, I have, directed the National Security Council staff not to participate in the actual operations associated with such activities pending the outcome of the report by the special review board. You will have the full cooperation of all agencies of the executive branch and the White House staff, in carrying out your assignment. And I want to assure you and the American people, that I want all the facts to come out. Upon learning about a possible transfer of funds from the sale of arms to Iran to those fighting the Sandinista government we acted to learn the facts. And we'll continue to share the actions we take and the information we obtain with the American people, and the Congress.[8]

The appointment of this Board, and the stature of its membership are a demonstration of a commitment to learn how this happened, and how it can be prevented in the future. The Department of Justice investigation is continuing with my full support and cooperation, and if they determine an independent council is called for I would welcome that appointment. If we're to maintain confidence in our government's foreign policy apparatus, there must be a full and complete airing of all the facts, and I am determined to get all of the facts out and take whatever action is necessary. The work of this Board, and the Department of Justice investigation will do, just that. Just as soon as your findings and recommendations are complete, they will be shared with the American people and the Congress. So, with that, I say, go to it!

Member of the Press: Mr. President, when ah, the Attorney General said you were not fully informed, and you said you were not fully informed, did that mean that you never knew anything about Contra funding with Iran sales money?

President Reagan: Helen,[9] I answered that question, I'm not going to take — we have a meeting now to go into, but ah, I answered that question a couple of times.

Helen Thomas: Well does that mean that you, you had no knowledge at all?

President Reagan: That's what I said. [sighs]

Member of the Press: Mr. President are you willing to call Congress back in for a special session? [Pause]

President Reagan: That is under discussion and there's been no decision yet, but we want to work with the Congress. [Voices overlap]

DECEMBER 2, 1986: PRESIDENT REAGAN'S ADDRESS TO THE NATION ON THE IRAN-CONTRA AFFAIR

President Reagan, responding to encouragement to get out in front of public opinion on the Iran-Contra Affair, took a series of measures to establish that he was in control of the situation. Not least among them were his efforts to speak to the American people. In a nationwide television address from the Oval Office on November 13, Reagan explained the affair as flowing purely from his concern to rebuild relations with Iran. That version collapsed with the revelation of the diversion of money to the contra rebels. Reagan made a second attempt in another address televised from the Oval Office at noon on December 2. This time his speech resulted from a report that morning by Attorney General Edwin Meese, who now argued that the appointment of a Watergate-style special prosecutor had become unavoidable politically and the president stood to gain credit by supporting such a move. Reagan also used the opportunity to announce his appointment of a new national security adviser, Frank Carlucci, to replace the ousted John Poindexter.

President Reagan had gathered senior administration figures and legislators prior to his speech to go over the ground he would cover. The group included Vice President George H.W. Bush; Senators Trent Lott (R-MS), Robert Dole (R-KS), and Alan K. Simpson (R-WY); Representatives Richard Cheney (R-MI) and Robert Michel (R-IL), the House minority leader. White House Chief of Staff Donald Regan also attended and took notes at the meeting that were subsequently given to the special prosecutor who investigated the Iran-Contra Affair. According to Regan's notes, the president had outlined the affair and the statement he was about to make. No one was satisfied, not even Don Regan, who put the key question, "Mr. President, what did you know—when did you know it? That's the question on these fellows' minds. Tell them what you know." Reagan spoke reassuringly but did not succeed in quieting fears among his party leaders, who asked questions about the arms shipments and the opposition to them by cabinet secretaries, and who insisted that the issue was huge and that sweeping changes would be necessary. Regan's notes cite Lott, Cheney, and Simpson as saying they needed better answers. Reagan denied knowledge of the diversion and maintained that only Poindexter and North had known about it.[10] The previous day in congressional testimony Oliver North had invoked his right to avoid self-incrimination to avoid answering questions on Iran-Contra, and John Poindexter would do the same on December 3.

Despite arguments from public relations experts who advised President Reagan to emphasize his active management of White House policy machinery, notably by assuming responsibility for all that had happened, the president's pronouncements remained oddly tentative. In his first speech, Reagan had said nothing of responsibility. At the press conference revealing the diversion and the NSC shake-up, Reagan had briefly mentioned that the responsibility was his and his alone (see the text that appears earlier), but answering a question had insisted, "I don't feel that I have anything to defend about at all."[11] This attitude extended into December, by which time there was even more pressure on Reagan. The president essentially took the position that his professions of determination to get to the bottom of the affair substituted for any need to take responsibility, and that was the case on December 2, when Reagan not only voiced support for a special prosecutor but also supported a congressional investigation and spoke again of the Tower Board.

On the larger issues of the diversions and of the illegal arms sales to Iran, Reagan's comments were ambiguous, and only led back to the emphasis on investigation. "I can appreciate why some of these things are difficult to comprehend," President Reagan said, "and you're entitled to have your questions answered" (see following text). The president declared, "I want to state again that it is my policy to oppose terrorism throughout the world, to punish those who support it, and to make common cause with those who seek to suppress it" (see text below). Reagan did not address how his declared policy could have led to arms sales to Iran.

President Reagan's Nationally Televised Speech from the Oval Office
December 2, 1986, 12:00 P.M.

Good afternoon. Since the outset of the controversy over our policy relating to Iran, I've done everything in my power to make all the facts concerning this matter known to the American people. I could appreciate why some of things are difficult to comprehend, and you're entitled to have your questions answered, and that's why I've pledged to get to the bottom of this matter.

And I have said earlier that I would welcome the appointment of an independent council to look into allegations of illegality in the sale of arms to Iran and the use of funds from these sales to assist the forces, opposing the Sandinista government in Nicaragua. This morning Attorney General Meese advised me of his decision, that his investigation has turned up reasonable grounds, to believe that further investigation by an independent counsel would be appropriate. Accordingly, consistent with his responsibilities under the Independent Counsel Act, I immediately urged him to apply to the court here in Washington, for the appointment of an independent counsel.

Yesterday, I had my first meeting with the Special Review Board. That review board is made up of three men of unquestioned integrity and broad experience in foreign and national security policy. In the meeting with the Board, they promised me a tough, no nonsense investigation, and I promised them the full cooperation of the White House staff and all agencies of the executive branch. No area of the NSC staff's activities will be immune from review. And when the Board reports to me, I intend to make their conclusions and recommendations available to Congress, and to the American people. With the appointment of an independent counsel, we will have in place a dual system for assuring a thorough review of all aspects of this matter. If illegal acts were undertaken, those who did so will be brought to justice. If actions in implementing my policy were taken without my authorization, knowledge, or concurrence, this will be exposed and appropriate corrective steps will be implemented.

I recognize fully the interest of Congress in this matter, and the fact that, in performing its important oversight and legislative role, Congress will want to inquire into what occurred. We will cooperate fully with these inquiries. I have already taken the unprecedented step of permitting two of my former national security advisors to testify before a committee of Congress. These Congressional inquiries should continue, but I do believe Congress can carry out its duties in getting the facts, without disrupting the orderly conduct of a vital part of this nation's government. Accordingly, I am urging the Congress, to consider some mechanism that will consolidate its inquiries. Such a step has already been requested by several members of Congress. I support the idea.

In closing, I want to state again, that it is my policy to oppose terrorism throughout the world, to punish those who support it, and to make common cause with those who seek to suppress it. This has been my policy and will continue to be my policy. If the investigative processes now set in motion, are given an opportunity to work, all the facts concerning Iran and the transfer of funds to assist the, anti-Sandinista forces, will shortly be made public. Then the American people, you, will, be the final arbiters of this controversy. You will have all the facts and will be able to judge for themselves, yourselves. I am pleased to announce today, that I am appointing, Frank Carlucci, as Assistant to the President for National Security Affairs. A former Deputy Secretary of Defense, Deputy Director of the CIA, and Ambassador to Portugal, Mr. Carlucci has the depth of experience in foreign affairs, defense, and intelligence matters, that uniquely qualify him to serve as my National Security Advisor. The American people will be well served by his tenure.

Thank you. God bless you.

DECEMBER 4, 1986: PRESIDENT REAGAN MAKES REMARKS AND ANSWERS A FEW QUESTIONS FROM REPORTERS AT HIS FIRST MEETING WITH NEW NATIONAL SECURITY ADVISER FRANK C. CARLUCCI

In the least scripted of our selections from President Ronald Reagan, two days following his announcement of the Carlucci appointment, Reagan meets with Carlucci in the Oval Office, and some of their conversation is recorded. Carlucci was a longtime government official whom Reagan brought back to Washington from private business, where he had been chairman of Sears World Trade Incorporated. Carlucci had been Reagan's first deputy secretary of defense and also deputy director of central intelligence during the Carter administration. He had been a diplomat from 1956 to 1969 and had then held a succession of senior jobs in the Nixon and Ford administrations. In their White

House meetings, Carlucci had a strong sense of where he had to go to establish a sense of proper organization for the National Security Council staff, and President Reagan appears entirely supportive of Carlucci's intentions.

Defense Secretary Caspar Weinberger separately told reporters on this day that it would have been highly unusual for President Reagan not to have been briefed on all aspects of U.S. activities and that he felt the president had acted upon poor advice. Simultaneously the Justice Department applied to the courts to permit the appointment of a special prosecutor in investigating Iran-Contra, while the Senate and House of Representatives each formed investigating committees (later combined into a single joint committee) to look into these matters.

As for the NSC staff, Frank Carlucci insisted on having his own people in key positions, beginning with his deputy, who would be Army General Colin L. Powell, an appointment the White House announced on December 18, after lawyers had vetted Powell's own role in the Iranian arms shipments (he had been a top aide to Caspar Weinberger). Powell's initial meeting with President Reagan occurred in early January, when he and Carlucci went to the Oval Office early in the morning to present the national security briefing. It was the occasion on which Carlucci presented his plan for reorganizing the staff in the wake of Iran-Contra. Carlucci explained that he was getting the NSC staff out of covert operations, that the political-military office Oliver North had headed would be abolished, and that Powell would review all ongoing CIA covert operations. On this and other occasions, Reagan said little until Carlucci had finished making recommendations, and then would merely nod his head, as if to acknowledge what would be done in his name. One time, after a session on nuclear arms reductions, Carlucci turned to Powell and complained, "My God, we didn't sign on to run this country!"[12]

President Reagan's Initial Meeting with Frank Carlucci
December 4, 1986

[Mumbling, laughter, and the sound of cameras.]

Frank Carlucci: I enjoyed [unintelligible].

President Ronald Reagan: [Unintelligible] this. [unintelligible]

[Cameras]

Frank Carlucci: It did not exist under, Truman or Eisenhower, I think.[13] Uh, I think it started to grow under Kennedy. I remember coming here

President Reagan: Yeah. When would that be?

Frank Carlucci: but it [the NSC staff] was very small.

Voice: Thank you. [Camera noises, door closing]

Voice: [Unintelligible—"Do you think it was failing"?] when you were here?

Frank Carlucci: What?

President Reagan: That's a good question.

Voice: [Technician comment, door closes]

Frank Carlucci: I wanted to let you know I have, I have selected a Deputy. It's someone you know. It's General Colin Powell, who was Cap's military aide, the two-star general, the, the black general. Always used to sit with Cap. He's a marvelous man. And,

President Reagan: Fine.

Voice: Fine.

President Reagan: I remember. He's a real smart guy.

Frank Carlucci: He's a very good man. Ah, I'm sure Don [Regan] will ask you at the appropriate time if you wouldn't mind sending him a message or giving him a call because this will hurt his military career, and ah, if he can say that he has been asked to do this by the commander-in-chief, he can put that on the record, ah, he will so—

[Tape ends.]

DECEMBER 6, 1986: PRESIDENT REAGAN MAKES NEW EXPLANATIONS OF THE IRAN-CONTRA AFFAIR IN A WEEKEND RADIO SPEECH

On December 5 Republican congressional leaders met with President Reagan to describe their doubts about public confidence in the wake of the Iran-Contra revelations. The congressmen were certainly correct to point out public skepticism that Ronald Reagan had known nothing about the operation. Reagan kept to his story. The president has been quoted as telling this group that "I could put my hand on the Bible and swear I didn't know it and I wouldn't jeopardize my ticket up there."[14] The leaders reiterated that President Reagan should make a full disclosure to the American people.

Just after noontime the next day, President Reagan made one of his weekly radio addresses, on this occasion from Camp David, where he had gone for the weekend. He had deliberately chosen the less formal venue to evoke some of the atmosphere that used to attend the "fireside chats" which President Franklin Delano Roosevelt had given on the radio. In the speech Ronald Reagan acknowledged for the first time that the execution of his policies "was flawed" and that "mistakes were made" (see following text). Reagan continued to insist that his policy, conceived broadly, was the correct one, that he had acted immediately upon learning of irregularities, and that everything was being done to deal with the consequences of the matter.

President Reagan's Radio Address to the Nation on Iran-Contra, Camp David, December 6, 1986, 12:06 P.M.

I'm speaking to you today from Camp David, and because the atmosphere here is a bit more informal than everyday Washington, I thought it would be a good opportunity to think and reflect with you about those crucial foreign policy matters so much in the news lately. It's also a chance to do something I've wanted to do throughout the course of these events and that's share some personal thoughts with you, to speak to you, the American people, from the heart.

I realize you must be disappointed and probably confused with all the furor of the last couple of weeks, you must be asking what were we doing in the Middle East, what was our policy, where was it wrong, were we engaged in some kind of shenanigans that blew up in our face? I can understand if these are the questions you're asking and I'd like to provide some answers.

First of all the Middle East is critically important to our nation's security. Right now it's a major trouble spot that could easily set off the sparks of a wider conflict. Much of our effort has been aimed at stopping terrorism, putting an end to the bombing of innocent civilians and the kidnapping of hostages, especially our own citizens, and bringing about an end to the bloody war between Iran and Iraq. When word came to me that individuals in Iran, including some members of the government there, had asked through an intermediary, in a third country, for a meeting with a representative of our government, I said yes. And even though these were responsible elements in Iran, that might be able to assist us in stopping the violence and possibly helping us get back the hostages being held in Lebanon, there was a risk involved. But I believed then, and believe now, there was a greater risk in doing nothing, of not trying.

So I gave the order to proceed. We had some notable success, there was some reduction in terrorism, and three of our hostages were released, one at a time, and others were about to follow. Then someone in the government of Iran, leaked information about our contacts, with Iran, to a newspaper in Lebanon. You know the rest. This effort to establish a relationship with responsible moderates in Iran came to light and was broken off. But I think you can see the purposes behind our policy, to end the war in the Middle East, to prevent Soviet expansionism, to halt terrorism, and to help gain release of American hostages.

But now, I want to speak to you about something else, not the policies themselves, but how they were carried out, and while we are still seeking all the facts, it's obvious that the execution of these policies was flawed, and mistakes were made. Let me just say it was not my intent to do business with Khomeini [Ayatollah Ruhollah Khomeini, supreme religious leader of Iran], to trade weapons for hostages, nor to undercut our policy of anti-terrorism. And let me say again, I know the stories of the past few weeks have been distressing I'm deeply disappointed this initiative has resulted in such a controversy, and I regret it's caused such concern and consternation. But I pledge to you I will set things right.

That's what I'm doing now. When our Iranian initiative came to light, I spoke to you from the Oval Office and explained it. When revelations regarding the transfer of money from Iran to those attempting to fight the Sandinista government, were reported to me they were immediately shared with you and the Congress. I then appointed a distinguished, independent board, chaired by former Senator and ambassador John Tower, to review our National Security Council, staff apparatus. And to insure a complete legal inquiry, I urged the appointment of an independent counsel. They used to be called special prosecutors, and that's what they are, they just, changed the title. And finally I have stated, we will cooperate fully, with the Congress, as they undertake their proper review.

If illegal acts were undertaken in the implementation of our policy, those who did so, will be brought to justice. If actions in implementing my policy were taken without my authorization, knowledge or concurrence, this will be exposed and appropriate corrective steps will be implemented. I will continue to make all the facts known, surrounding this matter. We live in a country that requires we operate within rules and laws, all of us. Just cause and deep concern and, noble ends, can never, be reason enough to justify, improper actions or excessive means.

In these past six years, we have done much together to restore the faith and confidence and respect of our people, and our country. We've done so, not by avoiding challenges, or denying problems, but when confronted with these problems, dealing with them directly and honestly. We will continue to do so. Until next week, thanks for listening and God bless you.

NOTES

INTRODUCTION

1. Betty Sue Flowers remarks at conference "Presidential Tapes," John F. Kennedy Library, National Archives and Records Administration (NARA), February 16, 2003.

2. All quotes from speakers at the Presidential Tapes Conference held by the Kennedy Library.

3. John Powers, "The History of Presidential Audio Recordings and the Archival Issues Surrounding Their Use," CIDS Paper (Lyndon Baines Johnson Library, NARA), July 12, 1996, quoted on p. 9.

4. Dwight D. Eisenhower, *Crusade in Europe* (Garden City, NY: Doubleday, 1948), p. 38.

5. "The Kennedy Tapes," *Newsweek* Magazine, July 4, 1983, p. 19.

6. "Special Supplement to the Register of Presidential Recordings of White House Meetings and Telephone Conversations, 1962–1963," John F. Kennedy Library, NARA, p. 53.

7. Dudley Clendinen, "Log Shows Kennedy Secretly Taped 325 Talks," *New York Times*, February 5, 1982, quoted on p. A12.

8. Martin Schram and Haynes Johnson, "Robert Kennedy Used Tapes for Book on Missile Crisis," *Washington Post*, February 5, 1982, quoted on p. A20.

9. Ibid.

10. These transcripts are important historical records but were created by harried secretaries who were simultaneously doing much other work for President Johnson. The secretaries were also not familiar with the subjects of many of LBJ's conversations, and the task was one they disliked. The resulting transcripts are incomplete and contain

numerous errors, to the degree that archivists advise against regarding them as authoritative sources. These records thus form a starting point and reference for transcription and need to be used with care.

11. Michael R. Beschloss, *Taking Charge: The Johnson White House Tapes, 1963–1964* (New York: Simon & Schuster, 1997), p. 549.

12. Richard M. Nixon, *RN: The Memoirs of Richard Nixon*, vol. 1 (New York: Warner Books, 1979), p. 621.

13. Ibid., p. 620.

14. H.R. Haldeman, "The Nixon White House Tapes: The Decision to Record Presidential Conversations" *Prologue* (summer 1988): 80.

15. Ibid., p. 83.

16. Ibid., p. 84.

17. Butterfield remarks at Presidential Tapes Conference, Kennedy Library, February 16, 2003.

18. Haldeman, "The Nixon White House Tapes," 86.

19. David Frost in *I Gave Them a Sword* (New York: William Morrow, 1978), reprints the contents of this and two other exclusive interviews and provides Frost's commentary as well as an account of how the series came about.

20. Nixon, *RN*, vol. II, p. 451.

21. Gerald R. Ford, *A Time to Heal: The Autobiography of Gerald R. Ford* (New York: Berkley Books, 1980), p. 178.

22. James Cannon remarks, Presidential Tapes Conference, Kennedy Library, February 16, 2003.

23. The president has an aide assigned directly to him from each of the armed forces. These individuals are personal assistants and are not to be confused with the so-called "military assistant," a senior officer who serves as a liaison between the White House and the Joint Chiefs of Staff and is usually located within the National Security Council staff. In addition, for somewhat over a year in 1961–62 President Kennedy employed General Maxwell D. Taylor as his "special military representative," heading a sort of mini–National Security Council staff focused on military matters. President Johnson brought Taylor back in this capacity in 1967–68. There is also an umbrella unit, the White House Military Office, which actually manages all the assorted things the military does for the president, everything from running the president's airplane and helicopter (Air Force One and Marine One), to providing telephone, radio, and other services through the White House Communications Agency (WHCA). The president's aides, the Military Office, and WHCA all figure in the story of the White House videotapes.

FRANKLIN D. ROOSEVELT

1. Secretary Stimson's diary indicates he did not attend the September 27 meeting, sending Assistant Secretary Patterson in his place, but President Roosevelt's appointment calendar for this date notes Stimson's presence. Incidentally, the Stimson diary is replete with entries that show his basic opposition to integration in the military.

HARRY S. TRUMAN

1. Robert Butler, U.S. ambassador to Australia from July 1946 to May 1948, was a Minnesota businessman appointed to this diplomatic post.

2. General George C. Marshall, secretary of state for President Truman from 1947 to 1949.

3. Robert A. Lovett, undersecretary of state from 1947 to 1951.

4. Roy Atherton, career diplomat, ambassador to Canada from July 1943 to August 1948.

5. Butler actually became ambassador to Cuba in 1948 and remained in Havana until early 1951.

DWIGHT D. EISENHOWER

1. Dwight D. Eisenhower, *The White House Years: Mandate for Change, 1953–1956* (New York: Doubleday, 1963), p. 282.

2. Robert A. Caro, *The Years of Lyndon Johnson: Master of the Senate* (New York: Alfred A. Knopf, 2002), p. 529.

3. Ibid., pp. 531–33.

4. Section One was the part of the bill that specified treaties and agreements were not automatically part of U.S. law. In Senator George's 1954 version, this section merely stated that treaties could not contravene the Constitution, a position that President Eisenhower was willing to accept.

5. Although this passage of about three minutes contains much that cannot be discerned, it is clear that Senator George is explaining what happened to the Bricker amendment, and with Senator Bricker, in the Senate during the 1954 term of Congress.

6. Probably senatorial terminology for locking pending legislation up in a committee, as would in fact happen in this case.

JOHN F. KENNEDY

1. Dan Balz, "Johnson's Tapes a Treasure Under Seal for Fifty Years," *Washington Post*, February 5, 1982, quoted on p. A22.

2. Robert E. Baker, "Leader Calls March 'Revolution,'" *Washington Post*, August 26, 1963, p. A1.

3. *Public Papers of the Presidents of the United States: John F. Kennedy, 1963* (Washington, D.C.: Government Printing Office, 1964), p. 645.

4. The National Association for the Advancement of Colored People (NAACP), founded on February 12, 1909, was the oldest of the civil rights organizations.

5. A reference to African American unrest, as will become clear later in this conversation.

6. The Congress on Racial Equality (CORE) was founded in 1942.

7. Taylor Branch, in his history of civil rights *Parting the Waters: America in the King Years, 1954–63* (New York: Simon & Schuster, 1988, p. 886), reports that Reverend King quipped of Eisenhower, "Isn't he a Democrat when he goes to church?" The word "church" can be made out at this point in the recording but the remainder of that quote is obscured by the laughter and the many voices speaking.

8. Just over a month earlier, General Taylor had made an inspection visit to South Vietnam together with Secretary McNamara (and a group that had included William E. Colby as well). Their report had observed that, "Although some, and perhaps an increasing number of GVN military officers are becoming hostile to the government, they are more hostile to the Viet Cong [the Vietnamese communists] than to the government and at least for the near future they will continue to perform their military duties." Memorandum from the Chairman of the Joint Chiefs of Staff and the Secretary

of Defense to the President, "Report of the McNamara-Taylor Mission to South Vietnam," October 2, 1963, *Foreign Relations of the United States, 1961–1963, vol. IV: Vietnam, August–December 1963* (Washington, D.C.: Government Printing Office, 1991), p. 337.

9. South Vietnamese generals had already approached the Kennedy administration in August 1963 about Washington's support for a coup to oust Diem, and Kennedy had approved, then rescinded, a cable giving a green light for U.S. support. The August cable episode became notorious among U.S. officials.

10. This is probably a reference to General Harkins' opposition to a coup within the U.S. Embassy, the root cause of differences between Ambassador Lodge and Harkins. The general had been effectively kept from knowledge of the coup plots through Lodge's reliance on the CIA-Conein channel to the South Vietnamese generals. One of them, however, had himself mentioned the plot to Harkins at a diplomatic reception a few days earlier.

11. Political Adviser, a designated position for diplomats in United States joint commands.

12. The cable as sent at this point reads: "On coup contacts we will maintain continuous guidance and will expect equally continuous reporting with prompt account of any important divergences in assessments of Harkins and [deleted—a probable reference to Conein or CIA]."

13. That is, for the ambassador to act upon ("Action"), but for the information of both men.

14. "Chops" is government shorthand for bearing responsibility to approve or act; the speaker wants to ensure that Lodge's primacy is recognized in the manner of dispatch of the cable.

15. Here Kennedy reads from General Harkins' cable to Washington (Harkins-Taylor, MAC 2028, October 30, 1963, 4:00 P.M., Paragraph 10).

16. The South Vietnamese 5th Division's loyalties were uncertain as of this date. Its refusal to intervene when the coup took place two days later would be decisive in the downfall of Diem.

LYNDON B. JOHNSON

1. Memo, Walt Rostow–Dean Rusk, January 10, 1964 (declassified August 19, 1993). Lyndon Baines Johnson Library, Walt Rostow Papers, box 13, folder: Southeast Asia.

2. Walt W. Rostow, *The Diffusion of Power, 1957–1972: An Essay in Recent History* (New York: Macmillan, 1972), pp. 505–6.

3. General Maxwell D. Taylor, "Memorandum of a Conversation between the Joint Chiefs of Staff and the President," March 4, 1964. In Department of State, *Foreign Relations of the United States, 1964–1968, vol. 1, Vietnam, 1964* (Washington, D.C.: Government Printing Office, 1992), p. 129. This source will be cited hereafter as "FRUS," together with a volume number and date.

4. In edited portions of this conversation President Johnson and Bundy discuss the possibility of appointing a woman foreign policy expert, Dorothy Fosdick, to the NSC staff and also a request made by former president Dwight D. Eisenhower to visit the Lawrence Livermore National Research Laboratory.

5. Memcon of 537th NSC Meeting, August 4, 1964: FRUS 1964–68, vol. I, p. 608.

6. Department of Defense Chronology, August 28, 1964. Ibid., p. 609.

7. Ibid.

RICHARD. M. NIXON

1. Alexander M. Haig Jr., Memorandum for the President's Files, March 26, 1971 (declassified April 19, 1974). National Archives: Nixon Library Project: White House Special Files, President's Office Files, box 87.

2. Bernard C. Nalty, *Air War Over South Vietnam, 1968–1975* (Washington, D.C.: Air Force History and Museums Program, 2000), p. 271.

3. Robert Mann, *A Grand Delusion: America's Descent into Vietnam* (New York: Basic Books, 2001), quoted on p. 679.

4. This is actually a reference to the Palestinian crisis of September 1970. The events took place principally in Jordan and included terrorist hijackings of aircraft to fields in Jordan, where they were destroyed, along with the attempted overthrow of the Jordanian royal government and certain Israeli moves intended to dissuade Syria from meddling (the Syrians had important influence in Lebanon, which may have triggered Nixon's thought in this instance).

5. A reference to U.S. diplomacy during the India-Pakistan War of 1971, in which the United States "tilted" in favor of Pakistan. Nixon's rendition here of his reluctance leaves unsaid the U.S. debt to Pakistan for its help in opening channels to China, which President Nixon was about to visit—a trip from which he counted on major political gains.

6. Nixon refers to a colloquialism then current in the language that denoted people who refused to exercise initiative, or were passive in damaging ways.

7. Nixon refers to the United States having already notified Beijing of the list of journalists who would be included in the president's entourage.

8. Richard M. Nixon, *RN: The Memoirs of Richard Nixon,* vol. 2. (New York: Warner Books, 1979), p. 109.

9. Nixon's personal secretary, Rosemary Woods, ultimately took responsibility for erasing the June 20 taped conversation at a later time when she was attempting to create a record from the audiotapes. Nixon's memoir (*RN,* vol. 2, p. 472–74) gives a version of how that could have happened. There is no way to establish exactly who erased the June 20 conversation, however, and Nixon is known to have listened to these tapes also. The tapes were normally kept locked in a cabinet. Investigators have established that erasure started and stopped at a number of points and was redone at least five, and perhaps as many as nine times.

10. Stanley I. Kutler, ed. *Abuse of Power: The New Nixon Tapes* (New York: The Free Press, 1997), p. 51.

11. H.R. Haldeman, *The Haldeman Diaries: Inside the Nixon White House.* (New York: G.P. Putnam's Sons, 1994), p. 474.

12. John D. Ehrlichman, *Witness to Power: The Nixon Years* (New York: Pocket Books, 1982), p. 315.

13. H.R. Haldeman with Joseph DiMona, *The Ends of Power* (New York: Dell Books, 1978), quoted on p. 63.

14. *The Watergate Hearings: Break-in and Cover-up: Proceedings of the Senate Select Committee on Presidential Campaign Activities as Edited by the Staff of The New York Times* (New York: Bantam Books, 1973), p. 786.

15. Ibid., p. 603.

16. Haldeman and DiMona, *Ends of Power,* quoted on p. 67.

17. *Watergate Hearings*, p. 787. John Ehrlichman writes that "Walter's memoranda of the June 23 meeting and subsequent events (written about a week later) are striking examples of selective recollection and ass-covering" (*Witness to Power*, footnote p. 319).

18. H.R. Haldeman, *Haldeman Diaries*, p. 475.

19. CIA headquarters, in Langley, Virginia, is across the Potomac River from FBI headquarters and from the White House.

20. The Watergate Special Prosecution Force transcript of this conversation, and that by Stanley Kutler, read at this point: "They, they were approached by the Cubans. That's what Dahlberg has to say, the Texans too. Is that the idea."

21. A few months earlier Director Helms had approached John Ehrlichman with the CIA's legal problem in attempting to deal with a forthcoming book by former CIA officer Victor Marchetti and State Department employee John Marks, titled *The CIA and the Cult of Intelligence*, which would have been highly revelatory on agency operations. Ehrlichman cooperated in legal maneuvers to suppress large portions of the text. This is the only instance in which the Nixon White House is known to have protected the CIA from anything.

22. Charles ("Chuck") Colson handled many White House activities of a questionable nature, such as supervising the "Plumbers" unit that had originally employed both Hunt and James McCord. Nixon here expresses relief that those "dirty tricks" operations will not be revealed as a result of the Watergate break-in itself.

23. The Watergate Special Prosecution Task Force transcript reads at this point: Nixon: "Well, not sure of their analysis, I'm not going to get that involved, I'm [unintelligible]."

24. One of our transcribers heard this as "And you see a time . . . ," making it a question, or at least an instance of Haldeman summarizing a Nixon view.

25. Presumably a reference to CIA's willingness to voluntarily go to the FBI, as Nixon wanted, to shut down the Watergate investigation.

26. Richard Nixon and H.R. Haldeman are known to have been present at this meeting, but the voice seems different from Nixon's. Ronald L. Ziegler was present for at least a portion of the meeting. The president may have turned away from the microphones or there may be a third person in the Oval Office.

27. A Senate Watergate Committee transcript of this conversation made in 1973 reads, at this point: "[unintelligible] here is the possibility that one of our guys—that probably has some significance to the question [unintelligible]."

28. This is a reference to 1960, when Allen Dulles led the CIA and the Eisenhower administration was planning a covert operation against Cuba in the midst of the presidential campaign that Richard Nixon lost to John F. Kennedy. That turned into the Bay of Pigs, which Dulles conducted on behalf of Kennedy and which Nixon is hoping to use now to help him get the CIA to suppress the Watergate investigation.

29. At the time of the Bay of Pigs, the operations directorate of the CIA that carried out the invasion was headed by Richard M. Bissell, with Helms a subordinate official. Helms is known to have deliberately avoided knowledge of the plan to avoid being implicated in what he evidently believed would be a failure.

30. This exchange continues Nixon's and Haldeman's colloquy on the Bay of Pigs, starting from the matter of CIA briefings for presidential candidates. Nixon believed he had been ambushed by Kennedy in their fourth televised debate during the 1960 campaign, on October 21, 1960, and in a subsequent press release. Kennedy argued in favor of supporting anti-Castro Cubans in the overthrow of the Castro government in Cuba. Nixon, as vice president in the Eisenhower administration, knew of the existence of the CIA plan and felt he had to remain silent. He believed this gave Kennedy an advantage

in the election and carried the grudge ever after. In 1960, Kennedy received CIA briefings covering worldwide matters on July 23 and September 19; Kennedy's vice presidential running mate, Lyndon B. Johnson, was briefed on July 28. CIA director Allen Dulles told Nixon in the summer of 1960 that Kennedy had been told some things about Cuba, but not too much. It cannot be established from the record exactly what Kennedy knew about what became the Bay of Pigs as of the time of the presidential debates. Kennedy received a detailed briefing on the Cuba plan only after the election, on November 27, 1960. Now, in 1972, Nixon discusses what briefings should be provided the Democratic candidates in the current presidential election campaign.

31. Nixon refers to his February 1972 visit to the People's Republic of China, the U.S. mining of Haiphong Harbor in North Vietnam on May 8, 1972, and his summit conference with leaders of the Soviet Union later that month.

32. Nixon is reciting public opinion polling data from the Eisenhower years, approval ratings for the president. Here and as the conversation proceeds, Nixon shows himself to be a master of the poll data.

33. The Senate Watergate Committee transcript at this point reads: "We can 48, 49 by the nearest count."

GERALD R. FORD

1. *New York Times*, September 8, 1974, p. 21.

2. Ibid., July 18, 1975, p. 1.

3. Gerald R. Ford, *A Time to Heal: The Autobiography of Gerald R. Ford* (New York: Berkley Books, 1980), p. 299.

4. Ronald L. Nessen, second press secretary to President Gerald R. Ford.

5. White House Communications Agency, pronounced "Waca."

RONALD REAGAN

1. *Public Papers of the Presidents of the United States: Ronald Reagan, 1986* (Washington, D.C.: Government Printing Office, 1989), vol. II, pp. 1521–2.

2. Ibid., p. 1548.

3. Ibid., p. 1575.

4. John Prados, *Keepers of the Keys: A History of the National Security Council from Truman to Bush* (New York: William Morrow, 1991), quoted on p. 535.

5. *Public Papers of the Presidents*, p. 1587.

6. Ibid., p. 1588.

7. Ibid., p. 1593.

8. Reagan's delivery of the last several sentences differs from the text printed in the official *Public Papers of the Presidents of the United States: Ronald Reagan, 1986*: "And I want to assure you and the American people that I want all the facts to come out about learning of a possible transfer of funds from the sale of arms to Iran to those fighting the Sandinista government. We acted to learn the facts, and we'll continue to share the actions we take and the information we obtain with the American people and the Congress" (vol. 2, p. 1591).

9. Helen Thomas, correspondent for the United Press International.

10. Lawrence E. Walsh, *Firewall: The Iran-Contra Conspiracy and Cover-up* (New York: W.W. Norton, 1997), p. 366.

11. *Public Papers of the Presidents*, 1986, vol. 2, p. 1574.

12. Colin L. Powell with Joseph E. Persico, *My American Journey* (New York: Random House, 1995), quoted on p. 334.

13. Carlucci is giving Ronald Reagan a brief account of the origins of the NSC staff. Actually, there was a tiny NSC staff under Truman, who first used a White House staff person (Averell Harriman) on a special mission. Eisenhower built a larger staff and regularized it, but it was in the administrations of John F. Kennedy and Lyndon Johnson that the NSC staff began to acquire an operational role, which was greatly expanded by Henry Kissinger during the Nixon administration. See John Prados, *Keepers of the Keys: A History of the National Security Council from Truman to Bush* (New York: William Morrow, 1991).

14. *Miami Herald*, December 6, 1986.

FOR FURTHER READING

Readers interested in more on the presidential tapes benefit from a growing body of literature. Television producer William Doyle is the first writer to produce an overview of the full range of the presidential tapes in his book *Inside the Oval Office: The White House Tapes from FDR to Clinton* (New York: Kodansha International, 1999). The same ground is explored in more scholarly fashion by National Archives analyst John Powers in his unpublished paper "The History of Presidential Audio Recording and the Archival Issues Surrounding Their Use" (ms., July 12, 1996), though Powers stops with the presidency of Richard M. Nixon. The present book is the first to make representative recordings of all the presidents available to the public and the only other one to cover all the modern presidents.

Beyond these accounts are sources that focus on only a single president. Indispensable for Franklin Delano Roosevelt is the work of historian Robert J.C. Butow. Best known as an historian of Pearl Harbor and the Pacific war, Butow recorded what he learned in two articles that were published in the magazine *American Heritage*: "The FDR Tapes" (February/March 1982) and "How FDR Got His Tape Recorder" (October/November 1982). There are no published sources on the Truman or Eisenhower tapes except for newspaper articles by journalist Ron Ostroff in the *Kansas City Times* in 1982.

The Cuban Missile Crisis provided the catalyst for coverage of the Kennedy tapes, which started with an effort to transcribe those related to the crisis. The first fruit of that effort was the book edited by Ernest R. May and Philip D. Zelikow, *The Kennedy Tapes: Inside the White House During the Cuban Missile Crisis* (Cambridge: Harvard University Press, 1997). Zelikow went on to help sparkplug the much more ambitious transcription project of the Miller Center of Public Affairs at the University of Virginia, which he now heads (Ernest May is a member of its board of advisers). The Miller Center aims to create transcripts of *all* Kennedy tapes and all those of Richard Nixon as well. Their initial efforts led to a three-volume set that covers President Kennedy's conversations from July 30 through October 28, 1962, edited in general by Zelikow and May, with individual installments by Timothy Naftali, Naftali and Zelikow, and Zelikow and May. The set is titled *The Presidential Recordings: John F. Kennedy*, vols. 1–3: *The Great Crises* (New York: W.W. Norton, 2001). Volumes two and three in the set represent a perfected version of the same transcripts May and Zelikow offer in their first book, which provides additional illustration for the point that transcription is an inexact process and that each transcription will come out differently.

President Lyndon Johnson's taped telephone calls are to be covered in a projected three-book series by historian Michael R. Beschloss. Two of the three books are currently available. The first covers the period from November 1963 through August 1964. This is *Taking Charge: The Johnson White House Tapes, 1963–1964* (New York: Simon & Schuster, 1997). The second of the projected series is *Reaching for Glory: Lyndon Johnson's Secret White House Tapes, 1964–1965* (New York: Simon & Schuster, 2001), which includes tapes up until July 30, 1965. The last of these volumes awaits the Johnson Library's opening of the full set of LBJ tapes to historians. So far openings have covered only the period through late 1965.

On the Richard Nixon tapes, the Senate Watergate Hearings provide testimony on their existence from Alexander Butterfield. Nixon chief of staff H.R. Haldeman comments in detail on the taping system in his article "The Nixon White House Tapes: The Decision to Record Presidential Conversations," *Prologue* 20, no. 2 (summer 1988). On the tapes themselves, the major source is the volume edited by Stanley I. Kutler, *Abuse of Power: The New Nixon Tapes* (New York: Free Press, 1997), which transcribes the group of tapes whose release was expedited by the National Archives as a series on Watergate-related matters. Kutler played a notable role in the legal struggle to bring the Nixon tapes to the public and is among the best historians of the Watergate affair. The full range of Nixon tapes is much broader and covers many policy issues, as shown by the Vietnam and Billy Graham tapes included in the present collection. There is no comprehensive source on the Nixon taping enterprise, and the broad range of tapes is so far open only through mid-1972.

In addition to these sources, many participants in the events of these years, for example, Richard Nixon, H.R. Haldeman, John Dean, and others, have commented on taping or the tapes in memoirs or accounts of their roles. Lyndon Johnson quoted from some of his telephone tapes without identifying them in his memoir *The Vantage Point: Perspectives on the Presidency, 1963–1969* (New York: Holt, Rinehart & Winston, 1971). Robert McNamara quotes from some of the Kennedy tapes in his Vietnam recollections, *In Retrospect* (New York: Times Books, 1995). There are other instances of this practice as well. Obviously many additional sources helped to establish the contexts for the conversations selected for the present collection.